THE EFFECTS OF STANDARDIZED TESTING

Evaluation

in

Education and Human Services

Editors:

George F. Madaus
Boston College

Daniel F. Stufflebeam
Western Michigan University

The Effects of Standardized Testing

Thomas Kellaghan
Educational Research Centre
St Patrick's College, Dublin

George F. Madaus
Boston College

Peter W. Airasian
Boston College

Kluwer·Nijhoff Publishing
Boston/The Hague/London

DISTRIBUTORS FOR NORTH AMERICA:
Kluwer·Nijhoff Publishing
Kluwer Boston, Inc.
190 Old Derby Street
Hingham, Massachusetts 02043, U.S.A.

DISTRIBUTORS OUTSIDE NORTH AMERICA:
Kluwer Academic Publishers Group
Distribution Centre
P.O. Box 322
3300 AH Dordrecht, The Netherlands

Library of Congress Cataloging in Publication Data

Kellaghan, Thomas.
   The effects of standardized testing.

   (Evaluation in education and human services)
   Bibliography: p.
   Includes index.
   1. Educational tests and measurements.
I. Madaus, George F. II. Airasian, Peter W.
III. Title. IV. Series.
LB3051.K188   371.2'62   81-13676
                           AACR2

ISBN 0-89838-076-6

Printed in the United States of America

CONTENTS

PREFACE

When George Bernard Shaw wrote his play, *Pygmalion,* he could hardly have foreseen the use of the concept of the self-fulfilling prophecy in debates about standardized testing in schools. Still less could he have foreseen that the validity of the concept would be examined many years later in Irish schools. While the primary purpose of the experimental study reported in this book was not to investigate the Pygmalion effect, it is inconceivable that a study of the effects of standardized testing, conceived in the 1960s and planned and executed in the 1970s, would not have been influenced by thinking about teachers' expectations and the influence of test information on the formation of those expectations.

While our study did pay special attention to teacher expectations, its scope was much wider. It was planned and carried out in a much broader framework, one in which we set out to examine the impact of a standardized testing program, not just on teachers, but also on school practices, students, and students' parents. In the study we addressed a range of issues relating to the effects of standardized testing that had arisen in the current controversy on the topic. While many effects have been attributed to testing in this controversy, surprisingly little empirical evidence about the effects of testing was available. A major reason is that the use of standardized tests has grown widely in the United States and Britain over the past fifty years. In this situation it would be extremely difficult to identify teachers or students who had no experience of standardized testing and who could be used as a reference group with which teachers and students who had experience of testing might be compared. Ireland suggested itself as a country in which the effects of standardized testing might be investigated experimentally because even though the country had a well-developed educational system, very little use was made of standardized testing. Thus, the conditions existed in which an experimental design could be implemented, in which some schools would test and receive test information while others would not; differences between schools following these two conditions should be attributable to the testing program.

We were primarily interested in the use of standardized norm-referenced tests and the information derived from such tests. For our study we simulated the main features of a school testing program in the United States. An external agency, in our case the Educational Research Centre at St Patrick's College, Dublin, provided standardized, norm-referenced tests of ability and achievement to schools. Classroom teachers administered the tests to their pupils and returned completed answer sheets to the Research Centre for scoring and processing. Test results were then returned by mail to teachers.

Although the principal focus of our study was on standardized, norm-referenced tests of ability and achievement used in combination, provision was made for examining the effects of variation in the type of test employed (norm-referenced ability and norm-referenced achievement, singly and in combination, and criterion-referenced achievement) as well as in the type of information supplied (normative information, diagnostic information, and criterion-referenced information).

Our objective was to assess the impact of standardized testing and test information over a wide range of variables. We sought to monitor possible effects on school organization, on teachers' attitudes, perceptions, and practices, and on pupils' attitudes, perceptions, and scholastic performance. We asked such questions as, Does the availability of standardized test information affect teachers' perceptions of pupils? Does it affect students' level of achievement? How much weight do teachers give to standardized tests relative to other types of evidence in making educational decisions about pupils? Do teachers perceive standardized tests as biased against certain types of pupils? Does the availability of test information affect teachers' grouping practices? Does the content of standardized tests affect the nature and emphasis of classroom instruction? Do standardized test results influence a student's self-perception? Is testing perceived by teachers as fostering fear and competitiveness? Does a testing program in schools have any impact on parents' perceptions of their children? The answers to these and other related questions have relevance primarily for the initiation, continuation, or elimination of school testing programs focused on providing the classroom teacher with ability and achievement information about individual pupils. They are also relevant to an assessment of many of the judgments about the effects of standardized testing that have been made in the current controversy on testing.

Our emphasis on within-school effects of testing should not be taken to imply that wider, extraschool effects are not also of interest. However, we would expect that such effects would take time to develop. Presumably they require a threshold of testing activity in a society. Given the fact that standardized tests were being introduced on a large scale for the first time in Irish schools, we were unlikely to obtain evidence of anything more than slight effects outside the school. Because standardized tests were new to schools and because it might take some time before the effects of their use might be detectable, we decided that our study should be longitudinal and run for a period of four years (1973 to 1977).

Chapter 1 provides an outline of the current controversy on the use of standardized tests as well as a review of empirical research on the effects of school-based, standardized testing programs. The procedures followed in the investigation described in this book are presented in Chapter 2. Results follow in Chapters 3 through 8. In Chapter 3 all treatment groups are included in analyses to examine school-level effects. The results in Chapters 4 through 7 are based on comparisons between the three major treatments of our study: an experimental group in which norm-referenced standardized tests of ability and achievement were administered to pupils and norm-referenced information was given to teachers, and two control groups, one in which norm-referenced standardized tests were administered as in the experimental group, but results were not given to teachers, and one in which no testing was carried out. For these groups Chapter 4 reports teacher-level effects, and Chapters 5 and 6 pupil-level effects, the latter focusing on the relationship between test information and teacher expectations. Chapter 7 describes parent-level effects. In Chapter 8 school, teacher, and pupil-level effects are considered for a variety of alternative treatments—the provision of diagnostic information on achievement in addition to norm-referenced information, the provision of only ability-test information, the provision of only achievement-test information, and the provision of criterion-referenced information. A general summary of our findings is presented in Chapter 9.

Our study was a very large one and required a great deal of support—financial, personal, and moral. The fact that it was brought to a successful conclusion indicates that our indebtedness to a large number of people is very great.

First, we wish to acknowledge the support of our funding organizations. The Russell Sage Foundation provided initial support for the planning of the study and, in supporting the actual study, was joined by the Carnegie Corporation, the National Institute of Education, and the Spencer Foundation. The Department of Education of the Irish government supported the development of tests and the administration of the testing program in schools. We wish to express our sincere appreciation to these bodies, not only for their financial support, but also for the personal interest and assistance of their staffs throughout the life of the study.

A large number of individuals from both the funding organizations and other institutions provided support for the study. We are particularly indebted to Donal F. Cregan, former President of St Patrick's College, and Vincent C. Nuccio, former Director of the Center for Field Research and School Services at Boston College, for their support from the project's initial conception to its conclusion.

At an early stage, the efforts of David Goslin, Roger Lennon, Fritz Mosher, and Sean O'Connor were crucial in getting the study under way.

Representatives of our funding organizations were of immeasurable assistance throughout the life of the study: Daniel Antonoplos, Marion Faldet, David Goslin, H. Thomas James, Fritz Mosher, Andrew Porter, Jack Schwille, Arnold Shore, and Ward Mason.

We were also fortunate to have been assisted in the planning and running of the project by a very distinguished Steering Committee: Daniel Antonoplos, Benjamin S. Bloom, Edgar Borgatta, Joseph G. Brennan, David K. Cohen, Donal F. Cregan, Jacob W. Getzels, David A. Goslin, J. Thomas Hastings, William Hyland, Roger T. Lennon, Patrick Lynch, Ward Mason, the late M. Donal McCarthy, J. D. Monan, Fritz Mosher, E. F. O'Doherty, T. O'Raifeartaigh, Andrew Porter, Lee Sechrest, Jack Schwille, Arnold Shore, and Michael P. Walsh.

A number of people joined the Steering Committee for a meeting late in 1971 to help in formulating the objectives and strategies of the investigation. To all of these, who gave generously of their time and advice, we express our gratitude: Robert M. Farr, Andreas Flitner, A. H. Halsey, Philip Jackson, John Macnamara, Vincent C. Nuccio, Matthew Salters, George Seth, James A. Wilson, and John A. Wilson.

During the study Albert Beaton and Andrew Porter acted as consultants and attended a number of meetings to discuss data analysis. Albert Beaton also carried out initial analyses of data for us and advised on and reacted to our own analyses as they were carried out.

In the execution of the study, Patricia Fontes had major responsibility for the collection of data. Both she and Joseph Pedulla were responsible for computer analysis. Michael Martin built the data tapes and also worked on computer analysis with John Byrne, Paul Kelly, Fionn Murtagh, Myra O'Regan, and Ronan Reilly. Andrew Burke was responsible for the administration of the project. Administrative assistance was provided by Suzanne Edwards, Marilyn Terry, and George Elford. Other assistance throughout the life of the project was provided by Simon Clyne, Peter Archer, Owen Egan, Carmel Finn, and Veronica O'Hehir.

Vincent Greaney directed the development of the tests that were used in the project. We are indebted to Harcourt Brace Jovanovich and to Roger Lennon for permission to adapt the Otis-Lennon test for use in the study. For assistance in the writing of the report on which this book is based, we are indebted to Patricia Fontes and Owen Egan.

For assistance in the production of the manuscript, we are indebted to Mary Rohan, Ruth McLoughlin, Teresa Bell, Christine Quirke, Nora Pat Slowey, and Edward Lynch, and for the preparation of the index to Nora Pat Slowey. Type setting was by Hilary Keenan.

Finally, we wish to express our sincere appreciation to the teachers, pupils, and fieldworkers who participated in the project.

1 THE EFFECTS OF STANDARDIZED TESTING: *Controversy and Research*

CONTROVERSIAL ISSUES

In recent years controversy about examinations and testing has reached a high level of intensity; writing in *The Common* in September 1976, Pamela Bullard noted that "whether testing is beneficial or inimical to the individual and to society is one of the major controversies in education today." Such controversy is not new. The possible effect of examination practices on individuals and social institutions has long been a cause for concern. In a historical survey of examinations from ancient times to the present, O'Meara pointed out that, over the centuries, examinations have been accused of being responsible for a wide range of ills including:

> carelessness, hatred, favoritism, labor unrest, unprogressiveness, defective art, dishonesty, discontent, poverty, fraudulency, laziness, a generator of mental defectiveness and physical degeneration, serfdom, radicalism, suffering, death, strikes, and war. [O'Meara, 1944, p. 10]

Many of these purported ills can readily be translated into contemporary terminology to fit today's controversy over testing. In a recent commentary on standardized testing, it was claimed that the

1

misapplication and misinterpretation of test results can injure individual
students and erode curriculum and instruction . . . create social and intellectual
segregation, foster elitism, fashion a punishment/reward syndrome, reduce
learning to rote and regurgitative modes, deprecate, stigmatize, exclude.
[Cooper and Leiter, 1980, p. 35]

Not surprisingly, examinations and testing are of interest to a large number of
people. We may assume that the vast majority of people who live in a Western
society have had some experience of some kind of examination, and, if they live
in the United States, it is most likely that the examination at some time took
the form of a standardized test (see Goslin, 1963; Houts, 1975b). Test experience
is not confined to school; a majority of adult Americans have taken a test outside
of school, most commonly in applying for a job (Fiske, 1967). In some cases
the decisions based on test performance may have seemed very important to
people: whether or not they would go to a certain college, whether or not
they would be hired for a job, or whether or not they would be promoted at
work. Furthermore, some will have failed in a test, or have a child who has
failed, so that they are likely to exhibit an emotional involvement that may
cloud or distort their views when they come to consider tests at a later date.
As one would expect, the importance of the decision made on the basis of
test results is related to the strength of people's sentiments about testing
(Neulinger, 1966).

Much of the current controversy about testing in schools focuses on the use
of norm-referenced standardized tests — that is, tests in which the procedure,
materials, and scoring have been fixed, and an individual's performance is
interpreted in terms of the "normal" or average performance of a reference
group (see Anastasi, 1954; Cronbach, 1949). Those who see such tests as
beneficial argue that, when used properly, they have many advantages since
they are more "objective" and reliable than other, more impressionistic measures
of student attainment. Thus, for teachers and counselors they are a source
of information about students, individually and in groups, that can be helpful
in teaching and in student guidance. Tests can also be of assistance to administrators as well as teachers in monitoring the educational programs of schools
and in evaluating the effectiveness of new curricula, instructional materials, and
teaching methods. Finally, when test information is given to students and
parents, it can act as a source of motivation and contribute to the improvement
of students' learning and the enhancement of their self-concepts (see Adams,
1964; Bloom, 1969; Ebel, 1977; Findley, 1963; Tyler, 1968, 1969).

Those who see tests as having these advantages are not unaware of criticisms
of and abuses of tests. Such awareness is perhaps most strongly represented in
Buros's *Mental Measurement Yearbooks,* to which a large number of people have
contributed criticisms of specific tests, even if such criticism was "with the

high-minded purpose of advancing the science and refining the art of testing" (Dyer, 1977, p. 2). Indeed, the response to criticisms of testing has emphasized the need to improve tests rather than abandon them (e.g., Ebel, 1966; Tyler, 1968; Tyler and White, 1979). After all, the superiority of standardized tests over more conventional means of assessment, such as essay-type examinations and teacher judgments, in their objectivity and reliability could hardly be doubted. What appeared to be needed was better-quality tests, ensuring that achievement tests were geared to curricula rather than curricula to tests, the development of tests that measured a wide range of characteristics (for example, creative ability and noncognitive characteristics), and a general improvement in the conditions of test administration (for example, better teacher training).

On the other side of the controversy, a formidable array of criticism ranged from charges of bias in test content (Clark, 1963) to criticisms of the functions for which tests were used, in particular, the selection and labeling of students (Pidgeon, 1970; Rosenthal and Jacobson, 1968). The effect of tests on the general educational environment was regarded as unsatisfactory, tests being perceived as "arousing fear" and "satisfying greed" in students (Holt, 1968); one commentator went so far as to describe some tests as being "pretty strong poison" (Houts, 1975a).

Even this sample of the supposed advantages and disadvantages of tests indicates that the questions surrounding the use of tests are many and complex (see Airasian, 1979). Several difficulties, all interrelated, arise when one attempts to discuss, organize, and evaluate criticisms of tests. First, many of the criticisms and arguments are diffuse. For example, critics frequently fail to distinguish between different types or uses of tests. While intelligence tests and the use of the IQ measure seem to be singled out for most criticism, comments are often generalized indiscriminately to other types of test. Second, empirical evidence to support statements about the nature of tests or their effects is rarely cited. The criticisms often seem to be based on political and ideological positions on the educational system in general; testing becomes the subject of criticism insofar as it is seen to support and reinforce the system. Finally, much of the criticism of testing comes from people outside the testing profession and is made in the public arena rather than within the confines of scholarly publications (Cronbach, 1975; Jensen, 1980). While this means that one should not expect the debate to abide by the canons that normally apply in scholarly publications, it also means that the issues must be regarded as being important by a wide range of publics.

In general, criticisms of standardized tests can be categorized as relating to the nature of tests, the use of tests in educational settings, and the effects of testing on participants in the educational process. Probably the criticisms most frequently made of tests concern their nature. Critics claim that test constructors build their tests on the assumptions that all students have a common culture and have had equal opportunity to learn while attending schools with a common curriculum. However, these assumptions have been challenged, and critics have argued that not all students share the middle-class culture that predominates in schools (Bartel, Grill, and Bryen, 1973; Gay and Abrahams, 1973; Herndon, 1975; Houts, 1975a; Meier, 1973; Quinto, 1977; Ryan, 1979; Samuda, 1975; Weckstein, 1973). If testing practices reflect only the dominant culture's knowledge, language, and behavior, then they will provide imperfect measurement instruments for other groups (Tyler and White, 1979). Further criticisms are that the content of tests, for students of any background, is often trivial and provides no basis for evaluating a range of pupil characteristics, such as ability to learn, ability to make informed judgments, creative ability, or imagination (Green, 1975; Quinto, 1977; Schwartz, 1975; Serebriakoff and Langer, 1977).

Most standardized achievement and intelligence tests are norm referenced; this means that a pupil's score on a test takes on meaning only in terms of how his or her performance stands relative to the performance of pupils upon whom the test was standardized. This is seen as being unsatisfactory because the score provides no information about what a student has learned in a particular subject area (a criterion-referenced interpretation), only how he or she stands relative to other students (Quinto, 1977; Resnick, 1977). Indeed, the whole question of the nature of intelligence and the validity (content, construct, and predictive) of tests has been raised, and some commentators have gone so far as to say that standardized tests are found to be deficient when these issues are considered because what tests claim to measure is in fact unmeasurable (Silberman, 1976).

The use of tests in educational settings is also seen as creating many problems. Critics point out that since administrative procedures vary from one test site to another, the testing is not really standardized. The problem of unstandardized procedure can arise from ambiguous test instructions as well as from the fact that administrators (usually teachers) may have little familiarity with testing (McKenna, 1975; Weckstein, 1973); further, conscious cheating may even take place (Weber, 1974). Problems may also arise in the scoring, interpretation, and application of test results, thus making any judgments based on them of doubtful value.

The application of test results is another aspect of testing that has attracted much critical comment. It is generally assumed that tests are widely used to select and classify students. The rigid grouping of pupils in an attempt to reduce variance in ability or attainment, either within the school or within the class, is an effect that is frequently attributed to testing (Pidgeon, 1970). While such procedures may not be carried out with the intention of "labeling" students, critics claim that this, in fact, is the most usual end result (Rist, 1977). Critics are particularly concerned with the effects of labeling on pupils who score below average on tests, among whom are likely to be a large number of minority-group pupils (Connell, 1978; Lazarus, 1975; Lewis, 1977; Perrone, 1977; Williams, 1971). Thus standardized tests are seen as encouraging and perpetuating distinctions on the basis of race, gender, and social class (Nibley, 1979; Simon, 1971). Particular problems are raised when pupils are mislabeled as, for example, when a student is classified as mentally retarded because he or she had problems with a test that is not in the child's first language (Samuda, 1977).

Beyond the focus of the classroom, other functions for which the use of standardized tests has been severely criticized and resisted are those of allocating funds and teacher accountability. Critics have claimed, for example, that tests are sometimes used for resource allocation to serve political purposes rather than to improve the educational level of pupils. Besides, the allocation of funds on the basis of need creates technical and logistical problems and may also be seen as rewarding failure (Madaus, 1979). As far as assessing teacher effectiveness is concerned, standardized tests are seen as giving rise to a form of simplistic accountability (U.S. Department of Health, Education, and Welfare, 1979) and have been denounced in this context as irrelevant, crude, unfair, and unreliable (McKenna, 1975; Weber, 1974).

The consequences of standardized testing have been seen as both educational and psychological. We touched on some of these when we considered the criticism that testing leads to labeling. Critics have pointed to other educational effects on school programs and participants. They claim, for example, that testing pressures teachers into teaching for the test and thus leads to a narrowing of the curriculum into score-producing areas. Testing is also seen as perpetuating a standard curriculum and discouraging diverse and innovative programs (de Rivera, 1974; Perrone, 1977; Quinto, 1977). At the pupil level, testing has been accused of dampening creativity on the one hand while encouraging conformity and fostering intellectual dishonesty on the other (Hoffman, 1962; Houts, 1975a). It has also been said that standardized testing lowers student achievement; instruction time is lost through testing (Brady, 1977; Hein, 1975), slow learners are neglected because teachers concentrate on better students whose scores are easier to raise (McKenna, 1975), and, in general, students, particularly minority-group members, may accomplish less because teachers expect less of them (Perrone, 1977; Ryan, 1979).

Critics also have described tests as being negative in their psychological effects on students (Bosma, 1973; Samuda, 1977). They encourage a competitive atmosphere in the classroom and may lead to negative emotional reactions (pupils may feel frightened and anxious) as well as causing specific psychological damage. A frequent accusation is that tests are potentially damaging to a student's self-concept; this will be most likely to happen when action, such as tracking or referral to a special class, is taken on the basis of a test score.

These criticisms clearly cover a very wide range of supposed defects and negative consequences of testing. In some cases, no doubt, the criticisms point to real weaknesses in tests; in other cases they identify misuses in their application. Such criticisms are not new, nor are they confined to what Dyer (1977) has called the "outside critics." Many people involved in the development of testing over the past half century (the "inside critics") have adverted to most, if not all, of these criticisms. One of the benefits of the recent spate of criticism of tests by people outside the testing industry may be that many of the things about testing (misconceptions and limitations, misuses, and abuses) that the inside critics have been saying for years will now get across to the test-using public (Dyer, 1977).

The consequences of testing have been subjected to fewer empirical investigations than has the nature of tests, particularly their content, construct, and predictive validity. For example, the extent to which testing contributes to the inequities of life is far from clear. To what extent does testing lead to social stratification, to the labeling of students, to self-fulfilling prophecies, to competitiveness, or to weak self-concepts? Or, we may ask, to what extent do tests reflect injustices rather than create them? Indeed, how many of the consequences that are attributed to testing would occur if testing never took place? Does less selection, less labeling take place in school systems (for example, in Western Europe) that make little use of standardized tests than in systems that use tests?

On the other hand, we may also ask whether standardized tests provide teachers and counselors with information that is helpful in their teaching and in student guidance. Does test information contribute to the improvement of a student's learning and the enhancement of his or her self-concept? Are teachers who do not have access to test results at a disadvantage in their work in comparison with those who have? And are students likely to be at a disadvantage if teachers do not have the kind of information that can be derived from standardized testing?

In criticisms of testing there has been relatively little recognition of the fact that there is a variety of different types of test and that tests may be used for very different purposes (see Merwin, 1973; Shepard, 1979). Tests may be designed to measure intelligence or achievements in a wide range of scholastic areas; they may also be designed to measure personality characteristics, though the use of such tests is not as widespread in schools as is the use of cognitive tests. Tests may be used to provide information about individuals—for the diagnosis of learning difficulties, placement of students, certification of students, or counseling. They may also be used at the institutional level—to study the effects of innovations, to monitor standards in the interest of general accountability (to provide information on the quality of schooling, to evaluate the performance of teachers) and for resource allocation, as was done in the Quie Amendment, which proposed that funds be allocated for education disadvantage as represented by low test scores (Madaus, 1979; Shepard, 1979). In assessing the possible effects of testing, one should bear in mind the type of test and the purpose for which it is being used. Criticisms of, or research findings about, one kind or use of tests may have little relevance to other kinds of test or other uses to which test results might be put. In assessing the effects of testing, one should also consider the source of the testing and the person or persons to whom test information will be provided. The situation in which testing is carried out within a school at the initiative and under the control of the school principal or a teacher is quite different from that in which the testing is carried out by an outside authority, such as a state or district education agency, as is the case with public examinations in Europe and minimum competency testing in the United States (Madaus and McDonagh, 1979). One would expect that the effects of external testing would be much more potent and far-reaching than the effects of an internal testing program. For example, on the basis of the eleven-plus selection test in Britain, a decision was made about the type of postprimary school that a pupil could attend, while in some of the United States the granting of a high school diploma was made dependent on a student's performance on a minimum competency test.

Little empirical research exists that can throw light on the consequences of testing in any of the areas in which test results are used to make decisions (see Airasian, 1979; Dockrell, 1980; Goslin, 1963; Ingenkamp, 1977; Kirkland, 1971; Madaus, Airasian, and Kellaghan, 1971; Mahler and Smallenburg, 1963; Womer, 1969). In the absence of such research, much of the debate on testing has been confined to statements deduced from ideological or political positions. Those who reject the use of tests often seem to base their opinions on a mixture of intuitive feelings about their effects, possibly on the basis of the critic's general personality characteristics or personal experience with tests (Brim, 1965), coupled with ideological views about social stratification. Ideological positions that oppose testing are strongly represented among people who hold egalitarian views of society, in particular, those who subscribe to theories of educational inequality based on Marxist and Weberian views of social dominance. For such people, testing and the selection procedures of schools are perceived as contributing to the maintenance of the dominance of some social classes over others (see Karier, 1973; Lawler, 1973; Montagu, 1975; Neander, 1973; Simon, 1971). The strong antitesting view of egalitarians may be in part a reaction to the kind of optimism that led to the use of standardized tests to promote meritocratic ideals in the past. This phenomenon was most obvious in postwar Britain, where standardized tests were used to select pupils at eleven years of age for secondary schools (see Vernon, 1957). Although less obvious in America, the relationship between meritocracy and testing has not gone unnoticed; Cohen (1972), in discussing people's reactions to "IQ," notes that some people perceive it as becoming the central criterion for distributing "the good things of life" and the basis on which society's rewards and punishments are being allocated.

EMPIRICAL RESEARCH ON TESTING

At this stage we provide an outline of the limited empirical evidence that is available on the effects of standardized testing in school-based testing programs. We do not deal with other issues that arise from the controversy on testing, such as the nature of tests, on which topic a voluminous literature already exists (see Jensen, 1980). Neither do we consider evidence relating to the use of tests for certification or for accountability. We shall consider separately studies relating to the effects of testing on schools, teachers, pupils, and parents.

School-Level Effects

A consideration of the possible effects at the school level of using standardized tests suggests that one might expect effects on school organization and in a number of school practices. Relatively little research, however, has examined the effects of using standardized tests on schools or teachers. The assumption is seemingly often made that certain decisions and actions, such as the tracking of pupils and the allocation of slow learners to remedial classes, are taken on the basis of standardized-test information. For example, Kirkland (1971), in her review of the effects of tests on students and schools, considers evidence relating to the effect of ability grouping on students' achievement; however, she provides no evidence that the grouping was carried out in the first place on the basis of test information. A variety of decisions relating to school organization and student placement can be and are taken in the absence of test information. Evidence on the role of standardized-test information in making such decisions is far from clear. An exception to this is the use of individually administered intelligence tests to place children in classes for the educationally mentally retarded (EMR) (see Mercer, 1973). This procedure was clearly documented in a recent court case in California (*Larry P.* v. *Riles,* 1980), in which a federal judge prohibited the use of such tests for this purpose.

The earliest study of the effects of standardized testing on school organization and practice was probably that of Haggerty (1918), who mailed a questionnaire to a selected group of school superintendents, most of whom were known to have used tests and scales. The purpose of the enquiry was to learn what changes in school organization and procedure had been made as a result of such measurement. Sixty-two of the 200 respondents reported "some conscious alteration in the work of the school following the use of a standardized test" (p. 25). The changes reported related to the classification of pupils, courses of study, methods of instruction, time devoted to subjects, and methods of supervision. More recent studies have noted a tendency on the part of some teachers to direct their attention toward areas they know will be covered by standardized tests in district or city testing programs (Brickell, 1962; Brickman, 1946).

While there seems to be general agreement that tests and examinations affect curricula and teaching methods when the examinations are set by an external agency and when important decisions are made on the basis of students' performance (Tyler, 1966), the influence of standardized testing when administered as part of an internal school testing program is less clear. In a number of surveys of teachers, the most important of which was the Russell Sage survey of the social consequences of standardized testing in the United States that began in 1962, varying minorities of teachers (usually less than 30 percent) considered that standardized tests had a strong influence on the curriculum. Examples of such influence are a change in a course or the inclusion of material that had appeared in tests (Goslin, 1967; Sandlin, 1959; Traxler, 1958). However, the majority of teachers did not see tests as having such effects.

In the Russell Sage study, the main use of tests in schools as reported by principals, was not directly in the context of the curriculum, but rather in the context of the diagnosis of learning difficulties of pupils (72 percent of principals) and of homogeneous grouping (46 percent). Less frequent uses reported were counseling of parents (29 percent), counseling of children (28 percent), and evaluating the curriculum (28 percent) (Goslin, 1967).

Teacher-Level Effects

The large-scale research that is available on teacher-level effects of standardized testing is based on surveys of teachers, most of whom had considerable experience with such testing. Goslin (1967) reported a number of general conclusions about teachers' attitudes, perceptions, and uses of standardized tests. First, teachers tended to perceive the tests as fairly accurate measures of a student's intellectual ability and achievement. Second, teachers viewed the kind of abilities assessed by standardized tests as relevant determiners of pupils' future academic success and, to a smaller degree, of their success in life. Third, teachers reported that substantial weight should be accorded to standardized test scores—along with other indicators—in making decisions about the selection and instruction of pupils. Fourth, teachers tended to believe that the kinds of abilities measured by standardized tests were more a result of learned than innate abilities. Fifth, teachers' opinions about whether pupils should be provided information about their test performance was divided, although all teachers felt that some children should be given information in some circumstances. Sixth, in spite of these attitudes and beliefs, teachers generally reported a low degree of use of test scores in grouping, planning instruction, and similar activities. We should note that Goslin's survey was carried out at a time when tests were not widely used for curriculum evaluation, high school promotion, or teacher accountability. Thus, while the survey provides useful information on teachers' attitudes toward standardized testing, its present-day relevance may be limited in a number of respects.

More recently, large-scale studies of teachers' views of standardized tests have been carried out by Beck and Stetz (Beck and Stetz, 1979; Stetz and Beck, 1978). In these studies approximately 3,500 American teachers in grades K–12 responded to a questionnaire that elicited their views about the amount of standardized achievement testing in their schools and the usefulness of test information for various purposes, as well as information about their actual use of test results in the classroom. In addition to the use of a teacher questionnaire, information was obtained from pupils about their reactions to tests. Since these studies were carried out in the late 1970s in the midst of the debate over the usefulness of standardized tests for various forms of pupil, teacher, and curriculum evaluation, they provide a more contemporary reflection of teachers' views toward the uses of standardized tests than does Goslin's earlier survey.

Over two-thirds of the teachers in the survey felt that the amount of standardized testing in their school system was about right. The vast majority (over 90 percent in all cases) characterized themselves as moderately or very comfortable with, interested in, knowledgeable about, and supportive toward standardized achievement testing. Sixty percent, however, felt that additional training of school personnel in test interpretation and use was desirable. The majority did not favor a moratorium on various types of tests. However, 26 percent favored a moratorium on standardized intelligence tests and 21 percent favored one on standardized achievement tests. More teachers (34 percent) favored a moratorium on state-mandated achievement testing than on any other type of testing; only 18 percent favored the increased use of test results for school accountability purposes. These findings may reflect a reaction to the growing use of state-mandated tests for teacher evaluation and pupil promotion and graduation.

In light of these results, teachers clearly seem to have believed that standardized test results were useful for some purposes but not for others. To provide additional information on the question of test usefulness, teachers were asked to indicate whether standardized achievement test results were or were not useful for seventeen different purposes. The usefulness of test results for the various purposes was viewed quite differently by teachers. Many of the teachers felt that test results were useful to measure the educational growth of individuals (77 percent), detect systemwide general strengths or weaknesses (73 percent), help plan instruction for class groups (65 percent), report to parents (63 percent), help plan instruction for individuals (61 percent), measure the educational status of individuals (58 percent), compare students with national peer groups (54 percent), and screen special education students (51 percent). Considerably fewer teachers felt that standardized test results were useful to report to news-papers (8 percent), to help evaluate teacher performance (19 percent), to compare classes in a school (26 percent), to compare schools within a system (33 percent), or to help evaluate teaching procedures or methods (36 percent). In general, teachers tended to view standardized test results as most useful for planning instruction and assessing the status of individual pupils in classes and as least useful for activities associated with teacher accountability. Interestingly, the teachers' negative attitudes toward the increased use of test results for account-ability decisions did not lead them to view tests in general or all test uses as harmful or bad.

Goslin's study and these recent studies present quite similar pictures of teacher perceptions regarding the usefulness of standardized testing for pupil-centered purposes; teachers tend to perceive such testing as useful for assessing individual and group status, for reporting to parents, and for planning instruction. The more recent studies indicate that teachers are less positive about the use of tests in the context of school or teacher accountability.

Goslin (1967) pointed to the difficulty of making inferences from this kind of survey data about the effects the possession of test information might have on teachers' behavior toward pupils. Some more recent studies have set out to address this problem by attempting to assess more directly teachers' reactions to actual test information. Most of the studies had as their impetus Rosenthal and Jacobson's (1968) study, *Pygmalion in the Classroom,* and were primarily concerned with possible effects of testing on pupils. However, effects on teachers were sometimes considered in the context of this work, since one can argue that if test information is communicated to teachers, some change in the teacher is a prerequisite to change in the pupil. These studies are of particular interest, not only because they aroused considerable public interest, but also because they attempted to present a model that describes how test results might interact with teachers' perceptions and overt behavior to influence student behavior.

The idea that our behavior is governed by beliefs and expectations of what will follow if we take one line of action rather than another recurs in the history of behavioral science (e.g., MacCorquodale and Meehl, 1948; Rotter, 1954; Tolman, 1932). The extension of that idea to one that an expectancy, whatever its relationship to "reality," may give rise to a self-fulfilling prophecy, also has wide currency and finds its classical expression in the Thomas theorem that "if men define situations as real, they are real in their consequences" (Merton, 1968). It was in this latter meaning that the term self-fulfilling prophecy was used by

Rosenthal and Jacobson (1968), who, in their study, manipulated test information to provide teachers with false information.

The view that expectations function as self-fulfilling prophecies is based on two assumptions: "First, that the act of making a definition about a situation is also an act of making a prophecy about it. Second, that the act of making a prophecy about a situation is also an act of creating the conditions through which the prophecy is realized" (Palardy, 1969, p. 370). Thus, a self-fulfilling prophecy will operate when a teacher forms an incorrect evaluation of a student and bases predictions or expectations about how the pupil will perform in school on that evaluation. These expectations will, in turn, affect the behavior of the student.

Criticism of the role of standardized tests in the formation of expectancies is not confined to cases where test information is inaccurate, or at least not intentionally so. A number of critics have claimed that knowledge of test scores can mislead teachers in their expectations for students. Clark asserted that "when a child from a deprived background is treated as if he is uneducable because he has a low test score, he becomes uneducable and the low test score is reinforced" (1963, p. 150). Similarly, Ravitz concluded that "the real damage of the IQ test is its subtle influence upon the mind of the teacher. Teachers, often unconsciously, expect the level of performance from the child that his IQ indicated" (1963, pp. 15–16). We might argue that in these cases the test score, because of the student's background and experience, is an inappropriate measure of his or her scholastic ability. However, we may ask whether tests are powerful influences in forming teachers' expectations in situations other than ones in which children from disadvantaged backgrounds are involved.

Teachers themselves report that they regard test results as important. In a national survey of elementary school teachers carried out by Austin and Morrison (1963), 80 percent of teachers reported that they used reading-readiness test scores either always or often in determining placement in a first-grade reading program. More direct evidence on the influence of test information on teachers' perceptions is not as compelling as this statistic on reported teacher use, however. The Rosenthal and Jacobson (1968) study, although it focused popular attention on teachers' expectations, did not provide any empirical data directly relating to those expectations; the data collected for analysis in the study were student test scores. While Rosenthal and Jacobson concluded that the teachers apparently interacted differently with the students who had been falsely presented to them as being "late bloomers" and thus likely to show unusual mental growth during the year, in fact no direct evidence was presented on this point.

Some other studies have suggested that test information may affect teacher perceptions (e.g., Beggs, Mayer, and Lewis, 1972). Rist (1977) cited a number of such studies, which he claims demonstrate the influence of standardized tests of intelligence and achievement on teacher expectations. Sanders and Goodwin (1971) compared the role of a number of variables in forming teacher expectancies. Teachers were presented with cumulative-record folders with information on each child's grade level, grade average, sex, age, IQ score, and standardized achievement test scores and were asked to predict the child's achievement. Teachers frequently used test scores to make predictions. Other investigators have reported similar findings (Long and Henderson, 1974). It is one thing for teachers to make judgments about hypothetical students or indeed even about students with whom they are not very familiar. In such cases a teacher might be glad to make use of the summarizing kind of information that a test score might be perceived as providing. It is quite another thing for a teacher to be supplied with test information about a student that he or she knows very well. A wide range of variables can influence teachers' perceptions of their students: the student's past educational history, gender, socioeconomic class, race, language, physical attractiveness, and personality. If a teacher has had time to gather this kind of information about a student over a period of day-to-day interactions, is the provision of test information likely to influence his or her perceptions very much?

In many cases, of course, we would expect the test information basically to confirm teachers' perceptions of pupils' scholastic achievements. There is considerable evidence that teachers' ratings of pupils' achievements and ability are formed early in the year (Rist, 1970; Salmon-Cox, 1981; Willis, 1972); further, they correlate reasonably highly with test scores (correlations of about .6 are common) (Scanlon, 1973) and are quite stable over time (Airasian, et al., 1977; Beggs, Mayer, and Lewis, 1972). The possibility that tests will alter teachers' perceptions and behavior will arise only in cases where the test information fails to agree with the already-formed perceptions. We would expect that teachers would react to that possibility in different ways, and there is no reason to assume that a teacher would automatically accept that a judgment based on a test score is superior to one based on other information. Indeed, when teachers are "surprised" by the test results of their pupils, they seem to be more likely to regard the tests than their own judgments as being incorrect (Archer, 1979; Jackson, 1968; Salmon-Cox, 1981).

In a real-life situation, then, test scores, as Leiter (1976) has pointed out, can be for teachers only what Husserl (1969) has termed "occasional expressions." They constitute data that cannot be interpreted by the teacher without recourse to additional information about the student—his or her home background and personal characteristics, and the circumstances under which the test was taken. Leiter takes up this point and goes on to note that while to the researcher a test may be unambiguous, since the questions and answers are clearly defined, it may be quite different for the teacher, whose task and interests are different:

. . . he must promote children into the next grade, and so must find out *what* each student knows. The test scores do not tell the teacher what he needs to know, so the scores are equivocal from the teachers' perspective. [Leiter, 1976, p. 59]

If Leiter's interpretation is correct, then we would not expect standardized test information to have a very great impact on teachers' perceptions or behavior. Even if teachers find test information to be more valuable than Leiter suggests, the information still has to be considered in the context of the network of constant evaluations made by teachers in their everyday work, some of which test information may serve simply to confirm.

Pupil-Level Effects

It seems reasonable to assume that standardized test score information has its most serious impact on the pupil. Thus, most research on the effects of standardized testing has not surprisingly been concerned with possible effects on pupils.

Goslin (1963) has suggested two levels at which information obtained from a typical standardized testing program might affect students. The first is the *direct* impact of additional information that the student receives about his or her own abilities. Bloom (1969) sees effects at this level as being important and argues that, if the tests are understood and utilized properly, they can do much to enhance a student's learning as well as his or her self-regard. On the other hand, it is not inconceivable that the results of a test might adversely affect an individual's self-concept, level of aspiration, or educational plans. Empirical evidence relating to this issue is surprisingly scant; however, one study carried out with university students indicates that knowledge of performance on intelligence and aptitude tests and a personality inventory leads to higher academic achievement (Flook and Saggar, 1968).

In Goslin's second level of effects, information about test performance comes to an individual in an indirect way; the test results are not told directly to the student, but some decision is made about him or her on the basis of test information. The decision could relate to a formal action, such as tracking, within-class grouping, or referral to a special class. It could also be less formal, as when, for example, it influences a teacher's perception of a student, and the teacher, even though he or she does not formally group the pupils in any way, proceeds to treat the student in accordance with the altered perception. This might have the effect of "suppressing" the learning of some students (Dusek, 1975).

From what we know of the communication of test results to students (Goslin, 1967; Brim, et al., 1969), if testing has an impact on them, it is more likely to be at the second rather than at the first level. Many investigators have assumed that teachers do in fact transmit test information in some way and so in their studies of the effects of testing have focused on student behavior, most usually as assessed by scores on standardized tests. Rosenthal and Jacobson's (1968) study was of this kind. This study was carried out in an elementary school in California and attempted to examine experimentally the influence of test results on pupils. At the beginning of the school year, a nonverbal IQ test was administered to a group of children. Teachers were then given the names of children who, on the basis of the test findings, could be expected to show dramatic intellectual growth. Actually, the names of the children were chosen randomly, and consequently the only difference between "high expectancy" and "ordinary" children was in the mind of the teacher and of the investigators. The investigators claim that group IQ tests administered by the teachers on three occasions during the year showed a significantly larger gain in score in the "high expectancy" children than in their classmates.

The results of this study have been strongly criticized on statistical and design grounds (Gephart, 1970; Snow, 1969; Thorndike, 1968). Further, most subsequent attempts to demonstrate the effects of test information on students' measured intelligence have failed (Claiborn, 1969; Fleming and Anttonen, 1971; Jose and Cody, 1971; Pellegrini and Hicks, 1972; Sorotzkin, Fleming, and Anttonen, 1974), though a small number have provided some evidence of an effect (Carter, 1970; Knill, 1969; Maxwell, 1970). On the assumption that students' achievements were more likely to be affected by teacher behavior than was students' intelligence, a number of investigators examined the effect on achievement of supplying teachers with achievement test information. Again, a small number of studies, which incidentally were not carried out in normal classrooms, did find an effect (Beez, 1970; Meichenbaum, Bowers, and Ross, 1969). Most studies that examined the effects of test information on student achievement, however, returned negative findings (Asbury, 1970; Broome, 1970; Carter, 1970; Dusek and O'Connell, 1973; Fleming and Anttonen, 1971; Goldsmith and Fry, 1971; Jose and Cody, 1971).

Studies of the possible influence of test information on variables other than intelligence or achievement are rare, even though the possible effects of such information on students' self-concepts have been regarded as important by more than one critic of standardized testing. While some evidence exists that teacher expectations are related to student expectations, self-esteem, and attitude to learning (Brookover, 1959; Carter, 1970; Keshock, 1970; Manis, 1955; Meichenbaum and Smart, 1971; Pitt, 1956), we have no evidence to indicate that test information plays a role in this. In a well-designed study, Torshen (1969) investigated the proposition that the form of evaluation that has the greatest impact on a person's immediate environmental context will also have the strongest effects on his or her personality, self-concept, and mental health. She hypothesized that in most classrooms, teachers' grades have a strong direct impact on students, while standardized achievement test scores have a more indirect influence. Underlying her hypothesis was the belief that achievement test scores do not play an important role in the daily routine of American classrooms since they are given at most once a year and the results are generally available only to the teacher or other school personnel. Further, she assumed that the teacher's grade incorporated nonacademic assessments not included in the standardized test information. Using a multiple-regression technique, she found that when the effects of teachers' grades and various control variables, such as sex and IQ, were removed, the remaining relationship between achievement test scores and measures of self-concept and mental health were not statistically significant. Further, she demonstrated a significant relationship between student grades and measures of self-concept and mental health that is independent of any influence of the control variables or of achievement test scores. Torshen concluded that grades contain an element that affects students' self-concept and mental health but is not related to purely academic achievement. This nonacademic element may be composed, at least in part, of teachers' evaluations of students on what Parsons (1959) has labeled the "moral" dimension of achievement. Torshen also concluded, however, that results of standardized tests may not be without impact, since such results may have affected teachers' grades, which in turn were related to mental health. These findings complement those of Goslin and Glass (1967), who concluded that test scores are of only minor importance in shaping students' estimates of their own ability, especially when the score contradicts other information.

In considering findings on the effects of test information on pupils, a number of investigators have reiterated a point made by Flowers (1966) that test information is of itself insufficient to overcome the effects of other factors such as the information teachers glean from assignments completed by students and from a knowledge of students' home backgrounds. As we saw in the previous section, test information is merely a part, and probably a relatively small part, of the pressure exerted on students by the educational environment (see Finn, 1972). Even if expectancy processes operate in the classroom, test information is only one factor in the network that creates such expectancies (Sorotzkin, Fleming, and Anttonen, 1974), and any possible role it may have to play in affecting students has to be considered in this context. The research findings to date, in contrast with what many critics may have had to say about standardized testing, indicate that that role is not a very major one.

Parent-Level Effects

Research on the effects of testing on parents in the context of school-based testing programs is even more scant than research on schools and teachers. While a little is known about how adults perceive the effects of tests they had taken themselves (Brim et al., 1969), we know next to nothing about how a parent's knowledge of a child's test performance affects his or her perceptions of and aspirations for a child.

Brim et al.'s (1969) findings support Goslin's (1963) observation that American parents are not aware of the extent of their children's exposure to standardized testing. Slightly over half the parents in the Brim study reported that their children took one or more tests; this contrasts with the approximately 80 percent of secondary school students who said they had taken such a test. Around a third of parents who said their children had been tested learned nothing about the child's test performance, while a similar number reported they had received "a very good idea" about it.

Brim and his colleagues feel that keeping parents ignorant of their child's test results is based on the school's assumption that such information may be injurious to the child's self-esteem, motivation, or mental health. They conclude that "it is shocking and astonishing to find so little solid social research testing this fundamental assumption" (Brim et al., 1969, p. 13). This assessment still stands.

THE PRESENT INVESTIGATION

Some of the problems in evaluating the effects of empirical testing during the debates of the 1960s and 1970s arose because tests had so long been part of the American educational scene that finding a group of teachers or pupils without experience with tests, who might have provided relevant comparative data, was impossible. Thus, inevitably, the kind of research that could be carried out and the range of questions that could be addressed was limited. With this situation in mind, the authors of this book proposed to carry out a study of the effects of standardized testing in the Republic of Ireland, a country that did not have a tradition of standardized testing in its schools. In the Irish school system, testing could be introduced on an experimental basis in a sample of schools, and at the same time a sample of schools in which testing would not be carried out could be maintained for comparative purposes. While there are obvious differences between the American and Irish systems of education, not the least of which is the fact that testing is an area of controversy in the United States while it is not in Ireland, the similarities that exist between the systems and the countries led us to expect that the results of a study of this kind carried out in Ireland would have relevance to the American scene.

In our study, which is described in this volume, we examined the effects of a classroom-based standardized testing program. As in a normal school-testing program, teachers administered standardized tests of intelligence and achievement to their students at the beginning of the school year. Thus, the test information was simply added to the many other sources of information available to the teacher. This seems a reasonable context in which to examine the impact of standardized testing, since it is the one most teachers will encounter in their use of tests.

While, strictly speaking, the source of the testing in the investigation was an external agency (a research organization), every effort was made to simulate a normal classroom-testing program in which teachers would control testing and results. Thus, teachers administered the tests in their own classrooms, and results were sent directly and only to teachers. The extent to which we were successful in this simulation, however, remains an important issue for the interpretation of our findings.

In the study we collected information that would allow us to examine the effects of testing on the institutional practices of schools, the perceptions and attitudes of teachers, the intelligence and achievement of pupils as measured by standardized tests, the self-concepts of pupils, and parents' perceptions of their children. Since the study was an experimental one, with experimental and control groups, isolating any unique effects that the availability of test information might have had should be possible.

Our testing program, it should be reiterated—whether or not it was perceived as such by teachers—was an internal, classroom-based form of assessment, one in which teachers tested their own students and, unless the teachers decided otherwise, one in which only they had access to information on students' performance. The testing was not mandated by any authority, and information was used only as teachers saw fit. This is a common form of testing situation, but it is one that obviously limits the possible effects of testing. Thus, the test information could not be used to make the radical kind of decision that might be made on the basis of a test administered by an external authority, as was the case with the eleven-plus selection tests in Britain or the Florida minimum-competency test. Further, since the purpose of our study was not to provide information on which to base judgments about school-level performance or teacher effectiveness, our findings do not relate to the controversial use of tests for accountability purposes.

2 AN EXPERIMENTAL STUDY OF THE EFFECTS OF STANDARDIZED TESTING: *Design and Implementation*

The purpose of this study was to examine experimentally the consequences of classroom-centered testing procedures on schools, teachers, pupils, and parents. We were primarily interested in the use of standardized, norm-referenced tests and the information derived from such tests. For the study the basic features of a school testing program in the United States were simulated. An external agency, in our case the Educational Research Centre at St Patrick's College, Dublin, provided standardized, norm-referenced tests of ability and achievement to schools. Classroom teachers administered the tests to their pupils and returned completed answer sheets to the Research Centre for scoring and processing. Test results were then mailed to teachers.

Since standardized testing was rare in Irish schools at the beginning of our study, we were able to select, in addition to the schools that would receive information on the performance of their pupils, two control groups of schools, one in which no testing at all would be carried out and another in which testing would be carried out but no information would be returned to schools.

Although the principal focus of our study was on standardized, norm-referenced tests of ability and achievement used in combination, provision was made for

19

examining the effects of variation in the type of test employed (norm-referenced ability and norm-referenced achievement, singly and in combination, and criterion-referenced achievement) as well as the type of information supplied (normative information, diagnostic information based on item data, and criterion-referenced information). It should be noted, however, that some of the newer testing approaches that endeavor to wed closely instruction and evaluation (for example, mastery learning and continuous achievement monitoring) were not examined.

The study was concerned with the impact of standardized testing and test information *within* schools—on school organization, on teachers' attitudes, perceptions, and practices, and on pupil attitudes, perceptions, and scholastic performance. We sought answers to such questions as the extent to which standardized test information alters teachers' perceptions of pupils; how much weight teachers give to standardized tests relative to other types of evidence in making educational decisions about pupils; whether teachers perceive standardized tests as biased against certain types of pupils; how accurate and stable an estimate of pupil performance standardized tests provide; how the contents of standardized tests influence the nature and emphasis of classroom instruction; and how standardized test results influence a student's self-concept and self-evaluation. The answers to these and other related questions have relevance primarily for the initiation, continuation, or elimination of school testing programs focused on providing the classroom teacher with ability and achievement information about individual pupils. Had testing been introduced into schools in a different form—for example, as a basis for making between-teacher and between-school comparisons in terms of pupil achievement—the same questions might have been asked, but with potentially different answers.

Our emphasis on within-school effects of testing should not be taken to imply that wider, extraschool effects are not also of interest. However, we would expect that such effects would take time to develop. Presumably they require a threshold of testing activity in a society. Given the fact that standardized tests were being introduced on a large scale for the first time in Irish schools, we were unlikely to obtain evidence of anything more than slight effects outside the school.

Because standardized tests were new to schools and because some time might pass before the effects of their use might be detectable, we decided that our study should be longitudinal and run for a period of four years (1973 to 1977). We tested in grades 2 through 6 only, partly because many elementary schools cater for only junior pupils (up to first grade) or only senior pupils (grades 2 through 6) and partly because the group testing of children in grades lower than second was not likely to be satisfactory. Teachers in other grades, however, were asked on some occasions to complete questionnaires.

THE LOCUS OF THE STUDY

The study was carried out in the school system of the Republic of Ireland largely because, even though the system is well developed, it did not have a tradition of using standardized tests. At this point, it may be useful to describe briefly some aspects of the system, particularly those related to evaluation.

As in other countries, there are three separate organizational levels of education: elementary or primary, postprimary or secondary, and third-level or tertiary. Traditionally, the postprimary system has been bipartite. The majority of students attend "secondary" or grammar-type schools, which emphasize an academic curriculum. The other main type of school is vocational; the curriculum in these schools is more practical than that in secondary schools. In recent years the number of comprehensive/community schools in the country has grown. (For more information on the Irish system of education, see Bell and Grant, 1977; *Investment in Education,* 1966; McElligott, 1966; Morris, 1968; Murphy, 1980.)

The curriculum for elementary schools is laid down by the Department of Education of the Irish Government (Ireland: Department of Education, 1971). While a wide range of activities in the school (including social and environmental studies, civics, music, and physical education) is provided, the main emphases in the curriculum are on English (the mother tongue of the vast majority of pupils), mathematics, and Irish (the traditional language of the country, which the government is committed to preserve). Thus all pupils are exposed to a second language at school.

How evaluation within schools is carried out is not well documented. One thing is clear, however: Up to very recently, practically no use was made of objective standardized tests, though this situation was changing, most notably in the area of educational and vocational guidance in secondary schools, for which American tests were introduced. Despite this increased use of tests, the situation without doubt differed markedly from that in Britain and the United States. Standardized tests did not form part of external or public examinations in Ireland; they were not used in a routine way by the school system, and they did not form part of selection or placement procedures in third-level education. At the beginning of our study, only three tests that had been developed specifically for use in Irish conditions existed. One was a group test of verbal reasoning ability, the use of which was restricted by the publishers; the second was an individually administered word-recognition test in English; and the third was an individually administered word-recognition test in Irish.

In the absence of standardized tests, how are students evaluated? This is a difficult question to answer, though the answer may not be very different from the case in which frequent use is made of standardized tests (Madaus, Airasian, and Kellaghan, 1971). The most usual formal means of assessment in the school (both primary and secondary) is a written (essay-type) examination, normally given at Christmas and summer. Such examinations, constructed by individual teachers, cover the content area covered in the various school subjects during the previous term or year. The results of examinations, often in the form of marks and place in class, are frequently sent to pupils' parents. Apart from the more or less formal type of examining that written examinations involve, there obviously must be considerable informal evaluation of pupils by teachers, based on day-to-day interactions, on knowledge of the pupil's background, his or her homework, how he or she answers questions, pays attention and so on.

While we have no overall picture of the evaluation procedures used by teachers in Irish schools, a few studies carried out in primary schools throw some light on the matter. Kellaghan, Macnamara, and Neuman (1969), in a study of teachers' estimates of the scholastic progress of a representative sample of eleven-year-old children, report the rather surprising finding that teachers regarded the general progress of 25 percent of their pupils as "unsatisfactory," while 66 percent were judged as having difficulty with at least one subject. The authors suggested that in the absence of norm-referenced tests, teachers seem to set a single (and for many children) unrealistic standard of progress.

What personal and background factors a teacher takes into account in forming informal judgments of a pupil's progress or expectations for scholastic perfor-mance is a matter that has attracted some attention, particularly in recent years. Obviously many factors might influence a teacher's judgment—his or her percep-tion of the child's "intelligence" or ability, physical appearance (cleanliness), social behavior, or home background (social status, parental interest). These factors are not unrelated, and the empirical information available from studies of Irish populations suggests that the relationships between intelligence and social class and intelligence and family size are much the same in Ireland as they are elsewhere (Kellaghan and Macnamara, 1972). So is the relationship between school attainment and home background (Cullen, 1969). Again, the incidence of children of high ability is related to social-class membership (Kellaghan and Neuman, 1971), as has been found in other countries.

The high level of selectivity that operates in the Irish educational system, probably at an early age (Kellaghan and Brugha, 1972) and certainly by the beginning of postprimary education (Kellaghan and Greaney, 1970), may be taken as indicating the operation of strong evaluative processes in schools. Some evaluation procedures, particularly the Leaving Certificate examination, taken on the completion of secondary schooling, are widely and explicitly used for selection (Madaus and Macnamara, 1970). But no doubt other, less formal methods of evaluation operate at a much earlier date.

While some form of student grading is implied in teacher ratings of pupils as "poor" or "excellent" and in the provision of marks based on term examinations, the formal granting of grades, which is a feature of American schools, does not occur. This is not to say that the evaluation procedures of Irish teachers are necessarily very different from those of their American counterparts. The day-to-day task of teaching groups of young students must inevitably involve the use of certain evaluative procedures and techniques, and, in the absence of evidence to the contrary, we may assume that these procedures and techniques will not be too different whether the teacher is in an Irish or in an American school. However, Irish teachers' evaluations are perhaps less formally communicated to students. From fairly superficial observation it would seem that, at the elementary level at any rate, within-class evaluation is less overt in Irish schools than it is in American ones. Further, the limited research evidence available suggests that primary school teachers are biased in their ratings of students, perhaps because they lack information on general standards in the country, of a kind that might be obtained from the use of norm-referenced tests.

THE SAMPLE

The sample was drawn from the population of elementary schools in the Republic of Ireland, as described by Department of Education statistics for 1971. All schools in the population, with a number of exceptions, were eligible for selection. At the time the sample was drawn, there were 4,220 elementary schools in the country. Of these, 3,877 were under Catholic management and 343 under Protestant management. (There were also approximately 200 private schools, which were not included in the study.) Because most Protestant schools are small and are largely confined to certain areas in the country, we decided not to include them in the sample. One-teacher Catholic schools were also excluded. The number of such schools was not very large (246); testing in them would have presented particular difficulties, and there was a government policy to amalgamate such schools into larger units.

After the above exclusions, the population of schools was stratified by sex composition of pupils attending (male, female, and mixed) and location (city, town, and rural). Within the categories formed on the basis of the stratification variables, schools were randomly selected. For each school selected, a further four schools matched on the basis of type of administration (religious, lay) and size (number of teachers) were also randomly selected. Each of the set of five matched schools was assigned at random to one of the five experimental or control groups. Altogether, thirty-five schools were selected for each treatment in this fashion. Over the five treatments, this gave a sample of 175 schools.

In fact, the actual sample with which the study began was not the same as the one that had been selected. Following the selection of schools, letters that described the project and invited participation were sent to school principals. This was followed by a visit from a fieldworker, who met with teachers in the selected schools and provided more information on the role that schools were expected to play in the project. Responses to letters and information gained during school visits soon indicated that the integrity of the planned sample could not be maintained. The main problem arose not from an unwillingness to cooperate in the study, but rather from changes in school characteristics from those described in the census data that were available in 1971.

When we found that the characteristics of a school had changed, the school was dropped and a replacement selected. However, we often found, especially in the case of small rural schools, that the replacement did not fit our criteria either. Over a period of two months, we tried to find schools that fitted our sampling needs. Eventually seeking further replacements became impossible, and a decision was made to retain selected schools even though their characteristics in terms of our stratification and matching variables no longer matched information contained in the population statistics that were used in selecting the original sample.

Altogether forty-five of the schools that were approached were not included in the final sample. A total of eight schools refused to participate in the study; a further four were "unable" to participate (e.g., because of accommodation problems); while three schools were found to be unsuitable from our point of view since they did not have complete cycles of pupils at the senior primary school level (grade 2 upwards). By far the largest number of losses (thirty) were the result of school closure or of a change in the size or sex composition of the schools. These changes in most cases were the result of a Department of Education policy of amalgamating small schools.

In the process of selection and replacement, five schools were lost from the planned total, reducing the number of schools in the final sample to 170. Apart from this loss, the sample was also disturbed in three other ways. First, the balance in the original sample in stratification and matching categories across treatments was not maintained in the final sample. Second, as many as fifty-two of the schools that appear in the final sample were not originally selected for the category in which they finally appeared. Twenty-two of these are in a stratification (location by sex composition) category for which they were not selected; twenty-eight have matching characteristics (number of teachers) for which they were not selected; and two represent overreplacement in the stratification and matching category for which they were selected. Third, some schools in the final sample appear in stratification categories that we had not intended to fill when the sample was first drawn. The effect of these changes was that the constitution of comparable control and experimental groups in terms of stratification and matching variables was not fully realized.

We recruited a further set of nineteen schools in the third year of the study to serve as a control group for the investigation of the effects of providing criterion-referenced information to teachers. The schools in this group were matched with schools already in the study on the sample strata characteristics—location and sex composition of schools.

Participation during the Study

The sample, as one would expect, did not remain static during the course of the study. In the first year seven of the 175 schools failed to cooperate at all. In the second year noncooperation was higher: twelve schools failed to participate. The number of noncooperating schools was reduced to five in the third year and one in the final year. Schools that failed to participate in a given year were not dropped from the study unless it was clear that they would not participate in the future. Some schools that failed to participate in one year participated at a later date. In the final year of the study, the number of participating schools was 155.

Not all the schools that were considered to be participating in the study actually met all the demands of the study. These demands varied from treatment to treatment, from year to year, and from grade to grade, but in general they involved test administration by classroom teachers and the completion of questionnaires by principals, classroom teachers, and pupils. Requests that were made for information in the course of the study can be distinguished as having three different targets: (1) the school, where only one questionnaire per school was to be returned; (2) the teacher, where one questionnaire per teacher was to be returned, as in the case of all Teacher Questionnaires; and (3) the class of pupils, where as many tests, Pupil Evaluation Forms, or Pupil Questionnaires were to be returned as there were pupils in a class. Full details of participation rates for each of these requests are provided elsewhere (Kellaghan, Madaus, and Airasian, 1980b); here we provide a general indication of these rates.

The School Questionnaire was completed by 158 schools at the beginning of the study and by 155 schools at the study's end. A high rate of return was also attained for pupil tests. This frequently exceeded 95 percent, though there was some falling off in the second and third year in the group that tested but did not receive results. Participation in testing at the end of the fourth year was also reduced in treatments where this was the second testing to be carried out in the school year.

The next most commonly returned items were Pupil Evaluation Forms completed by teachers at the start of the year and Pupil Questionnaires (completed by the pupils themselves); these were, with a fair degree of consistency across years and treatments, returned for about 75 to 85 percent of the classes for which they were requested. The return rate for both these instruments fell off somewhat in the fourth year compared with the third year, returns from about 10 percent fewer classes in the fourth year being typical across treatments. The rate of return of Teacher Questionnaires was fairly close to that for the pupil instruments.

The second Pupil Evaluation Form requested at the end of the third and fourth years of the study was the pupil instrument for which returns were poorest. About 60 to 65 percent of classes returned them in the third year, and about 50 to 60 percent returned them in the fourth year.

TESTS AND TEST INFORMATION

Two tests of ability and nine tests of achievement—eight norm-referenced and one criterion-referenced—were used in the study. The norm-referenced tests are similar in form to the type of commercially available standardized test used in the United States. All the achievement tests were constructed by the Educational Research Centre with the assistance of Irish teachers and were designed to reflect syllabi in English, Irish, and mathematics for Irish schools. The existence of national syllabi in these subject areas made the task of establishing the content validity of the tests easier than it would be in countries, such as the United States, that have less uniform syllabi. All the norm-referenced tests in ability and achievement were standardized and normed on Irish populations.

Tests

Ability Tests. Two ability tests were used—the Otis-Lennon Mental Ability Test, Elementary 1 Level, Form J (adapted Irish version) (Greaney and Kellaghan, 1973) for grades 2 and 3 and the Drumcondra Verbal Reasoning Test (Gorman, 1968; Kellaghan, 1976) for grades 4, 5, and 6. Reliability measures (test-retest and internal consistency) for the former test range between .83 and .91 and for the latter between .94 and .98.

Achievement Tests. The Drumcondra Attainment Tests were used to measure achievement in English, Irish, and mathematics. There are three levels for the English and mathematics test: Level I (grade 2), Level II (grades 3 and 4), and Level III (grades 5 and 6). The Irish test has two levels: Level II (grades 3 and 4) and Level III (grades 5 and 6). All tests have two parallel forms (Educational Research Centre, 1977, 1978a, 1978b, 1979a, 1979b, 1980a). For our analyses we use scores based on performance on the reading vocabulary and reading comprehension subtests of the English and Irish tests and performance on the total mathematics test or the computation subtest of the mathematics test. Test-retest reliability measures for these tests range between .70 and .96; internal consistency measures range between .77 and .96. The final achievement test used in the study was the Drumcondra Criterion-Referenced Mathematics Test, Level 6, which was administered only to grade 6 pupils (Educational Research Centre, 1980b). This test was designed to provide achievement measures that are referenced to specific behavioral objectives of the curriculum for fifth and sixth grades in primary schools (Ireland: Department of Education, 1971).

Test Information

Norm-Referenced Information. Norm-referenced information was provided for the performance of each pupil on the ability and achievement tests. For the Otis-Lennon Mental Ability Test, raw scores, standard scores (M:100; SD:15), and percentile ranks based on norms derived from a standardization within grades were provided. For the Drumcondra Verbal Reasoning Test, raw scores, standard scores (M:100; SD:15), and percentile ranks based on norms derived from a standardization by age level were provided.

The information provided for performance on the norm-referenced achievement tests in English, Irish, and mathematics was based on grade-level standardizations. In addition to raw scores, standard scores and percentile ranks were provided for performance on all subtests. Further, total "reading scores" based on total score on vocabulary, word analysis, and comprehension on the English test at Level I and on vocabulary and comprehension on the English and Irish tests at Levels II and III were provided.

Information on the test performance of pupils was provided on a test-score report form. Additional materials were also sent to teachers to assist them in understanding and interpreting results.

Teachers who had administered norm-referenced tests were given a booklet called *Interpreting Your Test Results.* This booklet contained a review of the testing program and of the basic concepts of standardized testing. It also contained a detailed explanation of each item of information (raw score, standard score, percentile rank) appearing on the report form and a brief description of some ways in which norm-referenced test results might be used. In addition, fieldworkers visited schools to explain the results and the interpretative material that accompanied the results.

Diagnostic Information. In addition to the norm-referenced information described above, some schools were provided with more detailed information on pupils' test performance in terms of the more specific skills and contents of the tests. Items were categorized to represent an area of skill or content, and information was provided for individual pupils on the number of items in the category, the number of items in the category attempted by the pupil, the number correctly answered by the pupil, and the national average correctly answered by pupils. The categories in the language tests covered aspects of comprehension (interpreting phrases, drawing inferences, identifying main ideas), spelling (errors involving consonants, errors involving vowels), and usage (errors involving noun forms, verb forms, prepositions, pronouns, and adjectives). For the mathematics test, information was provided on aspects of computation (operations on integers, addition and subtraction of fractions, multiplication and division of fractions, operations on decimals), concepts (properties of number systems, fractions, geometry, measurement), and problems (numerical operations, algebra, charts and graphs, measurement, costing).

Teachers who received diagnostic information on pupil performance also received a copy of the booklet on test interpretation, *Interpreting Your Test Results,* and a supplementary booklet dealing with the diagnostic scores on pupil skills. This latter booklet contained a detailed explanation of each item that appeared on the report form. Each skill area for which results were reported was described briefly, and the numbers of the test questions contributing to that area were identified. Information on how national averages had been calculated and suggestions about how the results might be used were provided. Assistance with interpretation was provided by fieldworkers.

Criterion-Referenced Information. Criterion-referenced information applied only to the criterion-referenced mathematics test used at grade 6. For each of the fifty-five objectives that the test attempted to measure, information was provided for each pupil on whether or not the pupil had achieved mastery.

A special test-interpretation booklet was provided for teachers. It dealt with the nature of criterion-referenced testing, the determination of objectives, and the setting and reporting of mastery levels. As with other groups, fieldworkers were available to assist in the interpretation of results.

TREATMENTS

In the original design of the study, schools were allocated to one of five groups. Two of these were to act as controls. We planned to carry out standardized testing in the third group and to provide norm-referenced results to teachers. In the fourth group, also, standardized testing would be carried out and, in addition to providing teachers with norm-referenced information, we also provided diagnostic information based on item data. We planned that the testing and reporting conditions in the fifth group would be the same as in the third group except that test results would also be provided to parents. In the more detailed description of treatments that follow, the first four of these groups are labeled Treatments 1, 2, 3, and 4A.

The treatment that involved the provision of test results to parents was never implemented since it became clear at an early stage that this procedure would not be acceptable to schools. A further problem in the implementation of the planned treatments, which arose in the first year of the study, related to the use of item data as a basis for diagnostic information. We found this not to be practical for tests that did not employ machine-scorable answer sheets. Since such answer sheets were not used in grades 2 through 4, the provision of diagnostic information had to be limited to grades 5 and 6 in the appropriate treatment group.

The effect of abandoning the parent-information treatment and our inability to provide diagnostic information in some grades allowed us to consider certain alterations to the original design in the second year of the study. The modifications permitted the examination of testing practices beyond those contained in our original design. These relate to criterion-referenced testing and the use of ability as opposed to achievement tests. We designated further treatment groups to allow an examination of these issues.

We now describe the main features of the treatment groups. The first three are the ones of major concern in this report, and major analyses were carried out on data collected from them.

Main Treatment Groups

Treatment 1 (Control). This treatment involved no standardized testing. However, pupils and teachers in grades 2 through 6 were involved in the collection of other data, which were obtained primarily through questionnaires.

Treatment 2 (Control). This treatment consisted of standardized testing of ability and of achievement in basic curricular areas (English, Irish, and mathematics) in grades 2 through 6. No feedback on the performance of pupils was provided. In the first year of the study, pupils in all grades (2–6) were tested. For financial reasons this practice was not followed in later years. In the second year grades 2 and 5 were tested; in the third year, grades 3, 4, 5, and 6; and in the fourth year all grades were again tested. Thus, treatment was not uniform for all grades in a school. For example, a pupil who entered second grade in the first year of the study was tested in grades 2, 4, and 5. However, a pupil who entered second grade in the second year of the study had experience of testing only in grades 3 and 4. The experience of teachers is more difficult to quantify; it depended on which grade a teacher happened to be teaching. For example, a teacher who taught fifth grade in a school throughout the study would have tested every year, while one who taught first grade, third grade, second grade, and third grade over the four years of the study would have had experience of testing only in the final year.

Treatment 3. This treatment consisted of standardized testing of ability and achievement in basic curricular areas (English, Irish, and mathematics) in grades 2 through 6. Norm-referenced information in the form of standard scores and percentile ranks on the performance of pupils was returned to all teachers. Pupils in grades 2 through 6 were administered tests in the first, second, and fourth years of the study. In the third year pupils in grades 3 through 6 were tested. Although conditions were more uniform across grades from year to year in this treatment than in Treatment 2, both pupil and teacher experience of testing still varied somewhat. The time of entry of the pupil or teacher to the school was the major factor affecting experience of the testing program.

Alternative Treatments

Treatment 4A. This treatment consisted of standardized testing of ability and achievement in basic curricular areas (English, Irish, and mathematics). As in Treatment 3, norm-referenced information in the form of standard scores and percentile ranks on the performance of pupils was returned to all teachers. In addition, teachers in this treatment received a more detailed breakdown of pupils' performance on tests in terms of the skills and contents assessed by the tests. Obtaining scores on sets of items was practical only for tests that employed machine-scorable answer sheets. Since such answer sheets were used only at grades 5 and 6, this treatment applied only at these grade levels. It was administered each year of the study. Lower grades in this treatment group, when tested, received only norm-referenced information, as in Treatment 3. This applied in grades 2 through 4 in the first year of the study and in grade 3 in the second year.

Treatment 4B. Since pupils in Treatment 4 schools who were in grade 2 in the second year of the study would not reach grade 5—the level at which diagnostic information was applied to teachers (Treatment 4A)—during the life of the study, it was decided to implement another treatment beginning with this grade. The treatment consisted of ability testing only, with norm-referenced information on pupils' performance being provided to teachers. An ability test was administered in grade 2 in the second year of the study, in grade 3 in the third year, and in grade 4 in the fourth year. Pupils in these grades had no other testing experience. A treatment group that received achievement testing only was constituted in a similar fashion from the original group of schools in Treatment 5 (cf. Treatment 5B).

Treatment 5A. This treatment consisted of achievement testing with a criterion-referenced mathematics test. The treatment was implemented only at grade 6 and only in the second and third years of the study. Pupils who were in grade 6 in the second year of the study had taken norm-referenced ability and achievement tests when they were in grade 5, and their teachers had received norm-referenced information. Pupils who were in grade 6 in the third year of the study had taken norm-referenced ability and achievement tests when they were in grade 4, and their teachers had received norm-referenced information; they were not tested in grade 5. Treatment 5A was divided into three groups, the first two of which were selected from the original Treatment 5 group of schools. Schools within sample strata (location and sex served) were randomly assigned to one of two groups. The third group of schools was recruited in the third year of the study to provide control information. These were matched to the schools in the other groups on the basis of sample strata characteristics. The treatments in the three groups were as follows.

1. Pupils in sixth grade were administered a criterion-referenced test of mathematics and a norm-referenced test of mathematics in the second and third years of the study. In the third year an ability test was also administered. Results of the tests were returned to teachers.
2. Pupils in sixth grade were administered a criterion-referenced test of mathematics in the second and third years of the study. In the third year an ability test was also administered. Results of the tests were returned to teachers.
3. Pupils in sixth grade were administered a criterion-referenced test of mathematics in the third year of the study. No information on pupil performance was provided to teachers. As noted before, the schools in this treatment had no other participation in the study.

Treatment 5B. This treatment parallels Treatment 4B. The treatment consisted of achievement testing only, with norm-referenced information on pupils' performance being provided to teachers. Achievement tests in English and mathematics were administered in grade 2 in the second year of the study and in English, Irish, and mathematics in grade 3 in the third year and in grade 4 in the fourth year. These pupils had no other testing experience.

Treatment 5C. This group does not, strictly speaking, constitute a distinct treatment group at all. It operated for only the first two years of the study and during that time was similar to Treatment 3. In the first year grades 2, 3, and 6 were administered norm-referenced tests of ability and achievement, and teachers were provided with information on pupil performance. In the second year grade 4 was administered norm-referenced tests of ability and achievement, and teachers were provided with information on pupil performance.

DEPENDENT VARIABLES

We obtained information on a large number of dependent variables. Most information on schools, teachers, and pupils was gathered by means of structured, closed-ended questionnaires. In most cases Digitek-type answer sheets containing questions, response options, and a place for the respondent to blacken in responses were used. The need for a closed-ended, optical scanning response format is evident when one considers that in each year of the study, multiple questionnaires were administered to thousands of teachers and pupils.

In a few cases, where the number of respondents was small or where the nature of the information sought was not amenable to a closed-ended, machine-scorable format, other, more open-ended techniques were used. For example, questionnaires completed by the principal of each school contained a number of open-ended questions and options that permitted the principal to add substantive remarks or explanations as needed.

Altogether, apart from the standardized tests that were administered to pupils, eight instruments were used to gather dependent variable information. A number of these basic instruments came in two forms: one that was administered in control groups and a second that contained questions about testing and test information and was administered in treatments that tested. In many cases, to obtain longitudinal data on perceptions, attitudes, and reported practices, questions asked on one instrument were repeated on another, subsequently administered instrument. Finally, each instrument contained many questions, each of which individually could serve as a dependent variable in analysis. In the following sections we present a brief description of the general, more important areas covered by each test or questionnaire.

Schools

At the beginning of the first year of the study and again at the end of the fourth (final) year, principals in all sample schools were asked to complete a School

Questionnaire that sought information on current school practices and organization. The School Questionnaire administered at the end of the study was similar to the one administered at the beginning except that for schools that had carried out testing, it was augmented by a series of questions dealing with the use of test results.

The School Questionnaire sought information in eight general areas: (1) background data on the school (name, address, phone number, and so on); (2) background data on school principal (sex, number of years as principal, and so on); (3) school information (enrollment, number of full-time teachers, basis for admitting pupils, basis for streaming pupils); (4) parent-teacher associations; (5) school progress reports (methods used to report pupil progress, frequency of reports); (6) standardized testing in school (name, time of administration, reasons for testing, and so forth, for all commercially available standardized tests used in the school); (7) school remedial facilities; and (8) school record files (type of file kept, information on file, access to file, and so on). Additional questions, included only on the second School Questionnaire and asked only in schools that had tested as part of the study, included more specific questions about the use of test results. For example, principals were asked to indicate and then describe in an open-ended question whether test results had been used to support a recommendation that a pupil transfer to another school, assign pupils to classes within the school, retain a pupil in a grade, identify pupils in need of remedial help, communicate with parents about pupil progress, and so forth.

Teachers

A total of five questionnaires was administered to teachers over the course of the study. Some of these questionnaires had multiple forms, and some were revised slightly for subsequent administration.

Teacher Questionnaire I and Teacher Questionnaire I Revised. These questionnaires were administered to all teachers in sample schools at varying times during the study. The questionnaires gathered the following types of information from teachers: (1) background data (name, gender, teaching experience, and so on); (2) knowledge, experience, and opinions about testing (participation in courses on standardized testing, familiarity with standardized tests, importance of standardized test information for making selection and instructional decisions about pupils, attitudes about the accuracy and relevance of standardized test information, and so on); (3) teacher attitudes toward examinations, streaming, and so on; and (4) whether inter- and intraclass grouping was practiced and the criteria used.

Teacher Questionnaire II.   Teacher Questionnaire II obtained information about teachers' attitudes and perceptions in a number of areas, including perceptions of the accuracy of estimates of pupil intelligence made by teachers, classmates, and parents, the frequency of use of various pupil-assessment techniques, the primary reasons for giving examinations, perceptions of the emphasis accorded various skills or content areas in instruction, opinions on the accuracy and stability of standardized test scores, the nature of the construct tapped by intelligence tests, and perceptions of the relationship between the kind of intelligence measured by standardized tests and the kind of intelligence required for success in school and work.

Teacher Questionnaire III.   This questionnaire was administered to teachers in treatments that received standardized test results and was intended to gather information about the tests and testing program. The first two sections of the instrument contained questions about the mechanics of testing (the timing of the testing, multiple-choice format, the use of separate answer sheets, and so on) and pupils' reactions to the test (had difficulty following directions, asked for test results, were interested in the test, and so on). The remainder of Teacher Questionnaire III sought information about teachers' perceptions of the adequacy of the coverage of the content in the tests, the accuracy of the test results, the number of pupils and parents to whom test scores were communicated, and the influence of the standardized achievement test results on the teacher's work.

Teacher Questionnaire IV.   This questionnaire had two forms, a shorter form administered to teachers who tested but did not receive results, and a longer form administered to teachers who tested and received results. All items in the shorter form were included in the longer form. The questionnaire was intended to provide detailed information on the processes associated with the implementation of the testing program in schools. In the case of teachers who had received test results, information on the use, distribution, and adequacy of the results was obtained. The first half of Teacher Questionnaire IV was administered to all teachers who tested their pupils as part of the study. Data were gathered about teachers' methods of preparing pupils to take the multiple-choice tests, teachers' eagerness to see test results, pupil and teacher reactions after taking the tests (pupils' questions, talking to other teachers about the test, and so on), scoring tests before returning answer sheets for processing, perceptions of the effects of tests on pupils (motivate them, increase competitiveness, increase anxiety, and so on), information about tests, test scores, or test use that would be helpful to the teacher (more detailed test scores, wider range of tests, test scores from previous years, and so on), and teacher perceptions of the types of pupils favored by tests (urban vs. rural pupils, high vs. low social class, good memorizers, and so on). The second half of the questionnaire was administered only to teachers who had received test results. Items in this section were focused on teachers' use and perception of the test results. Questions covered such areas as the frequency with which teachers used the test results, their access to results from prior years, the degree to which test results were shared with other teachers in the school, the relative usefulness of the different test scores reported, the use of test results to regroup pupils, the extent to which results were shared with pupils and parents, and the teachers' perceptions of the accuracy of the pupil assessment provided by the tests.

Teacher Questionnaire V. Teacher Questionnaire V overlapped greatly with Teacher Questionnaire II, but contained four additional items. The additional items sought information on the home background (parent education, family income, parental expectations for pupils, and so on) of the teachers' classes, teachers' perceptions of the amount of pressure placed on pupils for high academic performance, good classroom behavior, and good social development, teachers' descriptions of classroom organization and climate (accent on cooperative group work vs. accent on individual competition, frequent vs. infrequent class tests, and so on), and teachers' attitudes toward standardized, multiple-choice tests.

Pupils

Three basic sources of information comprised the data base on pupils: performance on standardized ability and achievement tests, teacher ratings of individual pupils on a variety of cognitive and affective behaviors, and a pupil questionnaire completed by sixth-grade pupils. Thus the standardized tests that were described above were used both as independent and dependent variables.

In addition to pupil test performance, teacher ratings of each individual in his or her classroom were obtained using an instrument called the Pupil Evaluation Form. There were two such forms, one administered at the start of the school year and a slightly different version administered at the end of the school year. Over the course of the study, the Pupil Evaluation Form changed somewhat, primarily to allow for the inclusion of new questions. It contained six sections for the teacher to complete: (1) pupil background data (name, gender, grade, father's occupation); (2) a rating of the pupil's general intelligence; (3) ratings of the pupil's general progress in eight subject areas; (4) ratings of the pupil's class position relative to his or her classmates in eight subject areas; (5) the teacher's perceptions of the appropriate postprimary school for the pupil; and (6) ratings of the pupil on a variety of school characteristics (participation in class, personal appearance and dress, speech/use of language, getting along with other children, and so forth). The Pupil Evaluation Form administered at the end of the school year contained these six sections as well as questions about whether the teacher had changed his or her rating of the pupil, the amount of parental interest in the pupil's schooling, and the amount of pressure the student was under to do well in examinations. Revision of the Pupil Evaluation Form added questions about whether the teacher had seen prior standardized test results on the pupil and about the teacher's contact with the pupil's parents.

A Pupil Questionnaire was administered to pupils in the sixth grade to ascertain their general attitudes, self-concept, and educational perceptions. There were two versions of the questionnaire, each with two forms: one for pupils who had not been tested and one for pupils who had. The second revised version of the questionnaire included a few items not present in the initial version. Items in five sections of the Pupil Questionnaire were completed by all sixth-grade pupils: (1) background information (name, gender, and so forth); (2) perceptions of the factors that help a pupil to get on well in class (hard work, asking questions in class, doing what the teacher tells you, luck); (3) comparison with other pupils in class on fourteen cognitive and affective areas (intelligence, memory, interest in school, and so on); (4) level of education expected and desired; and (5) general attitudes toward examinations, school, self-concept, and competition. Pupils who had taken tests were also asked for information about their attitudes toward sitting for the tests and their opinions about their test performance.

Additional Dependent Variable Information

In addition to the foregoing data on schools, teachers, and pupils gathered by means of questionnaires or tests, a number of other kinds of dependent-variable information were gathered in the study. Fieldworkers, who had visited schools a number of times each year over the life of the study, and other observers provided ratings of school and teacher cooperation and implementation of treatments. In the first and final years of the study, interviews with a sample of parents of children in participating schools were carried out to determine their attitudes toward education in general and their familiarity with standardized testing in particular.

PROCEDURE

At the beginning of the 1973–74 school year, a letter inviting each selected school to participate in the treatment to which it had been assigned was mailed to the school principal. Schools in all treatments received the same description of the purpose of the project, "to assess the value of tests which we have developed for the use of teachers in Irish schools." They were also informed of the study's intended duration of four years. Schools received different descriptions of the procedures in which the study would involve them, depending on the treatment to which they had been assigned. Principals and staff of schools in Treatment 1 were told that information about pupils' background and progress and their own views on assessment and examinations would be sought. Principals and staff of schools in Treatment 2 were told, in addition to the information given to Treatment 1 schools, that they would be asked to administer standardized tests to pupils each year and that the results from all tests would be sent to them at the end of the four-year period. The information given to teachers in schools in Treatments 3, 4A, 4B, 5A, 5B, and 5C was the same as that provided for Treatment 2, with the exception that teachers in Treatments 3 and 5 were told that "a report on the performance of each pupil would be sent to each teacher each year," while teachers in Treatment 4 were told that "a detailed report on the performance of each pupil . . . to provide sufficient information and guidelines to help teachers use the test results in planning and arranging their class-work" would be sent to each teacher each year.

Following a school's agreement to participate in the project, the school was visited by a fieldworker, whose task it was to acquaint teachers with the new form of test (objective, multiple-choice, standardized), to review the tests and manuals to be used in the study, to review the testing schedule, and to give directions for test administration. Fieldworkers also collected teacher lists (lists of teacher names and grade assignments) and class lists (lists of the name, date of birth, grade, father's name, and home address of each pupil in each class). Teachers were provided with a brief description of some of the other ways in which they would be asked to provide information for the study, particularly through teacher questionnaires and pupil-rating forms. Finally, the fieldworker reviewed in considerable detail with the principal the procedures for the distribution, collection, and return of completed test materials for scoring.

Test materials were sent to schools shortly after the visits of the fieldworkers. The tests were administered by classroom teachers in their own classrooms. In the first year, due to delays in the setting up of the project, testing was not completed in schools until the middle of the second term. In the subsequent three years, testing was carried out by the majority of teachers in the first two months of the school year. Schools were visited at the beginning of each year to review testing procedures and to induct new teachers into the program in a way roughly similar to that used with teachers in the first year.

Following the completion of testing, teachers were asked to complete a Teacher Questionnaire (TQI) and a Pupil Evaluation Form for each pupil in their classes, and each principal was asked to complete a School Questionnaire.

Test results were then returned to teachers in the treatment groups that were due to receive test information. This formed the pattern for subsequent years. Pupil Evaluation Forms were distributed to teachers when testing began at the beginning of the school year. This was followed shortly afterwards by the distribution of Teacher Questionnaire I in the second and fourth years. Later school visits combined the collection of these instruments and an explanation of the test scores that had been returned.

Beginning in the second year and continuing through the fourth year, we sent a new set of instruments to schools in the spring term. This included an end-of-year Pupil Evaluation Form to be completed by teachers in certain grades, a Pupil Questionnaire to be completed by sixth-grade pupils, and a number of Teacher Questionnaires—two in the second year and two in the fourth year.

In the second and third years of the study a special end-of-year testing took place in the criterion-referenced test treatment (Treatment 5A). At the end of the fourth (final) year of the study, a testing program was conducted in all treatments except Treatments 5A and 5C. Fieldworkers interviewed each principal and completed a second School Questionnaire. The fieldworkers also completed a rating of each school and of each teacher on degree of involvement in the study and on treatment implementation. Degree of involvement and treatment implementation were also assessed by staff from the Educational Research Centre in Treatment 3 and 4 schools.

3 EFFECTS OF TESTING ON SCHOOLS

Standardized tests, according to both their proponents and opponents, have a variety of uses, the effects of which should be discernible at the level of the school. Thus, we might expect to find the influence of test information in administrative decisions relating to the assignment of pupils to classes, in the operation of remedial and referral services, and in communications between teachers and possibly between teachers and parents. Further, whether testing is a useful aid to learning and achievement, as its proponents argue, or damaging to them, as its opponents contend, evidence of the effects of testing should be found in the school's achievement level.

Evidence relating to the possible impact of testing at the school level was sought in three ways. First, we monitored effects on school organization and practices by use of a School Questionnaire that was administered to school principals at the beginning and end of the study. We compared the practices of schools that had participated in the testing program with those of schools that had not participated. For schools that had tested, we obtained information on their use of test results. Second, we compared the performance on standardized tests of ability and achievement of pupils in schools that had participated in the testing program at the end of the study with the performance of pupils in schools that had not participated. Third, in the case of schools in which there was more than one class at a grade level, we examined variability in ability, achievement, and social class composition within classes at the end of the study; again we compared schools that had participated in the testing program with schools that had not.

It should be noted that the school is the analytic unit in all the analyses reported in this chapter. Further, all analyses, except some that are based on data collected only in schools that had tested, are experimental in the strict sense, comparisons being made between schools in control and experimental treatments.

EFFECTS ON SCHOOL ORGANIZATION AND PRACTICE

We examine the effects of testing on school organization and practice in analyses of the responses of principal teachers to a school questionnaire. For these analyses schools are categorized into five treatment groups only, on the basis of their designation in the original sample. This raises no problems in the case of Treatment 1 (no testing), Treatment 2 (norm-referenced testing of ability and achievement with no results), or Treatment 3 (norm-referenced testing of ability and achievement with norm-referenced results). However, because of modifications in the original design to allow for the introduction of additional treatments during the course of the study, schools originally designated as Treatment 4 schools actually came to represent two types of treatment, while schools originally designated as Treatment 5 schools came to represent three types of treatment (see Chapter 2 for details of subtreatments). Thus, treatment is a function of grade level as well as of school. For this reason we decided to retain the original treatment designation of schools in the school-level analyses.

Only schools that responded to the questionnaire when it was administered at the beginning and at the end of the study were included in analyses. There were 31 such schools in Treatment 1, 28 in Treatment 2, 34 in Treatment 3, 29 in Treatment 4, and 31 in Treatment 5—153 schools in all. (Treatment 5 included two schools, each of which had two divisions, with a separate head for each division. Each head completed a School Questionnaire. In the analyses reported in this chapter, the divisions are treated as separate "schools.")

Before examining differences between treatment groups at the end of the study, we looked at the responses of schools at the beginning of the study. We found that standardized tests did not figure greatly in school practice. One school reported that performance on a standardized test was used as a basis for admission. Sixteen percent of schools reported that they had purchased standardized tests, but less than 11 percent had used tests during the first year of the study. The test most frequently used was of the individual word-recognition type. The results of a standardized test—presumably a reading age based on a word-recognition test—were entered on record cards in 11 percent of schools. If this level of use seems somewhat higher than one might have expected, it should be pointed out that only one test—a relatively short, individually administered, word-recognition test—was used in most schools.

Most schools did not stream on the basis of ability or achievement in assigning students to classes when there was more than one class at a grade level. The practice of retaining pupils in a grade for a second year was rare.

Most schools (59 percent) had a referral agency to which pupils with learning and other problems could be referred. However, only 22 percent had a full-time or part-time remedial teacher. Record keeping existed in only slightly more than half the schools, and the information contained on record cards was limited to such matters as the students' home background (parents' names and occupations), scholastic progress in the form of marks or grades, and comments on pupils' application and deportment.

Our consideration of school principals' responses at the end of the study to questions relating to various aspects of school organization and practice—admission to the school, the content of school report cards, the use of standardized tests, streaming practices, provision for remediation and referral, communication practices and curricula—indicate that the overall impact of the provision of a standardized testing program and information derived from that program was slight. Schools in which testing had been carried out and information had been provided to teachers on pupils' performance did not differ from control schools in their criteria for admission, in the kind of information they recorded on school report cards, in their record-keeping practices, or in the kind of information on pupil progress they reported to parents. Neither was there any difference between treatments in the numbers of schools that employed remedial teachers.

For the most part, tests appear to be seen as something peripheral to the formal working of the school, though this is not to say that tests and the information derived from them were not attended to at all in schools. Permanent records of test results and the passing-on of results from one teacher to another occurred in more than half the schools. However, our test results, with the exception of one school, were not entered on pupil-record cards. Four percent of schools that received test information did include information from other standardized tests (mainly a word-recognition test) on their pupil-record cards. Though the number of schools involved in this practice was small, the finding is not without interest. Some teachers apparently found that another type of standardized test was of more value than the ones used in the project. Familiarity with the test might have been a relevant factor here; the one they used was older than ours, which of course had been developed for the project and were being used for the first time. The scores provided by the test used on record cards (reading ages) were perhaps more readily interpreted—correctly or incorrectly—by teachers.

Test information was also used in communicating with parents, though not in the context of the formal structures of the school, such as on pupil progress reports or at formal parent-teacher meetings. Indeed, the information seems to have come more as a response to parents' initiatives in asking about the purpose of the testing program (28 percent of schools reported such requests) or in asking for results (25 percent of schools had such requests). Interestingly, schools in which testing took place but that received no results had many fewer requests for information, even about the purpose of the testing. The provision of test results or its anticipation somehow seems to have affected parents' initiative in asking about the tests.

The use of test results also appeared in communications with other schools, most frequently at the point of transfer to high school. About 14 percent of schools reported that they had been asked for or had provided test results to postprimary schools that were considering applicants.

In organizational decisions within the school, very little use was made of test information. There was a very slight, not statistically significant tendency for schools that had more than one class at a grade level and that received test information to report that pupils were assigned to classes on the basis of "general intelligence" or "general achievement," even though, with one exception, school principals stated that standardized tests were not used in the assignment.

We also have some evidence, again not statistically significant, that schools (2 percent) that received test information moved pupils from more-able to less-able classes and vice versa more than did schools that did not receive test information. Likewise, schools that received test information tended to have a higher retention rate. Although retention rates were low in all schools, ranging from 0.32 percent to 3.55 percent, Treatment 3 schools at grade 3 showed a significantly higher retention rate than did other treatment schools. Decisions about retention may be regarded as organizational ones for a school. They may, however, also be considered as decisions relating to individual pupils. In contrast with the practice of tracking, a decision not to promote a pupil tends to be made by an individual teacher after careful consideration of an individual's performance. Tests were apparently more frequently used by individual teachers in the context of individual decision making than they were by schools in the context of school-level organizational decisions.

We might expect to find evidence of the use of tests at the level of individual decision making in decisions to refer pupils with learning difficulties for special treatment. There was a slight, though nonsignificant, tendency for schools that had received test information to refer more pupils to an outside agency—available to most schools in the sample—than did schools that had not received information. Further, "low IQ," a concept perhaps obtained from or reinforced in the testing program, was given as a reason for referral in 3 percent of schools that had received test information, but not at all in schools that had not received test information. In 5 percent of schools that had received test information, referrals were made on the basis of test results. Furthermore, 3 percent of such schools reported that teachers had made special provision for pupils on the basis of their test results.

The final area for which we can report some effects is in the area of the school curriculum. Effects in this area, though potentially of great importance, are difficult to assess. Our data are limited to school principals' perceptions of those effects in schools in which test results had been provided. It was reported for 8.5 percent of schools that tests had affected school curricula—what was taught or how it was taught—while for 15 percent a shift in curricular emphasis as a result of the use of tests was reported. These figures, if they are a realistic assessment of the extent of curricular change, are not insignificant. Seemingly, curricular changes would be most likely to occur when relevant information is given directly to teachers. Thus, while the provision of information directly to teachers might have reduced the probability of obtaining effects relating to the organization and practice of the whole school, it might at the same time have increased the probability of obtaining effects within individual classrooms. For whatever reason, our results indicate that school-level effects of our standardized testing program, even though they were never very great, are less likely to occur in the practice and organization of the school as an institution than in the practice of individual teachers dealing with individual pupils, particularly pupils experiencing scholastic difficulty.

EFFECTS ON SCHOOL ACHIEVEMENT

In this section we examine the schoolwide performance of students on standardized tests of ability and achievement at the end of the study. We were interested in determining if the exposure of schools to a testing program and the provision of information on individual pupil performance would affect the actual test performance of pupils. For these analyses, individual data within schools were aggregated to the level of the school. Thus, we are using measures of the mean performance of schools in a treatment rather than the mean performance of all the individual pupils in a treatment. (We also carried out analyses of test performance at the pupil level. The results of these analyses, while they differ in detail, basically confirm the results of the school-level analyses. See Kellaghan, Madaus, and Airasian, 1980b.)

Only three treatment groups are included in the analyses: Treatment 1, in which there was no testing; Treatment 2, in which ability and achievement testing was carried out but results were not provided; and Treatment 3, in which ability and achievement testing was carried out and norm-referenced results were provided to teachers. We will deal in a separate section with the other groups, which in the preceding school-level analyses were subsumed under Treatments 4 and 5. Students in all treatment groups were tested on a variety of measures at the end of the final year of the study: a general ability test and tests of achievement in mathematics, Irish, and English. The performance of pupils in grades 2 through 6 were compared by treatment at the end of the intervention period (i.e., the second testing in the final year of the study).

Before carrying out analyses for the final year, we confirmed that there had been no significant differences between treatment groups—with the exception of Treatment 1, for which we had no test information—at the beginning of the study. Treatments 4 and 5 were included in these analyses.

There were three steps in the analysis of data obtained from the testing at the end of the study. First, a multivariate analysis of variance (MANOVA) was carried out to test the hypothesis of overall differences between groups on the variables for which measures were obtained. When the MANOVA yielded a significant lambda value, univariate analyses of variance were carried out for each variable. If these analyses yielded significant F-values, we then performed Scheffé post-hoc analyses to examine the significance of differences between pairs of treatments. We also carried out a discriminant function analysis if a MANOVA yielded a significant lambda value. The position of treatment groups on the functions was determined, and the significance of differences between group centroids was tested. Some schools were lost from these analyses because they had not taken one or more of the tests in a battery. One school was lost in this way at each of grades 2, 3, and 4; there was no loss at grades 5 or 6.

These analyses were directed to two questions: First, does testing and the provision of information about pupil performance to teachers affect pupils' subsequent scores on ability tests? And second, does testing and the provision of information about pupil performance to teachers affect pupils' subsequent scores on achievement tests? A comparison of the performance of the three treatment groups should throw light on these questions. If the nontested group (Treatment 1) differs in performance from the group that was tested and received no information (Treatment 2), the difference should be attributable to experience with testing. If the performance of the group that was tested and did not receive test information (Treatment 2) differs from that of the group that was tested and received test information (Treatment 3), the difference should be attributable to the receipt of test information. If we assume that practice on tests improves performance and if we further assume that knowledge of results adds a further increment to test performance, we would expect the highest level of performance from the group that tested and received information, the next highest from the group that only tested, and the lowest level from the group in which no testing was carried out (Treatment 3 > Treatment 2 > Treatment 1).

Our results do not conform to this simple pattern. At the second grade, we found no significant differences between treatments (Table 3.1). Thus, at this level neither the experience of testing nor the availability of test results had an impact on pupils' test performance at the end of the school year. We should point out here that, as the pupils in Treatments 2 and 3 had entered the testing program in the final year of the study, their exposure to testing was limited to one occasion prior to the final testing. Thus, we might attribute the lack of effects at this grade level to the relative inexperience of all pupils with testing, although even here pupils in Treatments 2 and 3 had more experience with tests than did pupils in Treatment 1.

At all other grade levels, we found significant differences between treatment groups. We found differences between the nontested group (Treatment 1) and the tested group that did not receive information (Treatment 2)—our index of the effects of practice— at grades 4 and 6 on the multivariate tests of significance (Tables 3.5 and 3.9). While univariate tests did not yield statistically significant results, at these grades the nontested group generally tended to obtain the highest mean scores on the achievement tests (Tables 3.4 and 3.8). This is surprising, given that the nontested group was being administered tests for the first time at the end of the study, while by this time pupils in the tested no-information group had all taken tests before; the higher the grade level, the more frequent and varied had been the pupils' test experience. Such experience, however, was not translated into all-round superior test performance.

Differences between the two groups that were tested, one of which received test information (Treatment 3) and the other not (Treatment 2), should be due to the receipt of such information. We found no significant differences at any grade level between these two treatment groups (Tables 3.1 to 3.9). From this evidence we must conclude that the availability of test information to teachers did not affect students' scores on either tests of ability or on tests of achievement.

Before finally concluding that test information did not play a role in contributing to differences between groups, we should note that while Treatment 2 was planned as a no-information group, in practice teachers most likely obtained some information on pupils' levels of test ability and achievement through their observations of pupils taking the tests (see Kellaghan, Madaus, and Airasian, 1979). Further, in a few cases teachers scored tests before returning them for processing. Thus, while these teachers did not receive norm-referenced information on their pupils' performance, they did have access to some information on pupil test performance that was not available to teachers in the nontesting group. While the possibility that such information accounted for some of the results we obtained cannot be ruled out, it is not without interest that the effects of such information could not be clearly distinguished from the effects of norm-referenced information in our findings. This interpretation, of course, raises the problem of

Table 3.1. Final School Test Performance by Treatment, Second Grade

Test	Treatment 1 (N = 31)		Treatment 2 (N = 21)		Treatment 3 (N = 29)	
	M	S.D.	M	S.D.	M	S.D.
Otis-Lennon	45.73	6.09	48.60	5.26	48.83	5.13
Mathematics	74.12	9.30	74.82	8.69	74.21	8.65
English reading	70.10	8.46	70.27	8.20	70.69	8.66

Table 3.2. Final School Test Performance by Treatment, Third Grade (df = 2,81)

Test	Treatment 1 (N = 32)		Treatment 2 (N = 22)		Treatment 3 (N = 30)		F	p
	M	S.D.	M	S.D.	M	S.D.		
Otis-Lennon	54.78	5.27	55.69	4.58	55.21	5.30	0.21	NS
Mathematics	72.56	9.14	67.95	9.23	66.08	10.48	3.67	$<.05$*
Irish reading	42.60	10.44	41.39	9.19	35.80	8.07	4.53	$<.05$*
Irish usage	17.06	2.38	16.76	2.46	15.64	1.92	3.32	$<.05$
Irish spelling	20.06	4.18	20.09	4.64	17.72	4.47	2.75	NS
English reading	47.63	6.72	46.66	6.90	42.72	7.01	4.29	$<.05$*
English capitalization/ punctuation	19.98	3.41	20.38	3.27	18.52	2.51	2.77	NS
English usage	14.98	1.29	15.22	1.47	14.40	1.39	2.51	NS
English spelling	30.69	3.71	31.13	2.68	29.18	3.28	2.64	NS

Note: Lambda value of MANOVA = .667 ($p < .05$; df = 18).

*In Scheffé contrasts, Treatment 1 schools superior to Treatment 3 schools ($p < .05$).

Table 3.3. Discriminant Function Coefficients for Treatments 1, 2, and 3: Loadings for Grade 3

Variable	Weight
English reading	1.08
Mathematics	.88
Irish reading	.37
Irish usage	.27
English spelling	− .05
English capitalization/ punctuation	− .13
Irish spelling	− .39
English usage	− .70
Otis-Lennon	−1.08

Group	Centroid*
Treatment 1	.73
Treatment 2	− .27
Treatment 3	− .58

Note: One significant discriminant function accounts for 24.05 percent of total variance.
*Only centroids for Treatments 1 and 3 differ significantly (p = .01).

controlling what goes on in treatments in an experimental study of the kind we carried out. On paper, one can specify certain conditions, such as testing or not testing, information or no information, and go on to make predictions about the relative effects of these conditions. In practice, events may intervene to alter the conditions.

Most significant differences occurred between the nontested group (Treatment 1) and the group that had received test information (Treatment 3). We found these differences at all grade levels except the second in the multivariate analyses. Univariate analyses yielded significant differences only at the third and fifth grades. At grade 3 the nontested group was superior to the tested group with information on tests of mathematical computation, English reading, and Irish reading (Table 3.2). At grade 5 the tested group with information was superior to the nontested group on the test of ability (Table 3.6).

These differences should be attributable, in the light of our experimental treatments, to a combination of experience with testing and the availability of information. We have already seen that test experience seems to contribute more, even if only slightly, to differential test performance than does availability of test information. However, the combination of test experience and test information seems more potent than either condition on its own. We say this because most significant differences occurred between the nontested group and

Table 3.4. Final School Test Performance by Treatment, Fourth Grade (df = 2,83)

Test	Treatment 1 (N = 31)		Treatment 2 (N = 23)		Treatment 3 (N = 32)		F	p
	M	S.D.	M	S.D.	M	S.D.		
Drumcondra Verbal								
Reasoning	55.41	9.04	55.20	7.88	55.93	6.86	0.06	NS
Mathematics	86.02	7.52	81.84	9.19	81.09	8.88	2.98	NS
Irish reading	47.92	9.05	44.56	9.55	43.36	8.91	2.07	NS
Irish usage	18.15	2.38	17.23	2.30	17.15	2.12	1.84	NS
Irish spelling	23.24	3.94	21.53	4.55	21.24	3.89	2.11	NS
English reading	55.56	4.88	53.32	6.70	53.72	4.72	1.43	NS
English capitalization/ punctuation	22.06	2.80	22.42	2.74	21.81	2.59	0.34	NS
English grammar	16.20	1.16	16.06	1.28	16.11	1.04	0.11	NS
English spelling	34.36	2.78	33.79	3.00	32.90	2.68	2.15	NS

Note: Lambda value of MANOVA = .630 (p < .01; df = 18).

Table 3.5. Discriminant Function Coefficients for Treatments 1, 2, and 3: Loadings for Grade 4

Variable	Weight
English reading	1.30
Mathematics	.84
Irish reading	.54
English spelling	.44
Irish usage	.06
Irish spelling	− .27
English capitalization/ punctuation	− .65
English usage	− .94
Drumcondra Verbal Reasoning	−1.06

Group	Centroid*
Treatment 1	.76
Treatment 2	− .33
Treatment 3	− .50

Note: One significant discriminant function accounts for 23.06 percent of total variance. *Centroid for Treatment 1 differs significantly from centroids for both Treatments 2 and 3 (p < .05 in both cases).

the group that tested and received information. Furthermore, differences were found for individual tests only in these comparisons. Thus, test performance is to some extent a function of intensity of treatment.

The precise differences in performance between treatment groups came as something of a surprise, insofar as they did not consistently confirm our hypothesis that intensity of treatment would be accompanied by higher levels of test performance. On practically all univariate tests, differences between treatment groups were not significant. However, there was a general tendency evident in the multivariate analyses for the performance of the nontested group to differ from that of the tested group that had received information and, less frequently, from that of the tested group that had not received information. The difference was exhibited on a function that was weighted on one end by performance on tests of traditional achievement (reading and mathematics) and on the other by performance on tests of ability (Otis-Lennon and DVRT) and tests of achievement that employ a rather complicated format (language usage, capitalization, and punctuation).

The performance of the information group tended to weigh on the ability end of the function. We see the tendency for this group to perform better than the nontested group on ability in the significant difference between these

Table 3.6. Final School Test Performance by Treatment, Fifth Grade (df = 2,84)

Test	Treatment 1 (N = 32)		Treatment 2 (N = 23)		Treatment 3 (N = 32)		F	p
	M	S.D.	M	S.D.	M	S.D.		
Drumcondra Verbal								
Reasoning	61.76	8.82	67.92	10.47	68.75	8.65	5.33	< .01*
Mathematics	65.83	9.33	66.91	10.39	65.13	9.13	.23	NS
Irish reading	41.57	10.13	41.98	8.44	41.00	9.54	.07	NS
Irish usage	22.57	2.79	22.62	2.41	22.41	3.30	.04	NS
Irish spelling	20.45	3.29	20.00	3.59	19.36	3.76	.76	NS
English reading	57.61	7.31	57.43	8.04	58.03	6.38	.05	NS
English capitalization/								
punctuation	23.18	2.65	23.90	3.17	24.27	2.59	1.27	NS
English grammar	24.45	2.66	24.51	2.84	24.94	2.67	.30	NS
English spelling	37.35	3.73	37.90	3.29	37.09	2.87	.40	NS

Note: Lambda value of MANOVA = .581 (p < .001; df = 18).

*In Scheffé contrasts, Treatment 3 schools superior to Treatment 1 schools (p < .01).

Table 3.7. Discriminant Function Coefficients for Treatments 1, 2, and 3: Loadings for Grade 5

Variable	Weight
English reading	.99
Mathematics	.91
Irish spelling	.37
English usage	.18
English spelling	.10
Irish reading	− .05
Irish usage	− .27
English capitalization/ punctuation	− .68
Drumcondra Verbal Reasoning	−1.79

Group	Centroid*
Treatment 1	.98
Treatment 2	− .35
Treatment 3	− .73

Note: One significant discriminant function accounts for 35.71 percent of total variance.
*Centroid for Treatment 1 differs significantly from centroid for Treatment 3 ($p < .001$).

two groups that was found at grade 5, as well as the consistent, if not significant, trend at other grade levels. The performance of the nontested group, on the other hand, tended to weigh on the achievement end of the function. Although differences on the achievement tests between this group and the group that had tested and received information were statistically significant in univariate analyses only at one grade level (grade 3), the performance of the nontested group tended to be superior at all grade levels.

These findings might be taken as evidence that testing and the provision of test information lead to high levels of ability and low levels of achievement in students. The fact that our findings differ for different kinds of tests, however, should cause us to pause before accepting such a conclusion. One explanation that must be considered is that the experiment produced a kind of reaction in the nontested group that it did not produce in the tested one. Teachers and pupils in the control schools may have prepared themselves for their first testing (which was the final testing for other groups) and expended effort in a way that schools that had had four years of testing did not. Certainly, the testing should have created no anxieties for the schools that had become accustomed to the testing program. Perhaps teachers and pupils had even lost interest in it. If the schools being tested for the first time had made an extra effort, while the other schools were at best not concerned and at worst had lost interest, then the

Table 3.8. Final School Test Performance by Treatment, Sixth Grade (df = 2,85)

Test	Treatment 1 (N = 31)		Treatment 2 (N = 24)		Treatment 3 (N = 33)		F	p
	M	S.D.	M	S.D.	M	S.D.		
Drumcondra Verbal								
Reasoning	74.01	7.37	79.16	7.65	76.22	8.08	3.00	NS
Mathematics	77.78	8.56	76.43	10.26	75.41	11.46	.43	NS
Irish reading	48.72	9.44	48.84	9.09	45.11	10.12	1.50	NS
Irish usage	24.81	2.66	24.33	2.69	23.45	3.07	1.90	NS
Irish spelling	21.95	3.39	22.26	3.69	20.88	4.25	1.08	NS
English reading	64.82	4.97	64.44	5.60	62.89	6.27	1.04	NS
English capitalization/ punctuation	25.18	2.24	25.70	2.62	25.75	2.54	.51	NS
English grammar	27.07	2.85	27.14	2.86	26.67	2.95	.23	NS
English spelling	40.13	3.17	40.04	3.03	39.16	2.84	.99	NS

Note: Lambda value of MANOVA = .522 (p < .001; df = 18).

Table 3.9. Discriminant Function Coefficients for Treatments 1, 2, and 3: Loadings for Grade 6

Variable	Weight
English reading	1.98
Irish usage	.94
Mathematics	.81
English spelling	− .04
Irish reading	− .07
Irish spelling	− .41
English usage	− .64
English capitalization/ punctuation	−1.01
Drumcondra Verbal Reasoning	−1.65

Group	Centroid*
Treatment 1	1.15
Treatment 2	− .61
Treatment 3	− .64

Note: One significant discriminant function accounts for 41.09 percent of total variance.
*Centroid for Treatment 1 differs significantly from centroids for Treatments 2 ($p < .01$) and 3 ($p < .001$).

appearance in our findings of what has been called a "John Henry effect"— a reactive effect that may occur in control groups as a Hawthorne effect may occur in experimental groups (Anderson, Ball, Murphy, and Associates, 1976) —should not be too surprising.

The effect, however, was confined to achievement tests and did not extend to ability tests. Perhaps teachers were more concerned with their students' achievement test performance because they thought that such performance would reflect more on them than would the students' ability test performance. Or "naive" pupils in the nontested group, when faced with tests for the first time, may have been more easily able to cope with the achievement tests (in which the content, if not the format, of the test would be relatively familiar) than with the ability tests (in which both content and format would be unfamiliar). This interpretation receives some support from the finding that achievement tests that had complicated formats seemed to fall close to the ability tests on the function that discriminated between the nontested group and the group that had been tested and received information.

In conclusion, our answers to our original questions regarding the impact of testing and the provision of test information to teachers turn out to be not simple ones. We do not find that level of test performance increases linearly with intensity of treatment. While we find some evidence that performance is uniquely affected by practice, we do not find that it is uniquely affected by information. A combination of practice and information seems to have the strongest impact.

DISTRIBUTION OF ABILITY, ACHIEVEMENT, AND SOCIOECONOMIC BACKGROUND

One obvious way in which objective-test information might be put to use is in the formation of groups within schools. If a school is large enough to have more than one class at any grade level and if test scores are used to divide students at the same level into separate classes, then the variability within classes and between classes in ability, achievement, or social class may be affected. If we accept the view that test results are one of the bases on which pupils are stratified in schools, we would expect, on the one hand, that classes would become internally more homogeneous in terms of ability and achievement when test results are available. On the other hand, classes with respect to each other would become more heterogeneous in terms of ability and achievement (i.e., the class means would become more widely dispersed). The effect of such a use of test results on social-class composition might be quite different; homogenization within classes on a variable such as ability might have the effect of redistributing other characteristics, such as social class, across classes. If this were the case, we might expect classes to become more heterogeneous internally and more homogeneous with respect to each other in terms of social class.

We examined data on classes within schools to determine if the groups that did not receive test information (Treatments 1 and 2) differed from the group in which teachers received norm-referenced information on pupils' performance on standardized tests of ability and attainment (Treatment 3) in the distribution of ability, attainment, and social class over classes. A measure of the degree to which pupils are grouped together with respect to a given characteristic has been developed by Beaton (1980). The measure is an index of homogeneous classroom assignment (i.e., of the extent to which pupils in a class are quite alike with respect to a characteristic; in other words, the extent to which the variance among classroom means is large). The index is expressed in the following formula:

$$d^2 = \frac{\Sigma g \, Ng \, (\overline{Y}g - \overline{Y}t)^2}{S_t^2},$$

where

Ng = number of pupils in class g;
$\overline{Yg}$ = mean of class g on variable y;
Yt = mean of all pupils to be assigned to classes on variable y;
S_t^2 = variance of all pupils to be assigned to classes on variable y.

For the analyses pupils were first grouped into classes within schools. Only schools that had more than one class at a grade level could be included. At each of three grade levels—2, 4, and 6—test scores and socioeconomic ratings were aggregated to the level of school and to the level of class. From these aggregations we calculated the number of pupils and the mean and the variance on each variable for each school and each class.

The test scores selected for analysis were those for ability, mathematics, and English reading. Measures of socioeconomic class based on six categories of ratings were also used. Socioeconomic class was coded as 1 for professional/ managerial, 2 for white collar, 3 for farmers of fifty acres or more, 4 for unskilled manual workers, 5 for farmers of less than fifty acres, and 6 for unskilled workers. Pupils were excluded from analyses when information on their socioeconomic class was missing or was not classifiable into one of the above categories.

We then computed the index d^2 for each of the four variables for schools in Treatments 1, 2, and 3. Following Beaton's procedure, we converted these values to Z-scores using a table of normal curve functions. Two analyses were carried out. In the first we compared the Z-scores for the three test variables across treatment groups, using multivariate analysis of variance; we conducted separate analyses for each grade level. If the test scores had been used to group pupils of similar ability and achievement into homogeneous classes, the Z-score indices of homogenization should be higher in Treatment 3 than in Treatments 1 and 2. In the second analysis we compared the Z-scores for social class across treatment groups, using one-way analysis of variance; again we conducted separate analyses for each grade level. We would expect the pattern of social class distribution to differ from that for test scores, predicting that the effect of using test results would be reflected in Z-score indices of homogenization that would be higher in Treatments 1 and 2 than in Treatment 3.

The results of the multivariate analyses of variance for the three test score indices among the three treatments indicated that there was no significant difference between treatments at any of the three grade levels (Tables 3.10 to 3.12). There is, therefore, no evidence of greater homogeneity within classes in Treatment 3 schools on the characteristics measured by the mathematics, English reading, or ability tests. On the contrary, the largest means, and therefore the greatest degree of homogeneity of classes, appeared in Treatment 1 schools in

Table 3.10. Means and Standard Deviations of Z-Score Indices of Classroom Homogeneity across Treatments, Grade 2

	Treatment 1			Treatment 2			Treatment 3		
Variable	*N*	*M*	*S.D.*	*N*	*M*	*S.D.*	*N*	*M*	*S.D.*
Mathematics	7	2.54	.98	6	1.88	1.45	8	1.56	.77
English reading	7	1.03	1.38	6	.95	1.52	8	1.15	1.44
Otis-Lennon	7	1.50	1.07	6	1.89	.96	8	.89	1.55
SES	4	.07	.51	3	.32	1.58	7	-.02	1.66

Table 3.11. Means and Standard Deviations of Z-Score Indices of Classroom Homogeneity across Treatments, Grade 4

Variable	Treatment 1			Treatment 2			Treatment 3		
	N	M	S.D.	N	M	S.D.	N	M	S.D.
Mathematics	8	1.87	1.86	6	1.22	1.06	11	1.39	1.43
English reading	8	1.51	1.15	6	.35	1.59	11	1.42	1.92
Drumcondra Verbal Reasoning	8	1.83	1.46	6	1.55	.95	11	1.58	1.20
SES	7	1.01	1.29	7	-.27	1.82	13	.47	1.46

Table 3.12. Means and Standard Deviations of Z-Score Indices of Classroom Homogeneity across Treatments, Grade 6

	Treatment 1			Treatment 2			Treatment 3		
Variable	N	M	S.D.	N	M	S.D.	N	M	S.D.
Mathematics	10	2.36	1.10	8	1.76	1.36	10	1.15	1.56
English reading	10	2.01	1.33	8	.35	1.60	10	.91	2.03
Drumcondra Verbal									
Reasoning	10	1.94	1.54	8	1.04	1.06	10	1.34	1.47
SES	9	.14	1.09	7	.05	.79	9	-.25	1.49

seven of the nine comparisons (mathematics at grade 2 and all three test variables at grades 4 and 6), although none of these differences is statistically significant. Likewise, the univariate analyses of variance for socioeconomic status revealed no significant difference in the degree of homogeneity of classes with respect to social-class composition across treatments. However, the Z for socioeconomic status is always smaller (albeit not significantly) for Treatment 3 than for Treatment 2.

Thus, our hypotheses regarding the effects of test information on the assignment of pupils within schools were not substantiated by our analyses. Schools that had test information did not have classes with greater homogeneity in ability and achievement or greater heterogeneity in socioeconomic class than did schools without such information. If anything, the trend of our findings was in the opposite direction.

CONCLUSION

Our data on the effects of standardized testing at the level of the school indicate that such testing did not have a great deal of impact. As far as school organization and practices were concerned, the availability of test information did not affect to any extent the admission practices of the school, the content of school report cards, provision for the remediation or referral of pupils with learning difficulties, or the communication practices of the school. Principal teachers reported that tests were rarely used in a decision to assign pupils to homogeneous ability or attainment groups. By and large the principals' reports were corroborated in an analysis of the variance in test scores of pupils within classes in schools that had more than one class at a grade level. We did find slight evidence of a higher retention rate in one grade in schools that had received norm-referenced information on the ability and attainment test performance of their pupils. While our findings provide evidence of some slight, perhaps incipient, tendency for test results to affect some grouping practices within schools, the tendency is hardly sufficient to conclude that test information has much to do with grouping in schools.

School principals were more likely to report effects within classrooms than in the context of the organization of the total school. One in eight reported that tests had affected what was taught in classes and how it was presented, while almost a quarter reported a shift in curricular emphasis as a result of experience with tests. Though the precise amount of change that testing might have effected in any school is not known, the number of schools involved in some change is not inconsiderable. Some schools reported making referrals of pupils with learning difficulties and making special provision for such pupils on the basis of test results.

The fact that test results, when used, were employed more within the class than in the context of the organization of the school should perhaps not be surprising, given that in our project the teacher was the key individual in the testing program. Testing was carried out by the teacher, and test information was returned to individual teachers. Whether more powerful effects at the school level would have been obtained if results had been returned to principal teachers is, of course, a moot question.

The relationship between the availability of test information and student performance on standardized tests was complex and inconsistent across grades and types of test. There were differences between the group that had practice in testing over a number of years and the group that had no practice. But the effect was not as one might have expected—that is, a superior performance on achievement tests on the part of the group with practice. There were also differences between the group with testing experience and test information and the group with no experience of testing, but these were not consistent for type of test. The experienced group tended to perform better on ability tests but less well on achievement tests than the group that was having its first experience of testing. Nothing in our findings would lead one to believe that testing leads to higher levels of achievement. Whether our results can be interpreted as indicating that testing leads to lower levels of achievement depends on what weight one gives to the differential performance of the groups with varying experience of testing on the ability and achievement tests and to the possible reactivity of the experimental situation from which our findings are derived.

4 EFFECTS OF TESTING ON TEACHERS

Teachers play a central role in most school standardized testing programs. They administer the tests, and they receive the results of their pupils' performance. Thus their reactions to tests and to test results should be an important element in producing at least some of the effects that have been attributed to standardized testing. If testing affects pupils, presumably the effects often occur because teachers use test results in some way. Teachers may communicate test information directly to students or parents; they may use it as a basis for grouping students or for selecting subject matter to be emphasized in their teaching; or the information may affect their perceptions of and reactions to students. In any of these cases, the teachers' reactions to and use of information derived from testing may be the key element in producing effects on students' self-confidence, self-concept, or scholastic achievement.

In this chapter we examine teachers' reactions to standardized tests, including not only information on their reported use of test information but also their general attitudes toward and beliefs about standardized testing as a method of evaluation. Presumably, the ways in which test information is used in classrooms and the consequent effect that these uses have on pupils, curriculum, and classroom climate will, to some extent, be a function of the favorableness of teachers' attitudes toward tests. If teachers perceive standardized tests and the constructs measured by them to be inaccurate, biased, unstable, or unimportant, they probably will be less likely to utilize test results in a practical way than if they perceive tests in a more favorable light. Even in those cases where teachers do have favorable perceptions, we should consider the weight teachers say they accord to test information relative to other forms of evidence about pupils (e.g., observations, prior teacher recommendations, classroom tests) before we suggest a strong relationship between standardized testing and various classroom practices.

The chapter is divided into three main sections. The first provides a summary of the effects that testing and the provision of test information had on teachers' attitudes toward and beliefs about standardized tests. We elicited teachers' perceptions of the accuracy of standardized tests, the constructs measured by intelligence tests, and the relevance and effects of standardized testing; we also asked them to express opinions about the uses of test information and to indicate their attitudes toward general educational issues. We can make inferences about the effects of testing and of test information by comparing the responses of teachers in three groups: those who had tested and received norm-referenced results (Treatment 3), those who had tested but had not received results (Treatment 2), and those who had not tested at all (Treatment 1). Data on teachers' attitudes and beliefs about tests are available from two points in time: early in the study and at its conclusion.

In the second section of the chapter, we examine teachers' perceptions of the process of testing—their preparations for it and pupils' reactions to the tests—as well as their perceptions of consequences of testing and possible biases in tests. Obviously, the data for this section had to be confined to teachers in treatments in which tests had been administered—Treatments 2 and 3. Information for this section was obtained in the final year of the study.

In the third section we examine teachers' perceptions of the usefulness of tests and their reported uses of test information. Teachers were asked questions about the usefulness of the test information they obtained for making decisions about pupils, the influence of the test results on decisions they made about grouping and instructional content, and the dissemination of test results. Questions about the use of test results obviously had to be confined to teachers who had received results—that is, teachers in Treatment 3. However, we were able to use comparative data for most of these analyses, since teachers in Treatment 3 had answered many of the questions in the second year of the study as well as in its final fourth year. For a few questions we did not have data from the second year and so had no comparative data. We also obtained global ratings of teachers' use of tests, made by the teachers themselves and by outside observers. When numbers permitted, teachers' responses were stratified by teacher gender and the location (urban, town, or rural) of the school in which the teacher taught to allow us to examine possible effects associated with these factors.

All the data for the present chapter were collected in questionnaires, which were administered to teachers. A total of five teacher questionnaires was administered during the life of the study (see Chapter 2).

TEACHERS' ATTITUDES, BELIEFS, AND BEHAVIOR RELATING TO STANDARDIZED TESTS

In this section we compare teachers' attitudes and beliefs about standardized tests and test information across three treatment groups: the no-testing group (Treatment 1), the testing—no-information group (Treatment 2), and the testing—norm-referenced information group (Treatment 3). The data bases for the analyses are teachers' responses to two sets of questionnaires. In one set a questionnaire was administered in the first year of the study (Teacher Questionnaire I) before test results were returned and readministered in the final year (Teacher Questionnaire I-revised). A sample of 252 teachers (Treatment 1: 93; Treatment 2: 67; Treatment 3: 92) responded on both occasions. In the second set a questionnaire was administered at the start of the second year of the study (Teacher Questionnaire II), and a parallel and extended version of the questionnaire (Teacher Questionnaire V) was administered in the last year. A sample of 259 teachers (Treatment 1: 88; Treatment 2: 77; Treatment 3: 94) responded on both occasions. Larger numbers of teachers responded on each occasion on which one of these questionnaires was administered. However, for the present analyses we selected matched samples of teachers who had responded twice to parallel questionnaires. The actual number of teachers in each treatment who responded to particular items on the questionnaires varied from the figures provided above. However, rarely did the number of respondents within a treatment vary by more than ten from these figures.

We performed separate analyses of variance for each item, on both the questionnaire data gathered early in the study (year 1 or year 2) and the questionnaire data gathered in the last year of the study. For items that evidenced a statistically significant treatment difference early in the study, we performed analyses of covariance in which adjustments were made for initial treatment differences. When a statistically significant difference was observed, we carried out Scheffé post-hoc comparisons among treatment means. In addition to reporting the results of the various significance tests in terms of an F-value and the associated probability level, we calculated an estimate of R^2 or ω^2 (in the case of two-group comparisons) for each significance test. These indices provide information about the proportion of the total variance that is associated with between-treatment differences and thereby indicate the magnitude of the effect associated with each significance test.

In addition to the primary analyses that compared the responses of teachers in the three treatment groups, analyses of data by teacher gender and geographical location of school were performed. In the first set of these analyses, teachers within treatments were stratified by gender and a 2 (gender) by 3 (treatment) analysis of variance was carried out. In the second set of analyses, teachers were stratified within treatments according to the location of the school in which they taught—city, town, or rural—and a 3 (location) by 3 (treatment) analysis of variance was performed. When a statistically significant gender or location main effect was observed for the responses obtained early in the study, we performed an analysis of covariance on the final-year data. We report the results of these secondary analyses only if they were statistically significant.

Teachers' Perceptions of the Accuracy of Standardized Tests

A major rationale for administering standardized tests in schools is that the results provide teachers with information that helps them to evaluate their pupils more accurately and to guide their instructional decisions. The extent to which test results are used for these and other purposes should, it seems, be a function of teachers' perceptions of the accuracy of the information provided by the tests.

In the first and last years of the study, teachers were asked to judge the accuracy in measuring a pupil's scholastic ability of (1) intelligence tests, (2) standardized attainment tests, (3) the Irish Leaving Certificate public examination, and (4) classroom exams. Judgments were based on a 5-point scale: "very accurate" (coded 5), "accurate" (4), "uncertain" (3), "inaccurate" (2), and "very inaccurate" (1). At the beginning of the study, teachers in all treatments had generally favorable perceptions of the accuracy of standardized intelligence and attainment tests (Table 4.1). Over 65 percent of teachers in each treatment judged intelligence tests to be accurate or very accurate, while over 55 percent gave a similar rating to attainment tests. Less than 15 percent in each treatment judged intelligence or attainment tests to be inaccurate or very inaccurate in measuring a pupil's scholastic ability. The treatment means summarize teachers' generally positive judgments; any mean greater than 3.0 indicates that teachers on average perceived the tests to be more accurate than inaccurate. As might be expected, in light of the lack of teachers' prior exposure to such tests, comparatively large percentages of teachers responded that they were "uncertain" about the accuracy of standardized tests as measures of a pupil's scholastic ability. This was particularly true for the ratings of attainment tests, for which over one-quarter of the teachers in all treatments selected the "uncertain" response.

Table 4.1. Perceived Accuracy of Four Types of Tests or Examinations in Measuring a Pupil's Scholastic Ability, by Treatment

	Year	Treatment	N	Very Accurate	Accurate	Uncertain	Inaccurate	Very Inaccurate	M	S.D.	F	p	R^2
Intelligence tests	1	1	93	8.6	62.4	16.1	10.8	2.2	3.64	.87	3.27	.04	.026
		2	67	17.9	61.2	11.9	9.0	0.0	3.88	.81			
		3	92	4.3	60.9	22.8	7.6	4.3	3.53	.87			
	4	1	90	4.4	57.8	23.3	13.3	1.1	3.51	.82	6.82	.00	.052
		2	68	13.2	69.1	10.3	7.4	0.0	3.88	.72			
		3	95	13.7	69.5	8.4	8.4	0.0	3.88	.74			
Standardized attainment tests	1	1	90	10.0	53.3	26.7	8.9	1.1	3.62	.83	.82	.44	.007
		2	69	7.2	58.0	29.0	5.8	0.0	3.67	.70			
		3	90	7.8	50.0	28.9	12.2	1.1	3.51	.85			
	4	1	90	7.8	46.7	34.4	10.0	1.1	3.50	.82	5.27	.01	.041
		2	68	7.4	66.2	23.5	2.9	0.0	3.78	.62			
		3	92	9.8	72.8	9.8	6.5	1.1	3.84	.73			

Table 4.1. (Continued)

	Year	Treatment	N	Very Accurate	Accurate	Uncertain	Inaccurate	Very Inaccurate	M	S.D.	F	p	R^2
Leaving certificate exam	1	1	92	5.4	45.7	15.2	27.2	6.5	3.16	1.09	1.36	.26	.001
		2	67	6.0	50.7	19.4	22.4	1.5	3.37	.95			
		3	91	2.2	46.2	19.8	25.3	6.6	3.11	1.03			
	4	1	92	2.2	64.1	10.9	18.5	4.3	3.41	.96	.27	.77	.000
		2	69	5.8	50.7	20.3	20.3	2.9	3.36	.97			
		3	89	9.0	46.1	16.9	22.5	5.6	3.30	1.09			
Classroom exams	1	1	93	19.4	59.1	5.4	16.1	0.0	3.81	.93	.71	.49	.006
		2	67	16.4	70.1	7.5	4.5	1.5	3.96	.75			
		3	92	12.0	69.6	7.6	8.7	2.2	3.80	.84			
	4	1	94	17.0	68.1	4.3	9.6	1.1	3.90	.83	.06	.95	.000
		2	69	10.1	79.7	5.8	2.9	1.4	3.94	.64			
		3	93	10.8	75.3	9.7	3.2	1.1	3.91	.65			

Analyses carried out on the final year means for the two items indicate statistically significant treatment differences. Teachers in the test-information group (Treatment 3) perceived intelligence tests as more accurate than did teachers in the control groups (Treatments 1 and 2). Teachers in the test-information group also perceived attainment tests as more accurate than did teachers in Treatment 2. The percentages of variance associated with these significant effects were 5.2 and 4.1, respectively.

Teachers' own classroom exams were judged to be the most accurate measures of a pupil's scholastic ability by teachers in all treatments. In both years nearly 80 percent or more of the teachers in each treatment judged these exams to be accurate or very accurate indicators of scholastic ability. The treatment means on the item in the first year were all 3.80 or higher; in the fourth year they were 3.90 or higher. There were no significant differences between treatments on the item. Both at the beginning and at the end of the study, the Leaving Certificate examinations were perceived to be the least accurate measures of a student's scholastic ability.

We conducted analyses to ascertain changes over time in the perceived accuracy of one type of information relative to another (e.g., whether the perceived accuracy of intelligence tests changed relative to the perceived accuracy of teachers' classroom exams). To carry out these analyses, we created variables that expressed the change in pairwise accuracy judgments. For example, we examined the change in the perceived accuracy of intelligence tests relative to classroom exams by creating a difference variable (D) in the following form:

$$D = \left[\binom{\text{intelligence test}}{\text{accuracy, year 4}} - \binom{\text{classroom exam}}{\text{accuracy, year 4}}\right] - \left[\binom{\text{intelligence test}}{\text{accuracy, year 1}} - \binom{\text{classroom exam}}{\text{accuracy, year 1}}\right].$$

A positive value on this variable indicates that, from year 1 to year 4, intelligence tests gained in perceived accuracy relative to classroom exams. A negative value indicates that the perceived accuracy of intelligence tests diminished over time relative to that of classroom exams.

Variables were created for three pairwise comparisons: intelligence tests with classroom exams, standardized attainment tests with classroom exams, and intelligence tests with standardized attainment tests. We calculated the mean for each treatment on each of the three variables (Table 4.2), and carried out separate, one-way analyses of variance. We found significant treatment differences for the comparisons between intelligence tests and classroom exams and between standardized attainment tests and classroom exams, but not for the comparison between intelligence and standardized attainment tests. For both indices for which we recorded a significant difference, the increase in perceived accuracy for intelligence and attainment tests relative to classroom exams was greatest

Table 4.2. Relative Perceived Accuracy of Intelligence Tests, Standardized Attainment Tests, and Classroom Exams, by Treatment

Comparison	Treatment	N	M	S.D.	F	p
Intelligence tests—classroom exams	1	87	-.23	1.33	3.674	.027
	2	65	.05	1.19		
	3	89	.28	1.21		
Standardized attainment tests—classroom exams	1	85	-.22	1.30	3.330	.038
	2	67	.12	1.09		
	3	86	.26	1.30		
Intelligence tests—standardized attainment tests	1	85	0.00	1.23	.553	.576
	2	65	-.14	1.13		
	3	87	.07	1.26		

in Treatment 3, second greatest in Treatment 2, and least in Treatment 1. Post-hoc comparisons indicated that Treatment 1 teachers were significantly different from Treatment 3 teachers. Thus, over time, teachers who administered standardized intelligence and attainment tests and received test results evidenced an increase in their perceptions of the accuracy of such tests relative to their own classroom exams.

Teachers' Perceptions of the Constructs Measured by Intelligence Tests

In addition to perceptions about the accuracy of the information provided by standardized tests, the use of test results in the classroom would also seem to depend, at least to some degree, on what teachers believe the tests measure. Regardless of how accurate test information may be perceived to be, if the constructs underlying the tests are considered to be irrelevant or unimportant to classroom instruction or to the tasks of the school, the tests are unlikely to have a significant impact on practice. This issue was of particular interest. Because of teachers' lack of exposure to intelligence tests prior to the start of the study, examining how their understanding and perceptions were influenced by exposure to such tests was possible. To obtain information about the constructs that teachers believed intelligence tests measured, two questions were asked early in the study and again in the final year.

Responses to the question, "Do you think that the kind of intelligence measured by intelligence tests matters much in life?" were spread across five response options: "yes, it matters more than anything else" (coded 5); "it matters a good deal but no more than other things" (coded 4); "not familiar enough with these tests to make a judgment" (coded 3); "it does not matter as much as other things" (coded 2); "no, it matters very little" (coded 1) (Table 4.3). In the first year of the study, between 2 and 7 percent of teachers in the three treatments thought the intelligence measured by intelligence tests very important, while a further 35 to 40 percent thought it mattered a good deal, but no more than other things. Quite a large percentage (25 to 30) were not sufficiently familiar with the tests to make a decision. In the fourth year of the study, the same teachers evidenced a few small changes in their distribution of responses. Most notably, some Treatment 3 teachers who had responded "not familiar enough with these tests to make a judgment" in the first year had, by the end of the study, judged that the kinds of things measured on intelligence tests did matter a good deal.

We found no statistically significant treatment differences on this item in year 4. However, when the gender of the teacher was included as a stratifying variable in a covariance analysis, a statistically significant gender effect was found. In the final year of the study, male teachers, to a significantly greater

Table 4.3. Teachers' Perceptions of the Importance of Test Intelligence in Life, by Treatment

			Percentage									
Year	Treatment	N	More than Anything Else	A Great Deal	Not Familiar Enough to Judge	Not as Much as Other Things	Very Little	M	S.D.	F	p	R^2
Do you think that the kind of intelligence measured by intelligence tests matters much in life?												
1	1	93	2.2	38.7	32.3	20.4	6.5	3.09	.97	.298	.74	.002
	2	69	7.2	34.8	29.0	23.2	5.8	3.14	1.05			
	3	91	2.2	40.7	23.1	25.3	8.8	3.02	1.05			
4	1	94	1.1	30.9	35.1	27.7	5.3	2.95	.92	1.794	.17	.014
	2	70	5.7	44.3	14.3	30.0	5.7	3.14	1.09			
	3	94	1.1	59.6	7.4	24.5	7.4	3.22	1.07			

extent than female ones, believed that the kind of intelligence measured by intelligence tests mattered much in life.

Teachers' beliefs about the importance of learned and inborn factors for performance on an intelligence test were more unanimous than was the case when they considered the importance of intelligence, as measured by tests. On a 5-point scale, which provided the categories "completely inborn" (coded 1); "mainly inborn" (coded 2); "half inborn–half learned" (coded 3); "mainly learned" (coded 4); and "completely learned" (coded 5), 60 to 70 percent of teachers across treatments in both years believed that intelligence test results depend about equally on inborn and learned factors (Table 4.4). The bulk of the remaining responses accepted the "mainly inborn" option, a fact that is reflected in the finding that all of the treatment means are less than 3.00. Very few of the teachers in any treatment selected the "completely inborn" or "completely learned" options. There was no significant treatment difference on this item in the final-year responses of teachers.

When the gender of the teacher was included as a stratifying variable in the variance analyses, the item evidenced a significant effect. After adjusting for initial mean differences, we found that male teachers believed more than did female teachers that the results of intelligence tests depend more on inborn factors.

Teachers also completed a series of items that asked for their opinions about the similarity between the kind of intelligence measured by standardized tests and the kind of intelligence necessary for success at various educational and occupational levels. For each item teachers selected one of five response options that were coded 1 to 5, respectively: (1) "completely different"; (2) "more different than alike"; (3) "similar, but many differences"; (4) "basically the same"; and (5) "identical." In general, the response to the six items evidenced a marked tendency for teachers in all treatments, in both years, to perceive the kind of intelligence measured by standardized tests to be less related to the kind of intelligence necessary for postschool success in various occupational arenas than to the kind of intelligence related to in-school success. Across treatments, 65 to 75 percent of teachers selected the options "similar but many differences" and "basically the same" to describe the relationship between what intelligence tests measure and what is necessary for success in primary school, postprimary school, and university. The percentages of teachers selecting these same options dropped to 55 to 65 percent for success in the professions, 40 to 50 percent for success in the business world, and 30 to 40 percent for success in blue-collar jobs.

At the end of the study, significant treatment differences occurred only on the items dealing with primary and postprimary school (Table 4.5). Teachers who had received norm-referenced test results (Treatment 3) perceived a greater similarity between tested intelligence and the kind of intelligence necessary for

Table 4.4. Teachers' Perceptions of What the Results of Intelligence Tests Depend on Most, by Treatment

			Percentages									
			Completely Inborn Factors	Mainly Inborn Factors	Half Inborn– Half Learned Factors	Mainly Learned Factors	Completely Learned Factors	M	S.D.	F	p	R^2
Year	Treatment	N										
What do you think the results of intelligence (IQ) tests depend on most?	2	1	86	1.2	24.4	70.9	3.5	0.0	2.77	.524	3.103	.046	.024
		2	77	2.6	16.9	64.9	10.4	5.2	2.98	.769			
		3	94	1.1	30.9	59.6	7.4	1.1	2.77	.646			
	4	1	88	1.1	25.0	70.5	3.4	0.0	2.76	.525	.414	.66	.003
		2	78	1.3	24.4	66.7	6.4	1.3	2.84	.622			
		3	97	1.0	27.8	58.8	12.4	0.0	2.82	.646			

Table 4.5. Teachers' Perceptions of the Relationship between the Type of Intelligence Measured by Standardized Intelligence Tests and the Types of Intelligence Necessary for Success at Various Educational and Occupational Levels

	Year	Treatment	N	M	S.D.	F	p	R^2
Primary school	2	1	84	2.91	1.00	.576	.563	.005
		2	73	2.92	1.06			
		3	90	3.06	1.01			
	4	1	90	2.91	1.06	3.479	.032	.026
		2	81	3.01	.93			
		3	91	3.29	.96			
Postprimary school	2	1	81	2.83	.93	2.862	.060	.027
		2	59	2.95	.94			
		3	73	3.16	.76			
	4	1	81	2.93	.92	4.878	.008	.039
		2	77	3.05	.90			
		3	83	3.34	.77			
University	2	1	77	2.99	.99	.292	.747	.003
		2	59	3.00	1.22			
		3	74	3.11	.96			
	4	1	79	3.05	1.04	.463	.630	.004
		2	77	3.03	1.08			
		3	81	3.17	.99			

Table 4.5. (Continued)

	Year	Treatment	N	M	S.D.	F	p	R^2
Professions	2	1	76	2.75	1.19	.889	.413	.009
		2	55	2.82	1.28			
		3	73	3.00	1.07			
	4	1	78	3.08	1.08	.856	.426	.007
		2	75	2.87	1.10			
		3	77	2.90	1.06			
Business	2	1	78	2.42	1.19	.997	.371	.010
		2	57	2.21	1.26			
		3	71	2.51	1.17			
	4	1	80	2.61	1.22	2.275	.105	.019
		2	77	2.25	1.10			
		3	72	2.55	1.11			
Blue-collar jobs	2	1	77	2.36	1.17	.950	.389	.009
		2	57	2.46	1.21			
		3	72	2.64	1.31			
	4	1	81	2.33	1.08	1.967	.142	.016
		2	77	2.34	1.17			
		3	82	2.63	1.07			

success in both primary and postprimary schools than did teachers in Treatment 1, who had not administered tests to their pupils (Table 4.5).

To obtain an indication of the constructs that teachers perceived intelligence tests measured, they were asked: "How clear or definite an index about a pupil's performance, i.e., where a pupil stands compared to other pupils, do you get from the intelligence, IQ, or aptitude tests used in schools?" The teachers could respond "a very good idea" (coded 5); "a pretty good idea" (coded 4); "a general idea" (coded 3); "a fairly poor idea" (coded 2); or "a very poor idea" (coded 1). Early in the study and again at its end, teachers in all treatments believed that intelligence tests provide a "pretty good idea" of where a pupil stands compared with other pupils. In both years the grand mean of teachers' responses was around 3.75 on the 5-point scale. Although there were no significant treatment differences, there was a significant gender effect. Male teachers believed that intelligence tests provide a better idea of a pupil's intelligence than did female teachers.

Finally, we obtained information on teachers' judgments of the relative stability of intelligence and attainment test results. Teachers responded to two items that asked how much change there would be in the ranking of pupils if an intelligence test and an attainment test were administered that year and a similar test were administered three years later. Response options were: "no change," "small changes," "moderate changes," "fairly large changes," "very large changes," and "don't know." In calculating a measure of teacher perceptions on these two items, the first five response options were coded 1 to 5, respectively. Although data on the percentages of teachers who responded "don't know" are provided, these responses were not included in the calculations reported in Table 4.6. In interpreting the means in this table, it is important to note that the lower the reported mean, the more stable the test scores were perceived to be. Data in the table indicate that across years and treatments, teachers perceived the rankings provided by intelligence tests to be more stable than those provided by attainment tests.

The majority of teachers in all treatments and in both years in which the questions were asked judged that intelligence and attainment test results would evidence "small" and "moderate" changes if pupils were retested three years later (Table 4.6). However, the percentages of teachers selecting these two response options are somewhat smaller, of the order of 3 to 4 percent, for attainment test results than for intelligence test results. These differences were reflected in the larger percentages of teachers selecting the "fairly large changes" option for the item concerned with the stability of attainment test scores. Moreover, teachers' perceptions of the stability of either kind of test over time changed little. There were no statistically significant treatment differences on either item concerned with the stability of measurement. When the items

Table 4.6. Teachers' Perceptions of the Stability of Intelligence and Attainment Test Scores in Ranking Pupils over a Three-Year Period

Type of Test	Year	Treatment	N	No Changes	Small Changes	Moderate Changes	Fairly Large Changes	Very Large Changes	Don't Know	M	S.D.	F	p	R^2
Intelligence	2	1	88	1.1	44.3	33.0	3.4	1.1	17.0	2.51	.67	2.650	.073	.024
		2	77	3.9	29.9	41.6	5.2	3.9	15.6	2.71	.84			
		3	92	6.5	47.8	27.2	8.7	0.0	9.8	2.41	.77			
Intelligence	4	1	79	2.2	50.0	23.3	12.2	0.0	12.2	2.52	.77	.481	.619	.004
		2	72	5.1	44.3	29.1	6.3	2.5	12.7	2.49	.82			
		3	88	3.1	52.6	29.9	5.2	0.0	9.3	2.41	.66			
Attainment	2	1	86	1.2	24.4	40.7	15.1	3.5	15.1	2.95	.83	.140	.870	.001
		2	73	0.0	26.0	39.7	12.3	6.8	15.1	3.00	.89			
		3	89	1.1	18.0	50.6	14.6	3.4	12.4	3.01	.76			
Attainment	4	1	81	0.0	22.2	46.7	20.0	1.1	10.0	3.00	.73	.962	.384	.008
		2	72	2.6	28.8	41.0	15.5	1.3	11.5	2.83	.79			
		3	82	0.0	29.2	37.5	17.7	1.0	14.6	2.89	.77			

were analyzed by teacher gender and school location, the only significant difference occurred on the one dealing with attainment test stability. In the final year of the study, city teachers perceived attainment test scores to be significantly more stable than did town or rural teachers.

Use of Test Information in Making Decisions about Pupils

In light of the debate regarding the impact of standardized test results on teachers' perceptions of their pupils, it is of interest to examine the amount of weight teachers say that they would give to such tests in making various decisions about pupils. Teachers were asked to indicate the amount of weight ("no weight," "slight amount," "moderate amount," or "great amount," coded 1 to 4, respectively) that they would give to information derived from three sources—intelligence tests, attainment tests, and teacher recommendations—in making eight decisions about pupils: (1) assigning pupils to streams; (2) grouping pupils within a class; (3) assigning a pupil to a special class for slow pupils; (4) selection for admission to a postprimary school; (5) deciding who should take honors courses for public examinations; (6) guiding pupils in vocational decisions; (7) admission to third-level education; and (8) selection for employment. Separate principal components factor analysis with varimax rotation carried out for each of the four sources of information indicated that the eight items formed two factors: an instructional factor comprised of items 1, 2, and 3 and a selection factor comprised of items 4 through 8. All items on each factor had positive loadings, and a high score on a factor indicated that a teacher would assign weight to a particular kind of information in making either instructional or selection decisions about a pupil. For each type of information, we computed mean scores on the two factors for each teacher in the three treatment groups and used these data to obtain a treatment mean for each factor. We then compared mean treatment responses. We found no significant differences between treatments for type of test or for type of decision (Table 4.7).

A gender effect, however, was found on the item that asked teachers to indicate the amount of weight they would accord attainment tests in making instructional decisions. Male teachers reported that they would accord attainment tests significantly more weight in making instructional decisions about pupils than would female teachers.

To place the prior results in the broader context of classroom decision making, we may look at the weight that teachers say they would give to their own recommendations in making decisions about a pupil. Here we find great consistency in all teacher questionnaires administered during the study. Comparison of the mean weights in Tables 4.7 and 4.8 indicates that teachers report

Table 4.7. The Weight Teachers Report They Would Give to Intelligence and Attainment Tests in Making Instructional and Selection Decisions about Pupils, by Treatment

Test	Type of Decision	Year	Treatment	N	M	S.D.	F	p	R^2
Intelligence	Instructional	1	1	85	3.24	.60	.65	.52	.005
			2	65	3.31	.54			
			3	90	3.20	.57			
	Instructional	4	1	77	3.12	.63	1.30	.27	.011
			2	65	3.25	.54			
			3	92	3.25	.56			
Intelligence	Selection	1	1	78	3.09	.58	.16	.85	.001
			2	60	3.14	.69			
			3	77	3.07	.66			
	Selection	4	1	64	3.04	.64	.50	.61	.005
			2	55	3.10	.64			
			3	76	3.14	.56			

Table 4.7. (Continued)

Test	Type of Decision	Year	Treatment	N	M	S.D.	F	p	R^2
Attainment	Instructional	1	1	74	3.18	.59	.40	.67	.004
			2	58	3.17	.59			
			3	76	3.10	.58			
	Instructional	4	1	66	3.21	.58	.67	.51	.006
			2	60	3.10	.54			
			3	85	3.17	.55			
Attainment	Selection	1	1	74	3.12	.59	.10	.91	.001
			2	55	3.13	.63			
			3	67	3.09	.54			
	Selection	4	1	57	3.07	.61	.41	.67	.000
			2	53	3.14	.55			
			3	76	3.17	.56			

that they would accord considerably more weight to teacher recommendations than they would to intelligence or attainment tests. Since the maximum value the mean weights could attain was 4.0, teachers in all treatments evidently started the study with high confidence in the value of teacher recommendations as a basis for making decisions about pupils, and this confidence had altered little by the end of the study.

We undertook an additional set of analyses to examine the relative changes over time in weight accorded to teacher recommendations and that accorded to intelligence or attainment tests. As in previously reported analyses of relative gain in perceptions of the accuracy of various indices (see Table 4.2), we created new variables to examine relative gains in the weight accorded different types of data in making decisions about a pupil. For example, to examine changes in the relative weight accorded intelligence tests and teacher recommendations as a basis for pupil decision making, we created the following difference variable (D):

$$D = \left[\begin{pmatrix} \text{weight for} \\ \text{intelligence} \\ \text{test,} \\ \text{year 4} \end{pmatrix} - \begin{pmatrix} \text{weight for} \\ \text{teacher recom-} \\ \text{mendation,} \\ \text{year 4} \end{pmatrix} \right] - \left[\begin{pmatrix} \text{weight for} \\ \text{intelligence} \\ \text{test,} \\ \text{year 1} \end{pmatrix} - \begin{pmatrix} \text{weight for} \\ \text{teacher recom-} \\ \text{mendation,} \\ \text{year 4} \end{pmatrix} \right].$$

If D is positive, the weight accorded intelligence tests gained relative to the weight accorded teacher recommendations from year 1 to year 4; if D is negative, the opposite is true.

We created variables that compared teachers' relative weighting over time of (1) intelligence tests and teacher recommendations, (2) attainment tests and teacher recommendations, and (3) intelligence and attainment tests. We found no significant treatment differences for any of the three variables, indicating that the relative weightings obtained at the start of the study remained unchanged at its end. Teachers across treatments continued to indicate that they would give substantially greater weight to teacher recommendations than to test results in making both instructional and selection decisions about their pupils.

Further indication of the perceived importance of teacher judgments relative to other criteria can be found in two items administered only in the last year of the study. These items asked the teachers to rank from 1 to 5 the accuracy of the pupil, his or her teacher, standardized tests, classroom exams, and the pupil's parents in judging a pupil's intelligence and attainment. The lower the ranking, the more accurate the judgment was perceived to be by teachers. Across the three treatment groups, by a wide margin, a pupil's teacher was ranked as the most accurate judge of both a pupil's intelligence and attainment (Table 4.9). Standardized tests and classroom exams were ranked next most accurate; standardized tests were viewed as slightly more accurate than classroom exams

Table 4.8. The Weight Teachers Report They Would Give to Teacher Recommendations in Making Instructional and Selection Decisions about Pupils, by Treatment

Type of Decision	Year	Treatment	N	M	S.D.	F	p	R^2
Instructional	1	1	90	3.66	.52	.50	.61	.004
		2	67	3.67	.49			
		3	89	3.73	.50			
Instructional	4	1	89	3.70	.47	.79	.46	.006
		2	65	3.79	.42			
		3	91	3.75	.49			
Selection	1	1	81	3.46	.58	2.11	.12	.019
		2	62	3.59	.55			
		3	74	3.64	.53			
Selection	4	1	76	3.50	.57	.85	.43	.008
		2	57	3.59	.47			
		3	81	3.59	.47			

Table 4.9. Mean Ranks of the Perceived Accuracy of Five Judges of a Pupil's Intelligence and Attainment, by Treatment

Trait	Judge	Treatments		
		1	*2*	*3*
Intelligence	Pupil himself	3.59	3.72	3.68
	Pupil's teacher	1.53	1.49	1.58
	Standardized tests	2.60	2.54	2.56
	Classroom exams	2.69	2.74	2.84
	Pupil's parents	3.71	3.69	3.69
Attainment	Pupil himself	3.38	3.37	3.41
	Pupil's teacher	1.58	1.52	1.53
	Standardized tests	2.70	2.54	2.52
	Classroom exams	2.40	2.53	2.46
	Pupil's parents	3.70	3.71	3.76

in judging a pupil's intelligence, while the reverse was true for judging a pupil's attainment. On both items the pupil and the pupil's parents were ranked as the least accurate judges. Interestingly, teachers tended to perceive the pupil and his or her parents as being about equally accurate in judging the pupil's intelligence, but perceived the pupil as being more accurate than his or her parents in judging attainment.

Although there were no statistically significant differences between the three treatments, there were statistically significant differences in the ranking accorded standardized intelligence tests when teachers were stratified within treatments by gender and by school location. Teachers in city schools perceived standardized intelligence tests to be a more accurate index of a pupil's intelligence than did either teachers in town schools or teachers in rural schools. Teachers in rural schools accorded standardized intelligence tests the lowest ranking among teachers in the three strata. Perhaps more important, and consistent with other results we have presented, male teachers gave standardized intelligence tests a significantly higher accuracy rating than did female teachers.

Overall there is strong evidence to indicate that teachers perceived themselves as the most accurate judges of their pupils' intelligence and achievement and that they would give considerably more weight to their own impressions than to test information in making decisions about a pupil. The introduction of standardized testing and norm-referenced test information had little discernible effect on these perceptions. In spite of a significant increase in the perceived accuracy of standardized test information among teachers who had been given such information, we can detect little change in the weight teachers say they would assign to standardized tests in making selection or instructional decisions about their pupils or in their perceptions of the accuracy of tests in judging a pupil's intelligence and attainment relative to other people or measures.

Teacher Opinions regarding Who Should Have Access to Test Information

Another way in which differences in teachers' perceptions about standardized tests might be revealed is in questions asking to whom intelligence and attainment test scores should be reported. In year 2 and again in year 4, teachers were asked whether they thought that the results of standardized tests of intelligence and attainment should be reported to six publics: primary school pupils, post-primary school pupils, the pupil's teacher, the school principal, school inspectors from the Department of Education, and the pupil's parents. Each item was responded to by selecting "yes" (coded 1) or "no" (coded 2) for each public. Hence, the lower the reported mean score, the more that teachers agreed that the public should have access to the test information.

Teachers clearly made sharp distinctions as to which publics should have access to intelligence test scores (Table 4.10). The pupil's teacher, the school principal, and the pupil's parents were almost unanimously perceived as audiences who should receive intelligence test results. To a lesser extent post-primary pupils and inspectors from the Department of Education were perceived as groups that should see such results. Most teachers believed that primary school pupils should not receive them. Perceptions about access of each group to intelligence test information hardly changed from year 2 to year 4.

Except for the item relating to the report of test information to a pupil's teacher, there are no significant differences between treatment groups about the reporting of intelligence test scores. The significant difference probably does not have any practical significance. As the means for the item show, teachers in Treatments 2 and 3 unanimously believed that intelligence test information should be reported to a pupil's teacher. Eighty-five of the eighty-nine teachers in Treatment 1 believed similarly. Thus, for all practical purposes, virtually every teacher in each treatment believed that intelligence test information should be reported to the pupil's teacher.

A statistically significant gender effect was observed on the item concerned with the release of intelligence test information to pupils' parents. Male teachers, to a greater extent than female ones, believed that test score information should be reported to a pupil's parents. A significant gender effect was also observed on the item dealing with reporting intelligence test information to a pupil's teacher. While not shown in the table, this effect was attributable to three female teachers' replying "no" to the item in year 4 as opposed to the unanimous perception among male teachers that a pupil's teacher should have the pupil's test results. There was also a significant effect associated with school location on the item concerned with making intelligence test information available to school principals. Teachers in rural schools, to a significantly greater extent than teachers in either town or city schools, believed that the school principal should receive a pupil's intelligence test scores.

The results relating to the report of attainment test information are similar to those for intelligence tests (Table 4.11), with one notable difference. In general, teachers appeared to be considerably more inclined to release attainment test information to various publics than they were to release intelligence test information. For all publics except school inspectors, the means for attainment tests (Table 4.11) were lower than the corresponding means for intelligence tests (Table 4.10). Since school inspectors are employed by the Irish Department of Education to inspect the conditions, instruction, and learning in schools, teachers' failure to evidence a difference in their willingness to provide either type of test data to inspectors may reflect a general concern over accountability.

Table 4.10. Teachers' Perceptions of the Extent to Which Various Publics Should Receive Pupils' Intelligence Test Scores, by Treatment

Public	Year	Treatment 1			Treatment 2			Treatment 3			F	p	R^2
		N	M	S.D.	N	M	S.D.	N	M	S.D.			
Primary pupil	2	81	1.95	.22	63	1.83	.38	83	1.92	.28	3.347	.037	.029
Primary pupil	4	84	1.88	.33	78	1.85	.36	89	1.78	.42	1.809	.166	.014
Postprimary pupil	2	66	1.38	.49	44	1.48	.51	69	1.46	.50	.694	.501	.008
Postprimary pupil	4	79	1.37	.49	67	1.46	.50	78	1.40	.49	.701	.497	.006
Pupil's teacher	2	84	1.02	.15	73	1.01	.12	96	1.00	.00	1.102	.334	.009
Pupil's teacher	4	89	1.05	.21	80	1.00	.00	96	1.00	.00	4.099	.018	.030
School principal	2	75	1.11	.31	65	1.20	.40	83	1.11	.30	2.012	.136	.018
School principal	4	86	1.15	.36	77	1.17	.38	91	1.19	.39	.198	.821	.002
School inspectors	2	73	1.66	.48	58	1.55	.50	74	1.51	.50	1.657	.193	.016
School inspectors	4	33	1.63	.49	75	1.69	.46	88	1.52	.50	2.573	.078	.021
Pupil's parents	2	85	1.11	.31	67	1.08	.27	85	1.14	.35	.855	.427	.007
Pupil's parents	4	88	1.21	.41	78	1.14	.35	94	1:12	.32	1.407	.247	.011

Table 4.11. Teachers' Perceptions of the Extent to Which Various Publics Should Receive Pupils' Attainment Test Scores, by Treatment

Public	Year	Treatment 1			Treatment 2			Treatment 3			F	p	R^2
		N	M	S.D.	N	M	S.D.	N	M	S.D.			
Primary pupil	2	79	1.38	.49	61	1.34	.40	84	1.36	.48	.900	.906	.001
Primary pupil	4	84	1.41	.49	74	1.42	.50	87	1.39	.49	.065	.937	.001
Postprimary pupil	2	64	1.05	.21	42	1.12	.33	67	1.09	.29	.937	.394	.011
Postprimary pupil	4	79	1.10	.30	68	1.18	.38	78	1.10	.31	1.207	.301	.011
Pupil's teacher	2	80	1.01	.11	70	1.00	.00	94	1.00	.00	1.036	.357	.009
Pupil's teacher	4	88	1.01	.11	80	1.00	.00	95	1.00	.00	1.020	.362	.008
School principal	2	76	1.15	.35	60	1.18	.39	84	1.11	.31	.841	.433	.008
School principal	4	84	1.13	.34	74	1.20	.41	88	1.21	.41	.993	.372	.008
School inspectors	2	67	1.57	.50	56	1.57	.50	74	1.55	.50	.022	.979	.000
School inspectors	4	80	1.58	.50	71	1.68	.47	85	1.54	.50	1.542	.216	.013
Pupil's parents	2	84	1.04	.19	67	1.03	.17	88	1.02	.15	.127	.881	.001
Pupil's parents	4	90	1.08	.27	76	1.09	.29	92	1.07	.25	.209	.812	.002

Teachers' Grouping Practices

In examining the effect of testing on classroom grouping practices, we find two questions of interest. First, do more teachers who receive test information report that they group within their classes than teachers who do not receive test information? And second, to what extent do teachers report that they use test information as a criterion in forming instructional groups?

In years 1 and 4 of the study, teachers were asked a number of questions about their grouping practices. Respondents first indicated whether they divided their classes into groups for teaching and, if they responded affirmatively, whether they used any of nine criteria (teacher recommendations, standardized intelligence tests, standardized attainment tests, age, teacher's own observations, teacher's own tests, term or house examinations, interests of the pupils, no particular basis) in forming the groups. Teachers responded by indicating either "yes" (coded 1) or "no" (coded 0) for each item. If teachers grouped their classes, they were also asked how often individual pupils were changed from one group to another. There were four responses to this item: "frequently," "occasionally," "seldom," and "never," coded 1 to 4, respectively. The means for all but the last item in Table 4.12 indicate the proportion of teachers in each treatment who responded "yes" to the item; the higher the mean, the greater the reported incidence of grouping or the reported use of the nine grouping criteria.

At the end of the study, we found no differences between treatments in the proportion of teachers who reported that they grouped pupils in their classes. About 60 to 65 percent of teachers across treatments reported that they grouped their classes for instructional purposes. It is of interest that by the end of the study, the proportion of teachers in the test-information group who reported within-class grouping was less than the proportion early in the study. In light of these data, the decision about whether or not to group pupils within a class-room for instructional purposes appears to be made on the basis of factors not related to the availability of norm-referenced standardized test results. As in the school-level analyses (Chapter 3), our results provide no support for the contention that the availability of standardized test results leads to an increase in within-class grouping.

Analysis of the data by school location indicated a statistically significant difference in the incidence of within-class grouping. Not surprisingly, city teachers, who work in larger classes, reported grouping their classes to a significantly greater extent than did either town or rural teachers.

We did not find significant differences between treatment groups in the extent to which teachers used their own classroom tests and examinations as grouping criteria at the end of the study. (The means for each grouping criterion

Table 4.12. Teachers' Reported Classroom Grouping Practices, Grouping Criteria, and Movement of Pupils among Groups, by Treatment

Item	Year	Treatment 1			Treatment 2			Treatment 3			F	p	R^2
		N	M	S.D.	N	M	S.D.	N	M	S.D.			
Do you group within your classroom?	1	92	.77	.42	65	.51	.50	91	.70	.46	6.553	.002	.051
	4	86	.66	.48	65	.59	.50	86	.61	.49	.546	.580	.005
Grouping criteria													
Teacher recommendation	1	69	.74	.44	34	.65	.49	62	.73	.45	.495	.610	.006
	4	62	.87	.34	41	.66	.48	57	.79	.41	3.408	.036	.042
Intelligence tests	1	64	.14	.35	33	.18	.39	56	.25	.44	1.166	.314	.015
	4	54	.22	.42	36	.25	.44	57	.46	.50	4.167	.017	.055
Standardized attainment tests	1	64	.25	.44	35	.14	.36	57	.19	.40	.830	.438	.001
	4	55	.22	.42	37	.24	.44	54	.32	.47	.690	.503	.010
Age	1	64	.08	.27	34	.21	.41	59	.10	.31	1.872	.157	.024
	4	54	.07	.26	36	.14	.35	56	.07	.26	.725	.486	.010
Teacher observation	1	71	1.00	.00	36	.94	.23	67	.96	.21	1.830	.164	.021
	4	63	1.00	.00	42	1.00	.00	59	.98	.13	.889	.413	.011
Classroom tests	1	72	1.00	.00	34	.85	.36	63	.87	.34	5.543	.005	.063
	4	61	.98	.13	40	.95	.22	59	.88	.33	2.791	.064	.034

Table 4.12. (Continued)

Item	Year	Treatment 1			Treatment 2			Treatment 3			F	p	R^2
		N	M	S.D.	N	M	S.D.	N	M	S.D.			
Classroom	1	64	.61	.49	36	.25	.44	58	.45	.50	6.427	.002	.077
examinations	4	57	.54	.50	39	.33	.48	58	.47	.50	2.085	.128	.027
Children's	1	65	.39	.41	35	.46	.51	60	.48	.50	.646	.526	.008
interests	4	56	.36	.48	40	.55	.50	57	.42	.50	1.796	.170	.023
Random	1	62	.05	.22	34	.09	.29	54	.04	.19	.561	.572	.008
basis	4	56	.05	.23	39	.10	.31	54	.11	.32	.642	.528	.009
Incidence of	1	73	2.90	.67	37	2.97	.76	67	2.91	.69	.132	.877	.001
pupil changes among groups	4	65	2.85	.59	41	2.88	.81	57	2.97	.68	.476	.622	.006

in Table 4.12 indicate the proportion of teachers who said that they used that criterion in forming groups.) However, there were statistically significant treatment differences in the use of teacher recommendations and intelligence tests as grouping criteria. These differences accounted for 4.2 and 5.5 percent of the total variance, respectively. Treatments 1 and 3 teachers used teacher recommendations as a criterion for forming groups to a significantly greater extent than did Treatment 2 teachers. Treatment 3 teachers, as might be expected since they received intelligence test information as part of their treatment, reported using that information in grouping decisions to a significantly greater extent than did either Treatment 1 or Treatment 2 teachers. Interestingly, about one-quarter of the teachers in Treatments 1 and 2 reported that they used intelligence test results in forming groups. This finding is somewhat surprising since teachers in these treatments did not receive intelligence test results in our study. We know that some teachers in Treatment 2 scored the tests themselves, but this could not account for the fact that 22 percent of Treatment 1 teachers also reported using intelligence test results. While some Treatment 1 teachers possibly had access to intelligence test results from a source independent of the study, the most likely explanation for the high percentage of Treatment 1 teachers' reporting the use of intelligence test results is misinterpretation of the item.

The three most widely reported grouping criteria, regardless of treatment or year, were teachers' classroom tests, teachers' observations, and, to a lesser extent, teacher recommendations. Between 65 and 100 percent of the teachers who indicated that they grouped pupils for instructional purposes reported that they used one of these teacher-specific criteria to form groups. Even in the group in which test results were available, the reported use of these criteria greatly outweighed the use of standardized tests, indicating clearly that teachers rely more heavily on their own perceptions than on other "external" indicators.

For the final item relating to the intraclass grouping of pupils, teachers were asked if they moved pupils from one instructional group to another over the course of the school year "frequently," "occasionally," "seldom," or "never" (coded 1 to 4). On average, teachers reported that they seldom altered a pupil's initial group assignment (Table 4.12). There were no significant differences between treatment groups on this variable at the end of the study.

So far we have looked at the impact of testing on intraclassroom instructional grouping practices. The results of standardized tests may also be used for interclass grouping or streaming—that is, as a basis for assigning pupils to particular classrooms within a grade level. Teachers were asked in years 1 and 4 of the study whether pupils were selected and assigned to their classes on the basis of one or more of six ways: ability, attainment, to produce a class with a balanced mix of pupils, to distribute leaders and troublemakers across classes, randomly, or no selection process at all (e.g., all pupils in the same grade were in one classroom). Teachers responded to each of the six interclass grouping criteria by indicating "yes" (coded 1) or "no" (coded 2). Thus, the higher the mean on an item, the higher the percentage of teachers who responded "no" to the item.

Across treatments, the least utilized streaming criteria were clearly the distribution of leaders and troublemakers, ability, and attainment (Table 4.13), while the most frequent response was "no selection process" at all—that is, all pupils in the same grade were in one classroom. The fact that this response was cited most often reflects the fact that many schools in our sample, particularly town and rural ones, were small and had only a single class at a given grade level. Random allocation and allocation to produce a balanced mix of pupils across classes were identified by moderate numbers of teachers as ways of assigning pupils to classes, even though in both cases fewer teachers at the end of the study than at its beginning indicated that pupils were assigned in this way.

Analyses of variance and covariance as appropriate were carried out for each item. We found no statistically significant treatment differences for data obtained at the end of the study.

Analyses indicated that teachers in city schools to a greater extent than teachers in town or rural schools reported that pupils were assigned to classes on a random basis and that children with varying characteristics (leaders, troublemakers) were distributed across classes. A gender effect was also identified. Male teachers reported that pupils were assigned to classes on the basis of ability and attainment to a significantly greater extent than did female teachers.

Teachers' Perceptions of the Relevance and Effects of Standardized Tests

At the end of the study, teachers were asked to indicate the extent to which they agreed with thirteen statements about the relevance and effects of standardized, multiple-choice tests and test results. A comparison of teachers' responses by treatment group provides an indication of how different experiences with tests and test information influenced teachers' perceptions. The thirteen statements were selected to reflect issues that are of current interest and concern regarding test relevance and the use of tests in labeling pupils. The thirteen statements were: Standardized, multiple-choice tests (1) aid in the diagnosis of individual pupil needs and abilities; (2) provide teachers with important information about pupils not generally obtainable from classroom observation; (3) lead teachers to expect more or less of pupils than they had previously; (4) are generally unrelated to the objectives teachers consider to be important; (5) lead teachers to make more comparisons between pupils than they would

Table 4.13. Teachers' Reports of How Pupils Are Assigned to Their Classes, by Treatment

Criterion	Year	Treatment 1			Treatment 2			Treatment 3			F	p	R^2
		N	M	S.D.	N	M	S.D.	N	M	S.D.			
On the basis of ability	1	86	1.70	.41	61	1.93	.25	82	1.87	.34	3.081	.048	.027
	4	68	1.72	.45	54	1.88	.34	72	1.88	.33	3.546	.031	.036
No selection process; all pupils in same grade are in one classroom	1	86	1.36	.48	66	1.17	.38	90	1.23	.43	3.994	.020	.032
	4	83	1.30	.46	65	1.26	.44	89	1.15	.36	3.162	.044	.026
On the basis of attainment	1	79	1.79	.41	59	1.88	.33	80	1.85	.36	1.244	.290	.011
	4	66	1.77	.42	53	1.91	.30	72	1.90	.32	2.690	.071	.028
To produce a class with a balanced mix (bright, average, slow)	1	81	1.49	.50	63	1.48	.50	79	1.67	.47	3.610	.029	.032
	4	69	1.70	.46	54	1.67	.58	73	1.70	.46	.084	.919	.001
Distribution of leaders and troublemakers across classes	1	80	1.89	.32	61	1.85	.36	76	1.82	.39	.792	.454	.007
	4	67	1.88	.33	53	1.76	.43	73	1.86	.35	1.993	.139	.021
Random	1	76	1.55	.50	59	1.51	.50	75	1.48	.50	.400	.671	.004
	4	68	1.79	.41	54	1.74	.44	72	1.69	.46	.903	.407	.009

otherwise; (6) may attach a "label" to pupils that they carry with them throughout their school careers; (7) lead teachers to treat individual pupils differently than they would have in the absence of test results; (8) create pressures on teachers to teach toward the test; (9) lead teachers to attempt to teach low-scoring pupils less than they otherwise would; (10) have a "scientific" aura that gives them greater importance in teachers' eyes than they should have; (11) are so technical in nature that teachers do not pay much attention to them; (12) do not measure the kinds of skills, even in language and mathematics, that are actually taught in school; (13) are too dependent on a pupil's reading ability. Five response options were provided for each statement: "strongly agree" (coded 5); "agree" (coded 4); "uncertain" (coded 3); "disagree" (coded 2); and "strongly disagree" (coded 1).

We performed a principal components factor analysis with varimax rotation on responses to the statements. The coding of the five response options for items 1 and 2 were reversed ("strongly agree" was coded 1, "agree" was coded 2, and so forth), so that the directionality of the items would conform to the directionality of the remaining eleven items. Two factors were identified. Items 1, 2, 4, 11, 12, and 13 loaded on the first factor, which contained statements concerned with the relevance of standardized, multiple-choice tests in the classroom. The higher a teacher's score on the factor, the less strongly he or she perceived standardized tests as being relevant in the classroom. The remaining seven statements (3, 5, 6, 7, 8, 9, and 10) loaded on the second factor. These statements appeared to tap perceptions about an "expectation" effect that might be associated with standardized tests as well as perceptions about the extent to which such tests influence teachers' perceptions of and decisions about their pupils. A high score on the factor indicated that a teacher believed that standardized tests did not exert a powerful influence on teachers' perceptions of and decisions about pupils.

For each teacher we calculated a mean factor score on each factor. Analysis of variance revealed that there were no statistically significant treatment differences on the classroom relevance scale (Table 4.14). Experience with testing and test information did not influence teachers' opinions about the relevance of standardized tests for classroom use. There was, however, a significant treatment difference on the teacher expectation factor, accounting for 6.2 percent of the variance. Teachers in Treatment 3 were significantly *less* likely to view standardized tests as influencing the way teachers perceive and act toward pupils than were teachers in Treatments 1 and 2.

The percentages of teachers in each treatment who selected each of the response options on the seven items that comprised the expectation factor are of interest in a number of regards (Table 4.15). They indicate a tendency on the part of teachers who received test information, compared with other teachers,

Table 4.14. Mean Teacher Perceptions of Test Influence Factors, by Treatment

Factor	Treatment 1			Treatment 2			Treatment 3			F	p	R^2
	N	M	S.D.	N	M	S.D.	N	M	S.D.			
Classroom relevance factor	89	2.67	.61	78	2.69	.65	97	2.73	.66	.219	.803	.002
Teacher expectation factor	90	2.94	.50	82	2.84	.66	97	2.58	.63	8.825	.000	.062

Table 4.15. Breakdown of Responses to Items Comprising the Expectation Factor, by Treatment

		Response Options: Percentages				
Item	Treatment	Strongly Disagree	Disagree	Unsure	Agree	Strongly Agree
Standardized, multiple-choice tests						
Lead teachers to expect more or less from pupils	1	2.2	21.3	36.0	37.1	3.4
	2	2.5	28.7	22.5	42.4	3.7
	3	5.2	22.9	32.3	34.4	5.2
Lead teachers to make more comparisons between pupils	1	3.4	23.6	23.6	44.9	4.5
	2	6.3	23.7	16.2	45.0	8.7
	3	7.2	30.9	17.5	38.1	6.2
"Label" pupils	1	10.1	42.7	16.9	25.8	4.5
	2	16.0	43.2	16.0	17.3	7.4
	3	17.5	51.5	17.5	9.3	4.1
Lead teachers to treat individual pupils differently than in the absence of test results	1	2.2	21.3	25.8	44.9	5.6
	2	3.7	33.3	18.5	37.0	7.4
	3	7.2	38.1	15.5	36.1	3.1
Create pressures to teach to the test	1	6.7	38.2	23.6	25.8	5.6
	2	8.6	45.7	6.2	33.3	6.2
	3	20.6	58.8	8.2	12.4	0.0

Table 4.15. (Continued)

Item	Treatment	Response Options: Percentages				
		Strongly Disagree	Disagree	Unsure	Agree	Strongly Agree
Lead teachers to teach low-scoring pupils less	1	12.4	47.2	16.9	20.2	3.4
	2	18.5	46.9	13.9	16.0	4.9
	3	29.2	47.9	9.4	13.5	0.0
Have a scientific aura that increases their importance in teachers' eyes	1	10.1	40.4	19.1	28.1	2.2
	2	10.1	52.2	19.0	12.7	5.1
	3	18.6	39.2	21.6	16.5	4.1

to perceive standardized tests as having a smaller impact on expectations for and treatment of pupils. This tendency is most pronounced on the three items dealing with the influence of standardized tests on labeling pupils, creating pressures to teach to the test, and leading teachers to teach low-scoring pupils less. Further, across treatments about 40 to 50 percent of teachers agreed or strongly agreed that standardized tests help to increase teachers' recognition of individual differences between pupils. It is interesting to note that on all items except two (e and f) more than 15 percent of teachers in all treatments responded that they were "unsure." It is not evident why the percentages of unsure responses should be so high for these items. One possible explanation is that the items raised issues in teachers' minds that they had not considered previously and hence were, in fact, unsure about. The item that stated that "standardized, multiple-choice tests create pressure to teach to the test" revealed the largest disparity among treatments in the percentages of teachers who selected the "unsure" response. Almost one-quarter of Treatment 1 teachers responded "unsure," by comparison with 6 and 8 percent in Treatments 2 and 3, respectively. This disparity may indicate that familiarity with the content of the tests makes teachers perceive them as less likely to influence the selection of topics to be taught.

Finally, on all items across all treatments, sizable proportions of teachers associated standardized, multiple-choice tests with many of the negative effects attributed to them by their critics. For example, between 13 and 30 percent of teachers in the three treatments believed that standardized tests do lead to labeling of pupils. Between 12 and 40 percent believed that the tests can create pressures to teach to test content. While such negative perceptions clearly existed among teachers, experience with test results diminished rather than heightened them. Less than 14 percent of teachers in Treatment 3 felt that tests label pupils, as opposed to 30 and 25 percent in Treatments 1 and 2, respectively. Twelve percent of Treatment 3 teachers agreed, though none strongly, that tests encourage teaching to the test, as compared to 31 percent in Treatment 1 and almost 40 percent in Treatment 2.

TEACHERS' REACTIONS TO TESTING

In this section we describe the results of analyses carried out on responses to teacher questionnaires that were administered in the final year of the study only to teachers in treatments that administered tests. The questions dealt primarily with teachers' preparation for testing and their perceptions of pupils' reactions to the tests. A comparison of Treatment 2 (N = 110) and Treatment 3 (N = 143) responses provides an indication of differences between teachers who received

Table 4.16. Items Concerned with Teachers' Reported Preparations for Test Administration, by Treatment

Item	Treatment 2			Treatment 3			t	p	ω^2
	N	M	S.D.	N	M	S.D.			
Before test administration, did you prepare pupils to answer multiple-choice questions?	108	1.84	.37	140	1.90	.30	−1.35	.177	.003
Did you explain how to answer multiple-choice questions?	16	1.13	.34	17	1.29	.47	−1.18	.248	.012
Did you provide practice in answering multiple-choice items?	17	1.47	.51	14	1.50	.52	−0.16	.876	.000
Did you cover topics in class that were included in the test?	14	1.86	.36	16	1.81	.40	.32	.754	.000
Did you give other tests?	16	1.88	.34	17	1.65	.49	1.54	.135	.040

test information and those who did not. We also examine effects associated with teacher gender and the location of the school in which the teacher taught.

Preparation of Pupils for Testing

Teachers were asked whether, prior to test administration, they prepared their pupils to answer multiple-choice questions. If teachers responded that they did, they were then asked to indicate whether or not they engaged in four different types of preparation. Each item was answered either "yes" (coded 1) or "no" (coded 2). Thus, the higher the mean response, the higher the proportion of teachers who responded "no." The vast majority of teachers in both treatments indicated that they did not prepare their pupils to answer multiple-choice items (Table 4.16). A small group, however, provided assistance in dealing with multiple-choice items, while some covered topics in class that were included in the tests. There were no statistically significant differences between treatments on these items, nor were there any significant differences when the data were analyzed by teacher gender or school location.

Preparation for the tests could also be indicated in another way. Teachers in Treatment 3 who had received test results in earlier years of the study had an opportunity to examine their prior pupils' performance on the various content areas tapped by the achievement tests. Therefore, they might be aware of both the areas tested and the impact of their instruction on pupils' performance in these areas. Teachers in Treatment 2 might be familiar with the areas tested, but would not have received norm-referenced test results for students. We might expect this difference in the amount of information available to teachers about the tests in the two treatments to be reflected in the amount of content covered prior to testing by teachers. Teachers were asked, "How much of the content of the tests had your class covered by the time they were administered?" Separate items were provided for the tests in English, Irish, and mathematics. Teachers could choose from six response options: "very little" (coded 1); "less than half" (coded 2); "half" (coded 3); "most" (coded 4); "all" (coded 5); and "not applicable." The "not applicable" option was included primarily for second-grade teachers, who did not administer Irish tests to their pupils, and was not included in statistical calculations. In both treatment groups, across all content areas, the majority of teachers reported that they had covered most or all of the content of the tests by the time they had been administered (Table 4.17). Less than 10 percent of teachers in either treatment reported that they had covered very little or less than half the content prior to testing. We found no statistically significant treatment differences in the three content areas. However, teachers in rural and town schools reported that they had covered significantly

Table 4.17. Teachers' Reported Content Coverage, by Treatment

| Content Area | Treatment | N | Percentages | | | | | | M | S.D. | t | p | ω^2 |
			Very Little	Less than Half	Half	Most	All	Not Applicable					
English	2	107	2.8	0.0	10.2	61.1	25.9	0.0	4.08	.79	.03	.974	.000
	3	141	2.1	2.1	8.3	59.7	25.7	2.1	4.07	.79			
Irish	2	107	1.9	4.7	10.3	52.3	20.6	10.3	3.95	.87	1.08	.280	.001
	3	138	4.3	2.9	15.9	47.1	18.1	11.6	3.81	.97			
Math	2	107	1.9	3.7	10.3	64.5	19.6	0.0	3.96	.79	.74	.459	.000
	3	144	4.2	3.5	11.8	59.7	20.1	0.7	3.88	.91			

more of the content of the Irish tests than did teachers in city schools, suggesting that differences exist between schools in different locations in the emphasis that they place on Irish.

Teachers' Perceptions of Pupils' Reactions to Taking the Tests

Teachers in each treatment were asked to rate on a 7-point scale the seriousness with which their classes took the tests. This scale was arranged in terms of the seriousness of other types of tests in Irish schools. The most important tests that Irish students take are public examinations; next in seriousness are end-of-year school examinations, followed in order by end-of-term exams, smaller school tests, classwork that is corrected, classwork that is not corrected, and a competition not connected with school. These seven options comprised the scale on which teachers were asked to rate the seriousness with which their pupils took the standardized tests. The seven options were coded 1 to 7, with the most important tests (public exams) coded 7, and the least important 1.

We found no statistically significant treatment differences in the mean responses to this item. Teachers in both treatments reported that their pupils perceived the standardized tests to be about as serious as an end-of-term or a smaller school test. Over 50 percent of teachers selected one of these two response options. Less than a quarter reported that the tests were perceived by pupils to be less serious than a smaller school test. Overall, then, teachers in both treatments indicated that pupils approached the standardized tests with a moderate to high degree of seriousness. Male teachers in Treatment 2 (M = 4.75) perceived that their pupils took the standardized tests more seriously than female teachers in Treatment 2 (M = 4.00), while the reverse pattern was observed for male (M = 4.42) and female (M = 4.72) teachers in Treatment 3.

Teachers' Assessment of Pupil Test Performance without the Receipt of Test Results

Teachers were asked whether they scored their pupils' tests prior to forwarding them for scoring. Those who reported that they did were asked how and for whom this scoring was done. All items were responded to by selecting "yes" (coded 1) or "no" (coded 2). Some teachers (27 percent in Treatment 2 and 10 percent in Treatment 3) reported that they did correct some of their pupils' tests prior to returning them for scoring. The difference in the proportion of teachers in each treatment who scored tests was statistically significant; not surprisingly, teachers who expected to receive test results were less likely to score them themselves. Among those teachers who indicated that they scored tests, most indicated that they scored the tests on an item-by-item basis for some pupils in their class. Although the numbers are quite small on the items listed in the lower half of Table 4.18, teachers evidently employed a number of different selection strategies in picking the sample of pupils whose answer sheets they corrected. We found no statistically significant differences between treatment groups on these items. Significantly more teachers in city and town than in rural schools reported that they scored the tests before returning them for processing.

It is not surprising in light of the above findings that when teachers were asked, "After testing, do you think you had a pretty good idea, even without seeing the test results, of how your class and individual pupils in your class did?" a majority (over 80 percent) in both treatments responded in the affirmative. There were no significant treatment differences on these items. However, significant differences occurred when the teachers were stratified by school location. Teachers in rural schools, to a significantly greater extent than teachers in town or city schools, indicated that before receiving test results, they had a better idea of how both their classes as a whole and individual pupils in their classes performed.

Although most teachers reported that they had a good idea about class and individual pupil performance without seeing test results, when asked if they were eager to see the actual results, over 95 percent in both treatments indicated that they were "very" or "moderately" eager to do so. Forty-seven percent in each treatment group indicated that they were "moderately" eager to see the results, while 50 and 51 percent in Treatments 2 and 3, respectively, reported that they were "very eager." This reported eagerness most likely reflects teachers' curiosity to compare their informal impressions with actual test performance.

Teachers' Perceptions of Consequences of Taking Tests

Teachers were presented with a series of nine statements about the effects of test taking on pupils. Each statement referred to a possible consequence of test taking (e.g., tests motivate children, tests increase anxiety), to which teachers responded by indicating their agreement (coded 1) or disagreement (coded 2) with the statement. Whether teachers were in a treatment that received or did not receive test information did not influence their responses (Table 4.19).

Seventy percent or more of the teachers across treatments believed that test taking could have a number of beneficial effects on pupils: tests motivate children, provide intellectual stimulation, are useful for future education, and provide enjoyment to children. Similarly, most teachers (over 70 percent)

Table 4.18. Teachers Reporting Scoring Tests prior to Return of Tests for Central Scoring, by Treatment

Item			Treatment 2					Treatment 3						
	N	Yes	No	M	S.D.	N	Yes	No	M	S.D.	t	p	ω²
Before returning answer sheets did you correct any tests yourself?	105	27.4	72.6	1.72	.45	137	10.0	89.9	1.90	.30	-3.59	.000	.047
If "yes," did you correct them:													
Item by item?	33	67.6	32.4	1.30	.47	21	47.6	52.4	1.52	.51	-1.63	.109	.030
Item by item for every pupil?	29	46.7	53.3	1.52	.51	16	31.3	68.8	1.69	.48	-1.10	.279	.005
Item by item for some pupils?	22	73.9	26.1	1.23	.43	14	71.4	28.6	1.29	.47	-0.38	.703	.000
If you corrected tests for only some pupils, were they:													
The very best pupils?	16	41.2	58.8	1.56	.51	10	50.0	50.0	1.50	.53	.30	.767	.000
The very worst pupils?	16	35.3	64.7	1.65	.50	9	55.6	44.4	1.44	.53	.85	.404	.000
A few average pupils?	17	50.0	50.0	1.50	.50	10	30.0	70.0	1.70	.48	-1.14	.264	.011
One or two representative pupils?	17	55.6	44.4	1.41	.51	9	33.3	66.7	1.67	.50	-1.22	.233	.018

Table 4.19. Teachers' Perceptions of the Effects Test Taking Has on Pupils, by Treatment

Item	Treatment 2					Treatment 3					t	p	ω^2
	N	Agree	Dis-agree	M	S.D.	N	Agree	Dis-agree	M	S.D.			
Tests motivate children	106	78.3	21.7	1.22	.41	138	72.7	27.3	1.27	.45	−1.04	.298	.000
Tests provide intellectual stimulation	106	90.6	9.4	1.09	.29	134	88.1	11.9	1.12	.33	−0.62	.537	.000
The experience is useful for future education	106	89.6	10.4	1.10	.31	135	88.2	11.8	1.12	.32	−0.36	.720	.000
Children enjoy doing the tests	105	97.1	2.9	1.03	.17	137	93.5	6.5	1.04	.22	−1.32	.189	.003
Tests influence the child's self-concept	105	62.9	37.1	1.37	.49	139	56.4	43.6	1.44	.50	−1.06	.291	.000
Tests increase anxiety	107	16.8	83.2	1.83	.38	136	16.1	83.9	1.84	.37	−0.13	.893	.000
Tests get to be too much like exams	106	12.3	87.7	1.88	.33	138	18.0	82.0	1.92	.39	1.25	.213	.002
Tests increase competitiveness	104	26.0	74.0	1.74	.44	133	29.9	70.1	1.70	.46	.70	.487	.000
Tests seem inappropriate for younger children	106	34.0	66.0	1.66	.48	134	35.8	64.2	1.64	.48	.30	.766	.000

believed that testing does not increase pupils' anxiety and competitiveness. Male teachers, to a significantly greater extent than females, believed that tests increase competitiveness. Across the two treatments, teachers perceived a number of beneficial consequences of testing with few accompanying detriments. A majority (63 percent in Treatment 2 and 56 percent in Treatment 3), however, did agree that tests influence the child's self-concept. We cannot determine from the responses to this item whether teachers felt the impact of tests on self-concept was positive or negative, even though we may reasonably assume that teachers perceived effects in both directions. Despite generally beneficial perceptions regarding the effects of testing, about one-third of the teachers in both treatments believed that standardized tests were inappropriate for younger children.

Teachers' Perceptions of Pupil Characteristics That Affect Test Performance

Seven items were used to determine whether teachers who administered standardized, multiple-choice tests believed that pupils with certain characteristics were favored by such tests. Teachers were asked whether in their view standardized tests favored higher performance by boys compared to girls, by urban children compared to rural children, by high-social-class children compared to low-social-class children, by good readers compared to poor ones, by good memorizers compared to poor ones, by creative children compared to noncreative ones, and by superficial, glib children compared to reflective, thoughtful ones. The three response options, "yes," "uncertain," and "no," were coded 3, 2, and 1, respectively. In considering teachers' responses, one is struck by the high percentage who responded "uncertain" to most of the items (Table 4.20). Except for the item comparing the performance of good and poor readers, on which teachers in both treatments were virtually unanimous in their belief that good readers have an advantage over poor ones on standardized tests, considerable numbers of teachers indicated their uncertainty. Between 15 and 27 percent were uncertain in comparing social classes, good and poor memorizers, creative and uncreative children, and glib and thoughtful children; between 45 and 60 percent were uncertain in comparing boys and girls and urban and rural children. Moreover, the differences in the percentage of "uncertain" responses on any given comparison differed only slightly by treatment. We might have expected that teachers in Treatment 3, who had had access to test results, would have felt themselves to be in a better position to make a judgment about factors that might affect pupil performance. This, however, was not the case.

Table 4.20. Teachers' Perceptions of the Factors That Might Influence Test Performance, by Treatment

Item	Treatment 2						Treatment 3						t	p	ω^2
	N	Yes	No	Uncertain	M	S.D.	N	Yes	No	Uncertain	M	S.D.			
Does this kind of test favor higher performance by:															
Boys compared to girls?	110	1.8	38.7	59.5	1.64	.52	141	21.1	33.8	64.1	1.68	.51	−0.68	.498	.000
Urban compared to rural children?	110	14.4	40.5	45.0	1.75	.70	143	11.8	36.8	51.4	1.74	.65	.05	.961	.000
High social class compared to low social class?	110	40.5	37.8	21.6	2.02	.89	142	37.8	35.0	27.3	2.02	.85	−0.03	.979	.000
Good readers compared to poor readers?	110	92.8	6.3	.9	2.86	.50	144	92.4	1.4	6.2	2.91	.33	−0.88	.378	.000
Good memorizers compared to poor memorizers?	110	41.4	38.7	19.8	2.04	.90	143	37.5	47.6	14.6	1.90	.92	1.16	.246	.001

Table 4.20. (Continued)

Item	Treatment 2						Treatment 3						t	p	ω^2
	N	Yes	No	Uncer-tain	M	S.D.	N	Yes	No	Uncer-tain	M	S.D.			
Creative children compared to non-creative children?	109	45.5	33.6	20.9	2.13	.88	142	37.8	43.3	18.9	1.94	.90	1.69	.093	.007
Superficial, glib children compared to reflective, thoughtful children?	110	8.1	74.8	17.1	1.34	.63	142	16.1	65.7	18.2	1.51	.76	−1.91	.058	.010

Teachers in both treatments tended to believe that standardized tests favor pupils from higher social classes, pupils who are good readers, good memorizers, and creative. Gender, whether pupils are from urban or rural areas, and whether they are glib as opposed to thoughtful, were perceived not to influence test performance greatly. There were no statistically significant differences between treatments on the seven items. In considering these findings we should recognize a number of issues. First, a large proportion of Irish elementary schools, particularly in town and city areas, are single-gender schools. Teachers in such schools, despite receiving test information, might not have had a basis for comparing the performance of their pupils with the performance of pupils of the opposite gender. Second, the tables of norms for the standardized tests used in our study do not provide separate norms for gender, geographical location, or social class. Thus, the test norms would not have provided teachers with a basis for comparing the performance of different groupings of children. Third, and perhaps of most interest, standardized tests are not the center of a controversy in Ireland, and the public debate over the beneficial and detrimental effects of tests, sometimes related to gender, geographical, and social class differences, is not the focus of discussion. As a consequence teachers may not have been sensitized to such distinctions in the context of performance on standardized tests.

Despite this situation we found statistically significant differences when teachers were stratified by school location on three of the items that dealt with the performance of different types of pupil on standardized tests. Rural teachers, to a significantly greater extent than town or city teachers, perceived standardized tests as favoring boys compared to girls, urban compared to rural children, and high-social-class pupils compared to low-social-class ones. In the context of the perceived gender bias of tests, we may note that, in contrast with city and town schools, many rural schools serve both boys and girls. We also found a significant gender effect on the item that asked if standardized tests favored higher performance by good readers as opposed to poor readers. Female teachers perceived good readers to be favored on such tests to a significantly greater extent than did male teachers.

TEACHERS' PERCEPTIONS OF USEFULNESS AND REPORTED USES OF TEST INFORMATION

To obtain information on teachers' uses of test information, we obviously had to rely on the responses of teachers who actually received information—that is, Treatment 3 teachers. However, some comparative data on this topic were available since teachers had responded to most of the relevant questionnaire items in both the second and fourth years of the study. A total of ninety-six teachers who had responded on both occasions provide the data for our analyses. A number of questions, however, were asked only in the final year of the study. These relate to teachers' interest in different types of test results and the dissemination of test results within schools. Our information on these topics is restricted to the replies of teachers (approximately 140) in Treatment 3 at the end of the study.

One could speculate on a number of possible consequences of experience with tests. On the one hand, one might hypothesize that the introduction of test booklets and computer-printed output would assume importance in teachers' eyes simply because of the form and novelty of the procedure and of the information provided. Under such circumstances perceptions about tests as well as the use of test scores might reflect a "Hawthorne effect" in the early years of the study. Over time, as tests and test information became a yearly event in the classroom, perceptions might change and tests assume less importance in teachers' eyes. On the other hand, one might hypothesize that the very novelty of the tests, coupled with teachers' inexperience with norm-referenced test results, would create unfavorable perceptions and inhibit wide use of the results during the early years of the study. Familiarity gained through experience might make teachers more comfortable with tests and test results by the end of the study. Given these two competing hypotheses, we were interested in determining how increased exposure to tests did in fact affect teacher perceptions and reported use of test results.

Teachers were asked to provide information at two points in time about six topics. One of these related to pupils' reactions to tests, two to teachers' perceived usefulness of the tests, and three to actions that teachers had taken on the basis of test results. The six topics were: (1) pupil reactions to tests; (2) the usefulness of the test scores for making various decisions about pupils; (3) the accuracy of the pupil assessments provided by the tests; (4) the number of pupils and parents to whom teachers reported scores on the tests; (5) the number of pupils moved from one instructional group to another on the basis of test results; and (6) the influence of test information on the material covered or methods of teaching in the classroom. In the following analyses we compare the perceptions and reported practices of Treatment 3 teachers in the second and final year of the study. Analyses in which teachers' responses were stratified by gender of teacher and by school location were also carried out. In a few cases, as we have indicated, comparative data from the second year are not available.

Teachers' Perceptions of Pupils' Reactions to Tests

Questions were asked of teachers about pupils' reactions to the standardized tests in eight items. For each item teachers selected an index of the number of pupils in the class who manifested a particular reaction: "all," "most," "half," "few," or "none" (coded 1 to 5, respectively). Thus, the higher the mean presented, the *fewer* the number of pupils who were reported to manifest the reaction. The data in Table 4.21, which presents the results of correlated *t*-tests of the teachers' perceptions, show that between the second and fourth years of the study, teachers differed significantly in their report of four of eight pupil reactions to the test. In the fourth year, compared with the second year, fewer pupils were reported as feeling the test program was too long, as having difficulty following test directions, as being anxious about test results, or as asking the purpose of the tests. These findings could be the consequence of many factors—greater familiarity with the tests, perceptions of the importance of the tests and particularly of their impact on activities in the classroom and pupils' status in the class. There were no differences between the second and fourth years in the numbers of pupils who asked for test results (30 to 35 percent), who were interested in the tests (75 percent or more), who had difficulty using separate answer sheets, or who had difficulty keeping the right place on answer sheets.

In the fourth year rural teachers reported significantly more pupil anxiety than did city teachers. They also reported that their pupils were significantly more interested in the tests than either town or city teachers.

Usefulness of Test Scores for Making Decisions about Pupils

Before considering teachers' perceptions of the usefulness of test scores for making decisions about pupils, we may note that in the final year of the study, teachers reported a high interest in the test results; 97 percent of teachers said that they had examined their pupils' test scores either "immediately" (83 percent) on receiving them or "within a week" (13.6 percent). Ninety-two percent reported that they examined the test results on a pupil-by-pupil basis for all or most pupils in their class.

Also in the final year, teachers were asked about their relative interest in the different kinds of scores that were provided. About two-thirds of teachers indicated that the scores from the single ability and three attainment tests were about equally useful or interesting to them. One-third, however, reported that one of the scores was more useful or interesting than the others. Over three-quarters of those who identified one of the scores as being more useful or interesting than the others selected the pupil's intelligence test score.

Table 4.21. Teachers' Perceptions of Pupil Reactions to Standardized Tests (Treatment 3)

Item	Year	N	All	Most	Half	Few	None	M	S.D.	t	p	ω^2
						Response Options: Percentages						
Pupils asked about the purpose of the tests	2	92	9.8	32.6	10.9	30.4	16.3	3.12	1.31	-2.59	.011	.030
	4	92	5.3	26.6	4.3	46.8	17.0	3.46	1.21			
Pupils asked for test results	2	95	13.7	25.3	2.1	28.4	30.5	3.39	1.48	.08	.938	.000
	4	95	12.8	20.2	9.6	31.9	25.5	3.38	1.39			
Pupils felt the test program was too long	2	92	2.2	13.2	8.8	31.9	44.0	4.04	1.13	-3.26	.002	.050
	4	92	0.0	3.2	8.4	32.6	55.8	4.42	.77			
Pupils were interested in tests	2	96	30.4	45.3	18.9	5.3	0.0	1.99	.84	1.27	.208	.003
	4	96	38.9	46.3	6.3	7.4	1.1	1.87	.90			
Pupils were anxious about the test	2	92	12.1	22.0	18.7	36.3	11.0	3.13	1.22	-3.70	.000	.065
	4	92	2.1	17.0	8.5	48.9	23.4	3.71	1.06			
Pupils had difficulty following test directions	2	88	1.2	1.2	7.0	72.1	18.6	4.07	.64	-3.03	.003	.045
	4	88	0.0	1.1	3.2	56.8	38.9	4.33	.58			
Pupils had difficulty using separate answer sheets	2	49	0.0	8.8	10.3	66.2	14.7	3.98	.78	-1.18	.243	.004
	4	49	0.0	8.3	5.0	60.0	26.7	4.10	.90			
Pupils had difficulty keeping the right place on separate answer sheets	2	50	0.0	11.4	8.2	65.8	24.7	4.16	.62	-1.70	.095	.019
	4	50	0.0	1.7	3.3	60.0	35.0	4.34	.63			

The intelligence and attainment test results that were given to teachers in Treatment 3 contained each pupil's raw score, percentile score, and standard score for each test. Teachers were asked whether they gave more attention to one of the types of test score reported to them than to others. Two-thirds indicated that they attended most to the percentile scores, while an additional quarter reported that they attended most to the standard scores. When asked whether they retabulated test results in any way, only 16 percent said they did. Most of these teachers indicated that they retabulated results in order to make direct comparisons of a pupil's performance across different tests; small numbers of teachers calculated class means (6 percent of all respondents) or ranked pupils from highest to lowest on the basis of their performance on a test (10 percent of all respondents). The vast majority of teachers attended only to the results as they had been provided as part of the testing program.

The longitudinal sample's responses to eight statements about the usefulness of intelligence tests and the test information they received are presented in Table 4.22. There were five response options: "strongly agree," "agree," "uncertain," "disagree," and "strongly disagree" (coded 1 to 5, respectively). Inspection of the means indicates that across the eight items teachers generally tended to agree or strongly agree with each of the statements. We found no statistically significant differences over time on any of the items, indicating that increased exposure to the tests and test results did little to alter teachers' initial judgments about the intelligence tests. Substantial majorities of teachers in both years indicated that the ability test was a good measure of what the teacher considered to be intelligence, was a good measure of the kind of ability a pupil needs to succeed in school, provided scores that corresponded closely with the teacher's own estimates of pupils' intelligence, would be useful for assigning pupils to classes according to ability, and would be useful for ability grouping for instructional purposes within classrooms. As the locus of test use moves from the context of the classroom to more general decisions, such as admission to postprimary school or vocational and educational counseling, the teachers were more evenly divided in their perceptions of the usefulness of intelligence tests, even though they still tended to view the tests as useful. The percentage of "uncertain" responses also became larger on the last three items in Table 4.22, over 25 percent in most cases. These percentages did not change much over time. In general, while the majority of teachers agreed that intelligence tests and test scores were accurate and potentially useful within the classroom context, fewer teachers expressed such attitudes when the context shifted away from the immediate classroom situation to more remote educational contexts or decisions.

Teachers were also asked about the usefulness of the achievement tests in English, Irish, and mathematics that they had administered during the study.

Table 4.22. Teachers' Perceptions of the Usefulness of Intelligence Test Performance (Treatment 3)

Item	Year	N	Response Options: Percentages					M	S.D.	t	p	ω^2
			Strongly Agree	Agree	Uncertain	Disagree	Strongly Disagree					
The test is a good measure of what you consider to be intelligence	2	92	13.7	73.7	5.3	7.4	0.0	2.05	.70	.82	.417	.000
	4	92	12.9	69.9	9.7	7.5	0.0	2.12	.72			
The test is a good measure of the kind of ability a pupil needs to succeed in school	2	92	11.6	68.4	8.4	11.6	0.0	2.20	.80	1.29	.202	.004
	4	92	9.7	62.4	12.9	15.1	0.0	2.34	.86			
The scores reported for your pupils correspond closely to your estimates of their intelligence	2	92	23.2	58.9	1.1	14.7	2.1	2.13	1.02	.29	.776	.000
	4	92	12.9	72.0	4.3	7.5	3.2	2.16	.87			
The information provided by the test would be useful for assigning pupils to class according to ability	2	87	12.6	64.2	5.3	14.7	3.2	2.33	.99	.67	.502	.000
	4	87	7.5	61.3	14.0	16.1	1.1	2.40	.88			
The information provided by the test would be useful for grouping pupils for instruction within your class	2	91	16.5	62.6	5.5	14.3	1.1	2.22	.93	.98	.328	.000
	4	91	6.5	68.5	12.0	10.9	2.2	2.35	.86			

Table 4.22. (Continued)

Item	Year	N	Response Options: Percentages					M	S.D.	t	p	ω^2
			Strongly Agree	Agree	Uncertain	Disagree	Strongly Disagree					
The information provided by the test would be useful as an aid in counseling pupils about educational plans	2	91	12.8	45.7	23.4	17.0	1.1	2.46	.96	1.38	.171	.005
	4	91	7.5	44.1	26.9	18.3	3.2	2.65	.97			
The information provided by the test would be useful as an aid in counseling pupils about vocational plans	2	91	8.5	34.0	31.9	23.4	2.1	2.75	.98	−0.17	.862	.000
	4	91	4.3	41.9	32.3	17.2	4.3	2.73	.93			
This test would be useful as a screening device for admission to postprimary schools	2	91	14.9	40.4	18.1	18.1	8.5	2.67	1.19	0.00	1.000	.000
	4	91	4.3	48.4	28.0	15.1	4.3	2.67	.94			

For each of these three tests, they were asked to indicate how accurate an assessment of their pupils' achievement the test provided. Response options ranged from "very accurate" (coded 1) to "very inaccurate" (coded 4). A "not applicable" response option was also provided, primarily for teachers in the lower grades, who did not administer Irish tests, but this was not scaled or included in the calculation of the treatment means. Over 85 percent of teachers rated the three achievement tests as "accurate" or "very accurate" across subject areas and years. While the percentage of "accurate" or "very accurate" ratings tended to increase very slightly over time, this difference was not statistically significant for any of the tests (Table 4.23).

When these data were stratified by gender, analyses indicated that in the final year, male teachers, compared with female teachers, perceived the Irish and mathematics tests to be significantly more accurate. This finding agrees with earlier findings that male teachers were more favorably disposed than female teachers toward standardized tests and test information.

Two final questions asked of Treatment 3 teachers may provide some insight into teachers' perceptions of the usefulness of test information. First, teachers were asked whether, generally speaking, their class as a whole performed higher, lower, or about the same as expected on the tests. About 23 percent indicated their class attained higher scores than expected; 17 percent indicated that class performance was lower than they expected; and 60 percent indicated their classes performed about the same as they had expected. Second, teachers were asked to indicate whether the rank order of pupils on the tests was as they had expected—that is, whether those pupils teachers considered to be the best did best on the tests and those they considered to be poorest did worst. In responding to this question, teachers reported whether there were "many," "some," or "no discrepancies" between their ranking of pupils and the ranking provided by the test results. Only five teachers (3.5 percent) reported that there were many discrepancies between the two rankings. One hundred and two teachers (72.3 percent) reported some discrepancies, and thirty-four teachers (24.1 percent) reported none. It is evident from these results that teachers' assessments of pupils were perceived to correspond quite well with pupils' performance on the standardized tests. Therefore, for the majority of teachers, the test results could have held few surprises. In these circumstances they may have felt that no point would be served by referring back to test results.

Dissemination of Test Results

Teachers were asked to indicate whether they provided intelligence or standardized achievement test information to "all" (coded 1), "most" (coded 2), "half"

Table 4.23. Teachers' Perceptions of the Accuracy of Attainment Test Information (Treatment 3)

Test Information	Year	N	Response Options: Percentages					M	S.D.	t	p	ω^2
			Very Accurate	Accurate	Inaccurate	Very Inaccurate						
Standardized Irish test	2	78	7.1	83.3	8.3	1.2		2.03	.46	1.26	.211	.004
	4	78	11.1	82.9	6.1	0.0		1.94	.41			
Standardized English test	2	84	16.1	75.9	6.9	1.1		1.94	.52	.16	.871	.000
	4	84	11.1	84.4	4.4	0.0		1.93	.40			
Standardized mathematics test	2	84	15.9	70.5	12.5	1.1		1.99	.59	.61	.540	.000
	4	84	14.6	75.3	10.1	0.0		1.94	.48			

(coded 3), "few" (coded 4), or "none" (coded 5) of the pupils and parents of pupils in their classes. A "not applicable" option was also provided, but this was not scaled or included in the statistics. Since two different ability tests were used—the Otis-Lennon in grades 2 and 3 and the Drumcondra Verbal Reasoning Test in grades 4, 5, and 6—data regarding the dissemination of ability test information were presented separately for the two tests. Such a distinction did not seem necessary in the case of the achievement tests since a single test series was used at all grade levels.

A number of points emerge from an examination of Table 4.24. First, across intelligence and achievement tests, year, and public (pupils and parents), about one-half to two-thirds of the teachers reported that they did not disseminate test scores to any pupils or parents. Second, teachers reported disseminating intelligence test information more frequently to pupils in higher elementary grades than in lower grades. Third, few teachers selected the "half" response category. Rather, teachers' responses tended to divide on either side of the "half" category; a larger group of teachers provided information to few or no parents and pupils, and a smaller group provided information to all or most pupils and parents. The percentage of teacher responses that fell on either side of the dichotomy varied with time, test type, grade level, and dissemination group. Fourth, achievement test information was more widely disseminated among pupils than intelligence test information. This finding corroborates our earlier findings that teachers said they would be more prone to release achievement than intelligence test results to pupils. However, the reported dissemination of intelligence test information to pupils in grades 4, 5, and 6 closely parallels the figures for the reported dissemination of achievement test information to pupils in general. Slightly more parents were reported to have received achievement test information than intelligence test information. Fifth, although there were no statistically significant differences over time within categories, in general teachers were less likely at the end of the study to release test information to pupils and their parents than they were at an earlier stage; evidence for this is to be found in the increased percentages of teachers selecting the "few" or "none" response options in the fourth year as compared with the second year, as well as in the corresponding higher fourth-year means. The phenomenon is particularly pronounced for items related to the release of test information to pupils. Finally, although we saw earlier that teachers felt that parents should have greater access to test scores than pupils, in practice both achievement and intelligence test results were reported to be more widely disseminated to pupils than to parents.

Given that, as we have already seen, male teachers expressed more positive attitudes toward standardized tests than did female teachers, we should not be surprised to find that male teachers reported that in the final year they told

Table 4.24. Responses of Teachers to Items Concerned with the Dissemination of Intelligence and Attainment Test Information to Pupils and Parents (Treatment 3)

Dissemination	Year	N	Response Options: Percentages					M	S.D.	t	p	ω^2
			All	Most	Half	Few	None					
Intelligence test information												
Dissemination of scores to children												
Grades 2 and 3	2	38	17.9	10.7	0.0	16.1	53.3	3.87	1.56	-1.98	.055	.037
	4	38	8.5	4.3	0.0	14.9	72.3	4.40	1.24			
Grades 4, 5, and 6	2	54	34.3	4.5	1.5	14.9	44.8	3.24	1.83	-1.37	.176	.008
	4	54	25.4	6.0	1.5	10.4	56.7	3.59	1.75			
Dissemination of scores to parents												
Grades 2 and 3	2	35	9.1	3.6	1.8	23.6	61.8	4.43	1.09	-0.46	.646	.000
	4	35	2.3	4.5	0.0	27.3	65.9	4.51	.89			
Grades 4, 5, and 6	2	52	6.1	9.1	1.5	21.2	62.1	4.12	1.26	-1.41	.164	.014
	4	52	4.5	3.0	3.0	31.3	58.2	4.39	.99			
Attainment test information												
Dissemination of scores to children	2	83	32.2	8.0	2.3	13.8	43.7	3.34	1.80	-1.77	.081	.012
	4	83	25.0	3.4	2.3	13.6	55.7	3.71	1.72			
Dissemination of scores to parents	2	84	5.7	6.9	4.6	28.7	54.0	4.17	1.18	-0.23	.819	.000
	4	84	4.5	6.7	2.3	32.6	53.9	4.20	1.14			

their pupils their intelligence and achievement test scores to a significantly greater extent than did female teachers. Also in the final year town and city teachers provided achievement test information to more parents than did rural teachers.

In addition to disseminating test information to pupils and parents, teachers might also discuss their pupils' test results with other teachers. We have data on the issue only for the final year of the study, when a series of questions was asked of teachers to determine the extent to which test information was disseminated and discussed among teachers in the school. Such dissemination might occur by one teacher's directly passing test results on to another teacher or by formal or informal discussion among teachers regarding their pupils' test results. In response to a question that asked whether teachers had seen their current pupils' test results from the previous year, 56 percent (76 of 136 teachers responding) indicated that they had. Those teachers who reported that they had seen their pupils' prior test results indicated that the results came primarily from two sources: either they had taught the same pupil in a prior year (N = 44; 55 percent) or the pupils' prior teacher had passed the results on (N = 29; 35 percent). We should note that some teachers remained with a cohort of pupils for a number of years and that some small rural schools had only two or three teachers, necessitating that each teacher instruct at more than one grade level. Only about one-third of the teachers received test results directly from their pupils' prior teacher. Less than 10 percent of teachers who indicated that they had seen their pupils' prior test results obtained them from a central school file or by asking the prior year's teacher for them. The results that teachers received from an earlier grade were generally for all (68 percent) or for most (17 percent) of the pupils in their classes.

When asked when they had received their pupils' prior test results, the seventy-six teachers who said they had received pupils' prior results split roughly among the three response options: "before school closed in the prior year" (29 percent), "in the first month of school" (41 percent), and "after testing in the present school year" (30 percent). This last group probably obtained results either to anticipate performance on the tests they had just administered or to compare pupil performance over a two-year period. In fact, when asked how they used the results from a previous testing, 75 percent of the seventy-six teachers who had these results indicated that they used them to compare pupils' performance from one year to the next. Last, when the total sample of teachers were asked whether they had passed last year's test results on to any other teachers, 53 percent (N = 76) responded "no," 28 percent (N = 40) responded "yes," and 19 percent (N = 27) indicated that they did not have test results in the previous year.

Again in the final year of the study, each teacher was asked to indicate how many other teachers in the school knew the current test results of individual pupils in his or her class. About 52 percent (N = 51) responded that no other teachers knew the test results of individual pupils; 23 percent (N = 23) responded that one other teacher in their school knew the results; and 14 percent (N = 14) that a few other teachers knew the results. When asked how many other teachers had a general idea of how their class as a whole—as opposed to individual pupils—had performed, teachers' responses indicated that information about general class performance was more widespread. Thus, 37 percent of the ninety-four respondents said that no teachers in their school knew about the performance of their class as a whole; 23 percent said that one other teacher knew; 23 percent said that a few other teachers knew; and 16 percent said that most teachers in their school knew. These results show that standardized test information is disseminated among some teachers in a school but that this information is by no means widely or commonly available. Certainly, large percentages of teachers in the school are reported to be unaware of the performance of other teachers' individual students or classes.

Test results contribute to discussion among teachers, but not to a very great extent. About two-thirds of teachers said that they discussed their class test results with other teachers only once or twice a year. An additional 20 percent indicated that they never talked with other teachers in their school about their class test results. This comparatively infrequent discussion of test results is confirmed by teachers' responses to an item that asked how often teachers in their school talked among themselves about the test results. Over 80 percent of the reporting teachers indicated that teachers in their school talked about test results among themselves only "occasionally." Only 4 percent reported "frequent" teacher discussion of test results, and 12 percent reported that teachers never talked about test results. Teachers in rural schools, to a significantly greater extent than teachers in city or town schools, reported more frequent teacher discussion of test results. Whatever discussion there is among teachers is reported to take place in informal settings, such as in the staff room (96 percent of respondents), as opposed to formal meetings called for the express purpose of discussing test results (4 percent of respondents).

Movement of Pupils between Instructional Groups

Teachers were asked in the second and fourth year of the study how many pupils they had moved from one instructional group to another on the basis of intelligence test results and on the basis of results from each of the three achievement tests. Respondents were provided with a grid and for each type of test were asked to indicate the actual number of pupils moved among instructional groups. Since so few teachers, less than 10 percent over all variables and years, indicated they moved more than one or two pupils from one group to another on the basis of test results, responses were dichotomized into two categories, one indicating "no pupil change" and the other indicating "one or more pupils changed." In both years over 80 percent of the teachers indicated that they did not use test score information as a basis for altering pupils' instructional groups (Table 4.25). Teachers who indicated that in the second year they moved at least one pupil in the light of the test information reported that they relied slightly more heavily on intelligence test results (16.1 percent) than on results in English (9.6 percent), Irish (12.0 percent), or mathematics (13.0 percent). On all variables the percentage of teachers who reported moving pupils from one group to another decreased somewhat over time. Only the decrease in the reported use of intelligence test information as a basis for changing pupils' group assignments was statistically significant. There are at least two plausible explanations for this. First, and most simply, in later years of the study teachers may have relied less on test information relative to other criteria in making decisions to alter the membership of class groups. Alternatively, prior pupil test information could have had an impact on the formation of groups if teachers passed on test information or comments based on such information to pupils' subsequent teachers. Once groups were constituted, their constitution may have changed little from year to year. This latter explanation would assume a cumulative impact of test information, despite the fact that teachers reported they did not explicitly recognize that impact on their within-class grouping.

Virtually all of the movement of pupils in classroom groups, particularly in the final year of the study, occurred in city schools. When teachers were stratified and analyzed in terms of school location, there were statistically significant differences in the reported use of test results to move pupils among instructional groups. These differences were observed for intelligence, mathematics, and English test information. In each case city teachers moved significantly more pupils than did town or rural teachers. Indeed, in no case did rural teachers report having moved a single pupil. This is hardly an unexpected finding; classes in small rural schools would be grouped on the basis of grade, and one would expect that reallocation of pupils across grades within a class would be much rarer than reallocation between groups in the same grade.

Influence of Test Information on Material Covered in Class or on Methods of Teaching

It is a reasonable assumption that test results might influence the content teachers plan to cover in their classes and the methods they use to present these topics to their pupils. Questions designed to assess teachers' perceptions in these areas were asked. The general intent of the items was to determine the extent to

Table 4.25. Teachers Reporting Changing a Pupil's Instructional Group on the Basis of Standardized Test Results (Treatment 3)

Type of Test Information	Year	N	Percentage of Teachers Reporting		Corrected χ^2	p
			No Pupil Changes	One or More Changes		
Intelligence	2	93	83.9	16.1	4.456	.035
	4	86	89.5	10.5		
English	2	83	90.4	9.6	2.829	.093
	4	90	94.4	5.6		
Irish	2	92	88.0	12.0	1.089	.297
	4	89	93.3	6.7		
Mathematics	2	92	87.0	13.0	2.678	.101
	4	89	95.5	4.5		

which standardized tests and test information influenced the curriculum, either as regards "teaching to the tests" or reviewing topics that test results showed to be inadequately learned by pupils. We have already seen (cf. Table 4.15) that in the final year of the study, fewer than 13 percent of teachers in the test-information group believed that standardized, multiple-choice tests create pressure to teach to the test. In the present analysis we have an opportunity to see whether teachers' reported practices support this position and whether those practices changed from the second to the fourth year of the study.

Teachers were asked, "Do you feel that these attainment tests have influenced or will influence the material you plan to cover in class?" A similar question was asked regarding the influence of the attainment tests on the way in which the material would be taught. Teachers responded to each question by indicating the amount they thought tests influenced their practice: "to a great extent," "to some extent," "to a slight extent," and "not at all" (coded 1 to 4, respectively).

Less than 5 percent of teachers reported that the attainment tests had or would have a great influence either on the content they covered in class or the manner in which they presented that content (Table 4.26). About 40 percent indicated that the tests affected the content they covered to some extent, while 30 percent indicated that their teaching methods were affected to some extent. What is perhaps most striking about our results is the fact that the percentages of teachers selecting each response option on the two items is virtually identical in the two years in which data were obtained. Thus, the influence that the attainment tests had in the second year of the study was unaltered in the fourth year in spite of greater exposure to and experience with tests and test results.

Teachers' Overt Use of Test Material

In considering teachers' examination of and use of test results, their communication of test results to others, and the movement of pupils between instructional groups on the basis of test results, we got some indication of teachers' involvement in the study. We also had a more direct measure of teachers' overt use of test materials. We used three parallel scales. Teachers rated their own performance, regular fieldworkers from the Research Centre that was conducting the study rated performance on a second scale, and a group of six observers from the Research Centre rated it on a third scale.

The teacher rating was included in a teacher questionnaire that went to all teachers in treatments that had received test information (Treatments 3, 4, and 5). The fieldworkers' checklist covered the same population. The special observers' ratings were restricted to teachers in Treatment 3 (grades 2 through 6) and Treatment 4 (grades 4 through 6). For the teacher questionnaire there were

Table 4.26. Reported Influence of Attainment Tests on Content Covered or Method of Teaching (Treatment 3 Teachers)

			Response Options: Percentages								
Influence	Year	N	To a Great Extent	To Some Extent	To a Slight Extent	Not at All	M	S.D.	t	p	ω^2
Influence on content covered	2	89	3.2	38.7	33.3	24.7	2.82	.86	-0.46	.649	.000
	4	89	2.2	38.9	31.1	27.8	2.87	.86			
Influence on teaching method	2	87	2.2	29.7	30.8	37.4	3:04	.88	-1.08	.283	.001
	4	87	3.4	23.6	28.1	44.9	3.15	.90			

Table 4.27. Percentages of Teachers in Each Category of Use as Rated by Regular Fieldworkers, Research Observers, and Teachers Themselves

Category of Use	Rater		
	Fieldworker*	Research Observer†	Teacher‡
Regular user	36.8	16.4	15.5
Occasional user	37.6	44.0	33.2
Interested observer	19.7	26.1	45.8
Participant	5.9	13.4	5.4

*Number of teachers rated = 340.
†Number of teachers rated = 268.
‡Number of teachers rated = 367.

367 returns; fieldworkers rated 340 teachers, and the special observers rated 268 teachers. All ratings were made at the end of the study.

All forms of the use scale had the same four categories: regular user, occasional user, interested observer, and participant. On the fieldworkers' and observers' checklist, each teacher was to be described in relation to the materials supplied as a regular user (frequently brings out results and finds them helpful in class), an occasional user (who had made definite use of results at least once or twice), an interested observer (finding materials interesting but not really ever using them), or as a participant (perhaps very willing to cooperate, but with no real interest). The item that appeared on the teacher questionnaire was as follows:

As far as test results are concerned, which of the following statements best describes you? Mark one only.

I often bring out the results and find them helpful during schoolwork.

I brought out the results once or twice and found them helpful.

I find the results interesting, but I cannot honestly say that they have been of any great use to me. I have never referred back to them making a decision.

I did what I was asked but I am not greatly interested. I have glanced at the results, but that's about all.

I didn't look at the results.

The first four statements on the Teacher Questionnaire correspond to the four categories of the other instruments. The fifth statement describes a lower level within the participant category.

It is clear that the fieldworker's rating is strongly biased toward the positive end of the scale relative to the teacher's self-rating (Table 4.27). The observer's scale is also biased in this direction, though not to the same degree. Thus the percentage of users (i.e., regular or occasional) is put at 47 percent by teachers, while the observers put it at 60 percent and the fieldworkers at 73 percent. If we take teachers' own ratings as the most accurate criterion of use, then the outside observers seemingly failed, as in other studies, to differentiate between the "pleasantness" of experimental sites and the implementation levels of the treatment (see Lukas and Wohlleb, 1973).

CONCLUSION

Our examination of teachers' perceptions and attitudes toward standardized tests indicates that a number of differences were associated with the availability of norm-referenced test information. Teachers who had administered tests of ability and attainment and who had received information about their pupils' performance perceived both kinds of tests to be more accurate measures of a pupil's scholastic ability than did teachers who had not. Teachers who had received results also felt that the constructs measured by the tests were more similar to the constructs necessary for success in school work than did teachers in the other treatment groups. However, teachers with experience of tests and test results perceived standardized tests as exerting *less* influence on how teachers perceive and act toward pupils than did teachers without test experience. Finally, although no increase in the incidence of intraclass grouping was associated with the availability of test information, teachers who grouped pupils in the test-information group were more likely to assign pupils on the basis of intelligence test results than were teachers in no-information groups.

Differences associated with test experience, however, did not extend to areas not directly related to standardized testing. We found no treatment differences in beliefs about the extent to which the results of intelligence tests depend on inborn or learned factors, in perceptions of the degree of similarity between the kind of intelligence measured by intelligence tests and the kind of intelligence necessary for success in higher education or in work, in the weight that teachers reported that they would give to test information in making selection or instructional decisions about a pupil, in opinions about who should receive pupils' intelligence and attainment test results, in beliefs about the stability of intelligence and attainment test scores over time, or in the reported incidence of within-class grouping. Overall, exposure to standardized tests and norm-referenced results clearly did not alter radically or extensively the perceptions, beliefs, or reported practices of teachers.

We presented evidence that may provide some background for understanding these findings. We saw that regardless of treatment group, teachers perceived themselves to be much more accurate than a variety of other publics and criteria in judging pupils' intelligence and achievement. These perceptions were evident at the start of the study and remained virtually intact to its conclusion. Similarly, throughout the study teachers indicated that they would give considerably more weight to teacher recommendation in making decisions about pupils than they would to tests. While tests did gain the attention of teachers, relinquishing or at any rate giving less weight to existing evaluative practices is quite another matter, especially when the perceived accuracy of the new technique was less that the perceived accuracy of existing practices. The availability of standardized test information did lead some teachers to utilize that information in decisions involving the assignment of pupils to instructional groups. However, test information appeared to represent an auxiliary or secondary criterion in such judgments, since teachers were nearly unanimous in stating that the most commonly reported grouping criteria were the teachers' own observations and tests.

In competing with other criteria for the teachers' attention and use, standardized tests appear to be in a somewhat anomalous position. If the results of the tests are widely divergent from teachers' perceptions, the tests run the risk of being ignored on the grounds of inaccuracy. If, on the other hand, test results correspond quite closely to teachers' perceptions, the tests run the risk of being dismissed on the grounds of providing redundant information. To the extent that test results are perceived to provide accurate information about pupils—though not as accurate as teachers' own perceptions—the availability of test results is not likely to greatly influence practice.

Further, our findings indicate that while the cooperation of teachers in administering the test program was good, their commitment to using test results, even on their own admission, was not great. This is something that obviously has to be taken into account in interpreting results in which experimental groups are compared with control groups. In the light of information supplied by teachers themselves and by external raters, it would be surprising if we were to find large differences between experimental and control groups in the overt, conscious use of tests, such as in grouping practices or in the communication of test results to other possibly interested parties. This is not to say that differences between groups may not be detected in less overt, less conscious processes. Possibly, teachers who examined test results, and most did, altered in ways that were not detected in our questionnaire instruments. Possibly, too, their perceptions of pupils, and consequently their treatment of pupils, were altered, even if that treatment did not take the form of formally regrouping the pupils or other easily recognizable procedures.

In addition to general, treatment-level results, one additional set of results is worthy of attention. On numerous items analyses indicated that male teachers tended to have a significantly more positive view of standardized tests than did female teachers. Moreover, and of considerable importance, the observed male-female differences were at the level of main effects, not gender-treatment interactions, indicating that the differences were present in all treatments, not specific to particular treatments. Male teachers perceived standardized achievement tests to be more accurate, reported giving them more weight in making instructional decisions about pupils, and reported using these tests for within-class grouping decisions to a greater extent than did female teachers. Male teachers, to a significantly greater degree than female teachers, also believed that one obtains a clear idea of a pupil's intelligence from intelligence tests, that the kind of intelligence measured by intelligence tests matters much in life, that the results of intelligence tests depend more on what a person is born with than what he has learned, and that pupils' teachers and parents should have access to their intelligence test scores. In general, we found that male teachers were more favorably disposed to standardized intelligence and achievement tests than were female teachers.

We may note that teachers, irrespective of treatment group, perceived a number of benefits for pupils associated with test taking. In general, teachers believed that testing motivates pupils, provides intellectual stimulation, is useful for future education and that pupils enjoy taking the tests. Tests were not widely viewed as sources of anxiety or competitiveness. Over half the teachers felt that tests influence a pupil's self-concept; however, whether this influence was perceived as being positive or negative could not be ascertained from the questions that were asked. About one-third of the teachers in each treatment group felt that tests were inappropriate for younger children.

Teachers identified a number of pupil characteristics that they perceived as affecting pupil test performance. Almost all teachers believed that standardized tests favor higher performance by good as opposed to poor readers. Teachers were more evenly split on the effect of social class, memorizing ability, and creative ability on test performance and showed greatest uncertainty about the role of gender and geographical location in affecting pupil performance.

Teachers seemed to divide into two clusters regarding their reported dissemination of test information. A small group provided test information to most or all of their pupils and pupils' parents, and a larger group provided information to few or none of their pupils or pupils' parents. Very few teachers fell between these two extremes—that is, very few teachers reported the release of test information to about half their pupils or pupils' parents. Attainment test results were reported to be more readily released by teachers than intelligence test results. Male teachers disseminated intelligence and attainment test information to pupils to a significantly greater extent than did female teachers.

The dissemination of test results to other teachers was more common than dissemination to pupils or parents. About a third of teachers reported that they received from and passed on to other teachers their pupils' test results from previous years. Generally, test scores from earlier years were used to compare pupils' performance from year to year. Test results were not a great spur to discussion among teachers within schools. While some communication regarding the test performance of both individual pupils and classes as a whole was reported, this was infrequent and did not necessarily involve the whole school.

The use of attainment test results to reassign pupils among instructional groups diminished during the life of the study. Although tests were not widely used for this purpose at any stage—on average less than one pupil per classroom was reported to have been changed among groups on the basis of any given attainment test early in the study—by the end of the study the reported impact of tests on reallocation of pupils among instructional groups was practically nil. The primary impact of attainment test information on pupils' group assignments was in city schools. Over time, we found no reported increase in the extent to which the attainment tests influenced the content covered in classrooms or the way that content was presented. Few teachers, less than one in twenty, reported that the attainment tests influenced content or method of instruction to a great extent.

While we found some evidence that increased exposure to testing and test results affected teachers' uses of tests, overall the attitudes and uses expressed by teachers early in our study remained little changed at its end. While teachers seemed to like the tests and perceived a number of advantages as being associated with them, by and large the availability of norm-referenced tests and information did not substantially affect teachers' reported practices over a wide range of areas involving testing and evaluation.

5 EFFECTS OF
TESTING ON PUPILS

The issue of testing is most widely debated at the pupil level, for which a wide variety of possible effects of standardized testing has been posited. These include effects not only on the pupil's scholastic performance, but also on his or her attitudes, perceptions, self-concept, and life chances.

The precise effects that testing might have on pupils, however, are difficult to ascertain. For one thing, testing and test information are introduced into an environment in which considerable evaluative activity and information already exists. The informal evaluation and communication network that characterizes all classrooms informs students, virtually on a daily basis, about their capabilities, achievements, progress, and general "worth." When more formal, standardized testing and test results are introduced into such an environment, unambiguously disassociating their effect from that of ongoing classroom evaluation processes is difficult. Further, evaluative information, including test information, might have an impact on pupils in many ways. For example, the ease or difficulty a student finds in taking a test—apart altogether from formal information on performance—could provide information to a student regarding his or her capability, achievement, and scholastic progress. At a later stage pupils may obtain information about their test performance from their teachers and thus gain a further and firmer basis for self-evaluation and comparisons with other pupils. Even if teachers do not report actual test scores to pupils, they may take some action on the basis of the scores, such as grouping pupils in a particular way or behaving differently toward pupils with different test scores. If pupils become aware of these practices, even though the process may be indirect and subtle, test scores may affect them.

Information on the processes by which test information might have an impact on pupils would be valuable. However, that is not the focus of our study. We may regard such processes as really a secondary concern to the question of whether standardized tests and test information have an impact on pupils at all. That is to say, a concern that logically should take precedence over the study of transmittal mechanisms in the classroom is whether tests have any impact on pupils at all. Although assuming that tests can and do have an impact on pupils seems reasonable, and although the effects are claimed to involve a large number of student characteristics, clear empirical evidence regarding the impact of tests on pupils is scarce.

To obtain information about the impact of standardized tests and test information on pupils, we used a number of data-gathering procedures. Toward the end of the final year of the study, sixth-grade pupils in all treatment groups completed an instrument called the Pupil Questionnaire, which sought information about pupil perceptions in the following areas: (1) factors that help, hinder, or do not matter in getting on well in class (e.g., hard work, intelligence, luck); (2) pupils' self-rating of cognitive and affective characteristics (e.g., intelligence, English reading, exam results, originality); (3) factors that have changed a pupil's idea of how he or she was doing in school, either for the better or worse (e.g., test results, what teacher has said, what classmates thought); (4) agreement or disagreement with twenty-six statements about the pupil's educational experience (e.g., "I sometimes feel I just can't learn"; "Getting a high grade or mark in exams is very important to me"; "If I try hard enough, I will succeed in life").

In addition to questions in these four general areas, which were answered by pupils in all treatments, pupils in testing treatments responded to additional questions. They were asked to provide information on eighteen items that assessed their perceptions of and reactions to the tests (e.g., "Did you enjoy sitting for these tests?" "Did you feel afraid?" "Did you think the tests were fair?" "Did you try to do your best on the tests?"). Finally, pupils who were in a treatment in which teachers received test information were also asked a series of questions about their results (e.g., "Were you told how you did on the tests?" "Did you talk to your parents, teachers, or classmates about how you did on the tests?").

Analysis of the data involved examining differences in responses between the three main treatment groups of the study: the no-testing, control group (Treatment 1), the second control group in which ability and achievement testing was carried out but test information was not returned to teachers (Treatment 2), and the group in which ability and achievement testing was carried out and norm-referenced test information was returned to teachers (Treatment 3). Most of the analyses involve comparisons of the performance, attitudes, and perceptions of pupils in these three treatments. However, analyses concerned with pupils' reactions to taking standardized tests involve only Treatments 2 and 3, since Treatment 1 pupils were not tested until the end of the final year of the study.

A total of 2,967 pupils were included in analyses. However, the number fluctuates over the many analyses to be presented because of missing responses, absences on the day of testing, or an inability to match a pupil's responses on one variable to the pupil's response on another. The pupils were distributed across treatments as follows: Treatment 1: 820 pupils; Treatment 2: 819 pupils; Treatment 3: 1,328 pupils.

The chapter is divided into four sections. In the first section we describe pupils' perceptions of and reactions to the standardized tests that were administered. In the second section we present results of analyses that examined the types of activity that pupils perceived as important in getting on well in class and the extent to which different types and sources of information affect pupils' ideas of how they are doing in school. Pupils' self-perceptions of cognitive and affective characteristics are described in the third section, where we examine agreements between pupils' self-perceptions and both their teachers' perceptions of them and their actual standardized test performance. The fourth and final section provides a description of analyses that were carried out to ascertain whether testing in general, and test information in particular, affects pupils' self-concepts. The pupil is the unit in all the analyses. Thus, the analyses are quasi-experimental in nature, since they are based on a unit other than the one sampled for the study. Further, in this approach each pupil is counted as a degree of freedom for the tests of statistical significance; thus, the number of degrees of freedom in the analyses is quite large, with the result that small differences between groups may be statistically significant.

PUPILS' PERCEPTIONS OF AND REACTIONS TO
STANDARDIZED TESTS

Following four years of testing experience, sixth-grade pupils in Treatment 2 (no-information group) and Treatment 3 (norm-referenced information group) were asked to respond to a series of eighteen questions dealing with their perceptions of and reactions to the tests they took. A general introductory statement preceded the actual questions: "Last autumn you sat for several tests which were printed in special booklets. In these tests you picked the correct answer from among several answers given and marked the correct answer on a separate answer sheet. Answer each of the following questions about these tests." Pupils then were asked to respond to each question by marking "yes" (coded 3), "no" (coded 1), or "don't remember" (coded 2). Pupils in Treatment 1 were not asked to respond to these questions since in the preceding four years they had not been tested.

Most students remembered their reactions to the tests. On all questions, except the one inquiring about whether pupils "felt confident" while taking the tests, around 10 percent or fewer of the pupils responded "don't remember"; on the item regarding their confidence during testing, under 20 percent indicated that they could not remember their feelings (Table 5.1). The majority of pupils in both treatments clearly perceived the tests in favorable light. Across treatments, over 70 percent of pupils indicated that they enjoyed sitting for the tests, were not frightened by them, found them to be an interesting challenge, did not feel bored, did not think that the tests were too long or too difficult, thought they were fair, and liked picking out the right answer rather than writing out their own answer. Somewhat smaller percentages of pupils—although over 60 percent in all cases—reported that they felt confident about the tests, did not feel nervous, liked using a separate answer sheet, and did not think that the tests were too easy. Generally, fewer than one-quarter of the pupils in either treatment expressed negative feelings or reactions to the test-taking experience.

The largely positive reactions expressed by students are interesting in light of the fact that only about 60 percent of pupils reported that they cared whether or not they sat for the tests in the first place. In spite of this initial relative lack of interest, reactions to the tests and test-taking experience were positive. Moreover, more than 70 percent of the pupils indicated that they thought it was important to do well on the tests, and over 90 percent reported that they had tried to do their best. The fact that pupils viewed the tests as enjoyable and important is further confirmed by the data that indicate that about 80 percent across treatments reported that they told their parents about doing the tests. We do not know, however, what specific information pupils conveyed to their parents, either as regards the test-taking experience or the tests themselves.

Since pupils in the no-information group (Treatment 2) had never received test information, it is surprising that nearly 50 percent of them indicated that they expected to be told their marks on the tests. About 58 percent of pupils in the test-information group (Treatment 3) indicated that they had expected to be told their test results. This figure is about ten to fifteen percentage points higher than the approximately 45 percent of pupils in that treatment who,

Table 5.1. Pupils' Responses to Questions about Standardized Tests, by Treatment

Did you...	Treatment	N	Percentages			M	S.D.	F	p	R^2
			Yes	No	Don't Remember					
Enjoy sitting for these tests?	2	814	83.9	11.5	4.5	1.28	.66	10.981	.00	.005
	3	1316	77.6	15.7	6.7	1.38	.74			
Care whether you sat for them?	2	812	59.7	31.2	9.1	1.71	.91	.837	.36	.000
	3	1309	60.9	28.6	10.5	1.68	.89			
Dislike sitting for them?	2	811	10.0	85.9	4.1	2.76	.62	1.417	.23	.001
	3	1310	10.6	83.2	6.2	2.73	.64			
Feel afraid?	2	812	16.9	76.5	6.7	2.60	.76	5.145	.02	.002
	3	1311	20.6	72.2	7.2	2.52	.81			
Feel confident?	2	812	65.6	18.2	16.1	1.53	.78	1.568	.21	.001
	3	1305	62.3	19.3	18.4	1.57	.79			
Find them an interesting challenge?	2	813	78.8	13.9	7.3	1.35	.71	3.016	.08	.001
	3	1309	74.7	15.4	9.9	1.41	.74			
Feel nervous?	2	812	25.5	68.3	6.2	2.43	.87	2.950	.09	.001
	3	1310	29.1	65.1	5.8	2.36	.90			
Feel bored?	2	814	17.1	76.8	6.1	2.60	.76	.112	.74	.000
	3	1308	16.3	77.1	6.6	2.61	.75			

Table 5.1. (Continued)

Did you . . .	Treatment	N	Percentages Yes	Percentages No	Percentages Don't Remember	M	S.D.	F	p	R^2
Think the tests were too long?	2	813	12.1	82.7	5.3	2.71	.67	.419	.52	.000
	3	1309	12.1	80.7	7.2	2.69	.68			
Think the tests were fair?	2	812	88.9	7.4	3.7	1.18	.55	.664	.42	.000
	3	1303	87.0	7.4	5.6	1.20	.56			
Think the tests were too difficult?	2	808	5.6	89.7	4.7	2.84	.50	.221	.64	.000
	3	1303	5.1	88.2	6.8	2.83	.49			
Think the tests were too easy?	2	811	24.7	68.4	6.9	2.44	.86	2.471	.12	.001
	3	1300	20.4	70.0	9.6	2.50	.81			
Like using the separate answer sheets?	2	803	69.9	21.0	9.1	1.51	.82	11.599	.00	.005
	3	1300	63.1	27.4	9.5	1.64	.88			
Like picking out the right answer?	2	808	85.1	9.8	5.1	1.25	.62	.950	.33	.000
	3	1307	83.4	10.8	5.8	1.27	.64			
Try to do your best?	2	808	90.7	4.2	5.1	1.13	.45	.218	.64	.000
	3	1297	91.8	4.3	3.9	1.13	.44			
Expect to be told your marks?	2	810	48.8	45.3	5.9	1.97	.97	19.423	.00	.009
	3	1297	58.1	35.9	6.0	1.78	.94			

Table 5.1. (Continued)

Did you . . .	Treatment	N	Percentages			M	S.D.	F	p	R^2
			Yes	No	Don't Remember					
Tell your parents about the tests?	2	806	79.7	14.4	6.0	1.35	.72	2.062	.15	.001
	3	1302	82.5	12.7	4.8	1.30	.68			
Think it was important to do well on these tests?	2	810	75.6	16.8	7.7	1.41	.76	3.443	.06	.002
	3	1304	72.1	19.9	8.1	1.48	.80			

when asked on the Pupil Questionnaire whether they actually had been told their test results, reported that they had.

Questions about test results were asked only of Treatment 3 pupils, and their answers shed additional light on the extent to which test information was disseminated. Of the 45 percent of pupils who said their teachers had told them their test results, 69 percent indicated that they had talked to their parents about how they had done, 74 percent had talked to their classmates, but only 33 percent had talked to their teachers.

One finding on pupils' reactions to the tests is worthy of note. Although the majority of pupils indicated that they did not feel afraid or nervous in taking the tests, between 17 and 30 percent did indicate such reactions. More pupils reported being nervous (over one-quarter in each treatment) than being afraid (about a fifth in each treatment). Thus, although the majority of pupils viewed the tests favorably and reported no adverse emotional reaction to taking them, a significant minority did approach the testing situation with some trepidation. How severe the reported fear or nervousness was and whether it was based on pupils' knowledge of their performance on prior tests or on some other factors is not clear. However, the tests were a source of some emotional discomfort for some pupils.

Statistically significant mean differences between treatments were found for four of the eighteen items dealing with pupils' perceptions of and reactions to the standardized tests. Significantly fewer pupils in the test-information group reported that they enjoyed sitting for the tests than did pupils in the no-information group. Similarly, a greater proportion of pupils in the information group felt afraid while taking the tests. On the other hand, a greater proportion of pupils in the no-information group reported that they liked using the separate answer sheet. As might be expected, significantly more pupils in the test-information group expected to be informed about the results of their test performance.

From these findings we might infer that the receipt of test information by teachers had an adverse effect on some pupils by comparison with pupils whose teachers did not receive results. However, this conclusion must be tempered by a number of considerations. First, the treatments did not have a differential impact on a wide variety of other reactions and emotions. Thus, if the treatments had a differential impact on pupils' perceptions of some aspects of the tests and testing situation, the impact was by no means universal. Second, the significant differences observed involved differences in responses of about 4 to 6 percent of the pupils in the treatments, indicating that while the differences in pupil responses were large enough to reach statistical significance, in absolute terms they were not large. Thus, the practical significance of the observed differences should not be overestimated.

PUPILS' PERCEPTIONS OF FACTORS THAT AFFECT
SCHOLASTIC PROGRESS AND GETTING ALONG WELL IN CLASS

In one set of items, students' perceptions were elicited about the factors they believed were important in getting on well in their classes. If teachers who tested and received test results stressed to their classes the importance of standardized tests and the traits they are presumed to measure, we might expect that their pupils would perceive the importance of intelligence and exam results in a different light from pupils whose teachers had not received test information. In a second set of items, information was obtained on the extent to which seven factors influenced pupils' perceptions of how well they were doing in school. In particular, the reported impact of test results on pupils' perceptions should provide some indication of how important pupils felt test results were.

To obtain information on pupils' perceptions of factors that affect getting along well in class, the pupils were presented with the following statement: "Some items on the list below might help a pupil who wants to get on well in class, some might hinder, and some might not matter one way or the other. For each item mark what you think about whether it would help, hinder, or not matter." For analyses, "would help" was coded 3, "would hinder" was coded 1, and "does not matter" was coded 2.

Across the three treatments, the vast majority of pupils, over 80 percent in all cases, clearly perceived that hard work, being well behaved, attaining good exam results, paying attention in class, doing what the teacher tells one, intelligence, good memory, and doing homework are all helpful in getting on well in class; very few pupils, in most cases less than 10 percent, perceived such activities or behaviors as hindrances (Table 5.2). Behaviors such as neatness in homework, taking part in class discussions, having a good personality, and asking questions in class were also perceived by the majority of pupils as helpful, although to a somewhat lesser extent than the previously noted behaviors. Luck and getting asked a lot of questions by the teacher (which pupils may perceive as a chance or "luck of the draw" process) are not seen as particularly helpful for in-class success. From these results it is evident that pupils perceived that most of the behaviors listed were important and helpful to their getting on well in class. We should note that the behaviors endorsed as helpful span a wide gamut of areas, including cognitive behaviors (e.g., good exam results, intelligence), social behaviors (e.g., being well behaved, doing what the teacher tells you), and personal characteristics (e.g., neatness in homework, good personality). Thus, from the pupils' point of view, getting on well in class depends on a host of behaviors and characteristics, not all of them cognitive.

When we examined differences between treatment groups on the mean values of pupils' responses, differences were not found on eight of the items: hard

Table 5.2. Pupils' Perceptions of the Extent to Which Various Factors Influence Their Getting on Well in Class, by Treatment

| Perceived Factor | Treatment | N | Percentages | | | M | S.D. | F | p | R^2 |
			Help	Hinder	Doesn't Matter					
Hard work	1	819	93.9	4.2	2.0	1.10	.42	.335	.72	.000
	2	818	92.5	4.5	2.9	1.12	.44			
	3	1328	93.4	4.4	2.3	1.11	.43			
Being well behaved	1	820	90.2	6.3	3.4	1.16	.51	10.806	.00	.007
	2	816	87.1	9.3	3.6	1.22	.60			
	3	1325	83.8	12.4	3.9	1.27	.67			
Good exam results	1	816	89.1	6.3	4.7	1.17	.52	4.577	.01	.003
	2	813	90.0	5.0	4.9	1.15	.48			
	3	1323	87.5	9.5	2.9	1.22	.60			
Neatness on homework	1	811	80.1	16.5	3.3	1.36	.25	2.012	.13	.001
	2	811	81.0	14.5	4.4	1.34	.72			
	3	1317	76.9	17.0	6.1	1.40	.76			
Luck	1	813	31.5	53.1	15.4	2.22	.89	.840	.43	.001
	2	809	30.3	52.5	17.2	2.22	.88			
	3	1312	32.4	50.1	17.5	2.18	.89			
Paying attention in class	1	816	94.9	2.8	2.3	1.08	.36	.296	.75	.000
	2	813	93.6	3.0	3.4	1.09	.38			
	3	1322	94.2	2.6	3.2	1.08	.36			

Table 5.2. (Continued)

Perceived Factor	Treatment	N	Percentages			M	S.D.	F	p	R^2
			Help	Hinder	Doesn't Matter					
Taking part in class discussion	1	814	77.1	16.0	6.9	1.39	.75	3.827	.02	.003
	2	813	71.8	19.3	8.9	1.47	.80			
	3	1320	71.7	19.7	8.6	1.48	.80			
Good personality	1	813	69.4	24.1	6.5	1.55	.85	1.219	.30	.001
	2	819	66.3	27.7	6.1	1.61	.89			
	3	1315	67.3	26.2	6.5	1.59	.86			
Doing what the teacher tells you	1	811	92.0	5.3	2.7	1.13	.47	1.399	.25	.001
	2	814	91.4	6.0	2.6	1.15	.50			
	3	1324	89.7	6.6	3.8	1.17	.52			
Intelligence	1	816	90.2	5.9	3.9	1.16	.50	8.451	.00	.006
	2	807	90.1	4.6	5.3	1.15	.46			
	3	1321	86.2	9.5	4.2	1.23	.61			
Asking questions	1	815	84.5	10.8	4.7	1.26	.64	7.253	.00	.005
	2	812	80.4	11.8	7.8	1.31	.67			
	3	1320	76.7	14.4	8.9	1.38	.72			
Good memory	1	813	88.3	8.1	3.6	1.19	.57	4.321	.01	.003
	2	815	87.2	8.5	4.3	1.21	.58			
	3	1322	83.6	10.6	5.8	1.27	.64			

Table 5.2. (Continued)

				Percentages						
					Doesn't					
Perceived Factor	Treatment	N	Help	Hinder	Matter	M	S.D.	F	p	R^2
Doing homework	1	810	89.0	7.4	3.6	1.18	.55	.478	.62	.000
	2	805	87.8	7.3	4.8	1.20	.55			
	3	1312	87.3	8.2	4.5	1.21	.57			
Getting asked a lot of	1	809	57.7	27.1	15.2	1.69	.87	2.658	.07	.002
questions by the teacher	2	803	60.0	22.0	17.9	1.62	.82			
	3	1292	57.4	28.1	14.5	1.71	.88			

work, neatness in homework, luck, paying attention in class, good personality, doing what the teacher tells you, doing homework, and getting asked a lot of questions by the teacher. Six items did reveal significant treatment differences. Scheffé post-hoc comparisons indicated that, on four of the items, Treatment 3 responses differed from those of Treatments 1 and 2. Pupils in the test-information group to a lesser extent than pupils in the control groups perceived that being well behaved, having good exam results, being intelligent, and having a good memory were helpful in getting on well in class. Of particular interest is the finding regarding the role of intelligence. Why pupils, whose teachers had received intelligence test results, should have perceived intelligence as being less helpful in getting on well in class than pupils in other groups is not immediately apparent. Perhaps some teachers who received results played down the role of intelligence in school work.

Two other items evidenced statistically significant treatment differences. Both (taking part in class discussion and asking questions in class) were related to participation in class. Treatment 1 pupils were more inclined than pupils in the other groups to perceive participation in class discussions as a helpful way to get on well in class. In their responses about the helpfulness of asking questions in class, Treatment 1 pupils viewed this behavior as more helpful than did Treatment 3 pupils. How these findings might relate to the availability of test information is not evident.

To obtain information on pupils' perceptions of the factors that indicate how they are doing in school, the pupils were asked to say whether any of seven factors had changed their ideas on this matter. Three response options were provided: "Yes, made me feel I am doing better than I thought"; "Yes, made me feel I am doing worse than I thought"; and "No, made no difference about what I thought." The seven factors were: exam results, test results, what a teacher has said to me, the class I was put in, what classmates thought about me, the place I sat in class, and how well I could learn something. "Yes, better" responses were coded 1, "yes, worse" responses were coded 3, and "no difference" responses were coded 2.

All of the factors, with the exception of the pupils' seat location, were perceived by the majority of pupils as influencing their idea of how they are doing in school, either for the better or the worse (Table 5.3). Even the place in which a pupil sits in class was perceived as providing information about school progress by about 45 percent of pupils. It is also evident that some characteristics have more influence on pupils' academic self-concept than others. More pupils reported that the class they were put in and what their classmates thought of them made less difference on their perceptions than did how well they felt they could learn something, exam results, test results, and what a teacher had said to them. A reported change in pupils' academic self-perception

Table 5.3. Pupils' Perceptions of Factors That Had Changed Their Idea of How Well They Were Doing in School, by Treatment

Have any of these things changed your idea about how well you have done at school?

	Treatment	N	Percentages			M	S.D.	F	p	R^2
			Yes, Better	Yes, Worse	No Difference					
Exam results	1	804	69.7	12.7	17.7	1.43	.71	4.723	.01	.003
	2	807	66.8	11.5	21.7	1.45	.69			
	3	1290	62.7	14.7	22.6	1.52	.74			
Test results	1	813	65.9	13.2	20.9	1.47	.71	4.078	.02	.003
	2	806	64.4	15.1	20.5	1.51	.74			
	3	1280	59.2	15.6	25.2	1.56	.75			
What a teacher has said to me	1	805	53.9	19.9	26.2	1.66	.79	.08	.92	.000
	2	803	52.2	18.9	28.9	1.67	.78			
	3	1285	52.2	17.6	30.2	1.65	.76			
The class I was put in	1	806	52.9	8.1	39.1	1.55	.64	1.573	.21	.001
	2	795	49.9	6.7	43.4	1.57	.62			
	3	1275	48.0	8.0	44.0	1.60	.63			
What classmates thought about me	1	806	46.8	7.7	45.5	1.61	.63	2.483	.08	.002
	2	800	44.6	8.5	46.9	1.64	.63			
	3	1285	42.9	10.1	47.0	1.67	.65			
The place I sat in class	1	802	34.9	10.2	54.9	1.75	.63	.022	.98	.000
	2	803	33.3	9.0	57.8	1.76	.60			
	3	1277	35.2	11.1	53.6	1.76	.64			

Table 5.3. (Continued)

Have any of these things changed your idea about how well you have done at school?

			Percentages							
	Treatment	N	Yes, Better	Yes, Worse	No Difference	M	S.D.	F	p	R^2
How well I could	1	810	79.1	4.4	16.4	1.25	.53	17.112	.00	.012
learn	2	802	67.8	7.0	25.2	1.39	.62			
	3	1288	68.6	9.2	22.2	1.41	.65			

is much more likely to be a change toward a more positive self-concept than toward a more negative one. Respondents showed a marked degree of optimism in interpreting signs about their performance. On six of the seven items, over 40 percent across treatments reported a change for the better; in no case did more than 20 percent report a change for the worse. On items such as exam results, test results, and how well I could learn something, considerably more pupils reported a change toward a more positive academic self-concept than toward a more negative one. The factor that the greatest number of pupils reported as lowering their academic self-concept was what a teacher had said. While exams and tests clearly appeared to decrease some pupils' perceptions of their academic progress, they equally clearly increased such perceptions for many more students.

The impact of exam results and the impact of test results were perceived differently by the treatment group. Pupils in the test-information group (Treatment 3) differed from pupils in the two control groups in not perceiving examination results as providing information that they were performing better in school than they had previously thought. Pupils in the test-information group also differed from other pupils in their perceptions of the impact of test results. Compared with other pupils they were less likely to see such results as having a positive impact on their perceptions of school progress; inspection of the frequencies in Table 5.3 indicates that they were more likely to see the results as making no difference. Interpreting these findings creates some problems since the questionnaire items were stated simply in terms of "exam" or "test" results, not in terms of "standardized test results." Pupils with no experience of testing during the course of the study may not have interpreted the item correctly.

Finally, pupils' judgments of the extent that their school progress was affected by how well they could learn something varied by treatment. The mean for the group with no experience of testing was significantly lower than the means for the other two groups.

PUPILS' RATINGS OF THEIR SCHOLASTIC BEHAVIOR AND ABILITIES

Pupils were asked to rate their own standing relative to classmates on fourteen cognitive and affective variables. Data were also available on teachers' ratings of the pupils on a number of these variables and on pupils' test scores. Thus comparisons between pupils' self-ratings and these other indices were possible. Such comparisons should throw some light on the effect of the availability of standardized test information on pupils' self-appraisals.

The first topic we examined concerns pupils' self-perceptions of their standing in relation to their classmates on a number of cognitive (e.g., intelligence,

English reading) and affective (e.g., interest in reading, keenness to do well in school) variables. Pupils were asked to "compare yourself to other pupils in your class" on each variable. There were five response options; "at the top" (coded 1), "well up" (coded 2), "around the middle" (coded 3), "well down" (coded 4), and "at the bottom" (coded 5). In this system of coding, higher scores are associated with lower self-perceptions.

On all the variables rated, with the exception of spoken Irish, the distributions of pupil self-perceptions are skewed (Table 5.4). Substantially larger proportions of pupils rated themselves "at the top" or "well up" rather than "well down" or "at the bottom." High self-ratings were most pronounced on the variables English reading, English composition, interest in school, interest in reading, sport, and keenness to do well in school. On each variable over 50 percent of pupils rated themselves as being either "at the top" or "well up" compared to their classmates. Over 70 percent perceived themselves in the top two rating categories in keenness to do well in school and over 65 percent in English reading and interest in reading. High self-ratings were least in evidence for the three variables relating to Irish (spoken, reading, and writing). About 40 to 45 percent of pupils rated themselves as being "in the middle" relative to their classmates on these variables. Overall, pupils' perceptions of their performance and capabilities were very positive.

We found no statistically significant differences between treatment groups on seven of the variables on which pupils rated themselves: intelligence, mathematics, English reading, interest in reading, exam results, sport, and memory. Represented among these seven areas are all but one of the areas in which standardized tests were administered as part of the study treatment—intelligence (verbal ability), mathematics, Irish reading, and English reading. We might expect that if standardized tests or test results were to have an impact on pupils' self-perceptions, this would be most evident in ratings corresponding to the areas actually tested. Statistically significant treatment differences were found in seven areas: spoken Irish, Irish reading, written Irish, English composition, interest in school, originality, and keenness to do well in school. In each area except keenness to do well in school, the mean of the test-information group (Treatment 3) was higher than those of the two control groups (Treatment 1 and 2), indicating lower self-perceptions among pupils in the former group. The differences, though statistically significant, were often very small and accounted for less than 1 percent of the explained variance.

The Scheffé post-hoc comparisons that were carried out to identify the locus of statistically significant mean treatment differences revealed no consistent type of difference among the three groups that might serve as a basis for interpreting the observed differences in a meaningful manner. For example, on four of the variables (spoken Irish, Irish reading, interest in school, and originality),

Table 5.4. Pupils' Ratings of Their Performance and Abilities Relative to Their Classmates, by Treatment

Rating	Treatment	N	Percentages					M	S.D.	F	p	R^2
			Top (1)	Well Up (2)	Middle (3)	Well Down (4)	Bottom (5)					
Interest in reading	1	805	34.5	35.2	24.0	4.3	2.0	2.97	.97	2.232	.10	.002
	2	806	30.9	36.2	24.2	5.6	3.1	2.17	1.02			
	3	1314	32.4	34.7	23.7	6.3	2.8	2.12	1.03			
Exam results	1	803	8.7	34.5	48.6	7.2	1.0	2.57	.79	.161	.85	.000
	2	803	11.0	32.3	47.6	7.3	1.9	2.57	.85			
	3	1301	11.5	31.3	46.3	8.5	2.4	2.59	.89			
Sport	1	813	33.6	33.1	24.4	5.4	3.1	2.12	1.04	2.49	.08	.002
	2	814	33.8	31.9	25.9	6.7	2.0	2.11	1.01			
	3	1308	27.8	34.2	30.6	5.4	2.0	2.20	.97			
Memory	1	807	12.1	38.2	42.0	6.6	1.1	2.46	.83	1.426	.24	.001
	2	808	13.1	39.5	39.2	6.6	1.6	2.44	.86			
	3	1293	12.9	35.0	43.2	6.8	2.2	2.50	.88			
Originality	1	794	15.9	36.6	40.6	5.9	1.0	2.40	.86	7.19	.00	.005
	2	788	15.5	35.5	39.7	7.4	1.9	2.45	.91			
	3	1288	13.7	31.4	43.6	9.5	1.7	2.54	.90			
Keenness to do well in school	1	812	38.8	35.8	21.4	3.2	.7	1.91	.89	3.569	.03	.002
	2	813	32.8	38.3	24.2	3.1	1.6	2.02	.92			
	3	1314	34.6	37.6	22.3	3.9	1.7	2.01	.94			

Table 5.4. (Continued)

Rating	Treatment	N	Percentages Top (1)	Well Up (2)	Middle (3)	Well Down (4)	Bottom (5)	M	S.D.	F	p	R^2
Intelligence	1	811	7.6	33.3	53.0	5.2	.9	2.58	.74	.678	.51	.000
	2	809	8.5	32.1	49.9	8.0	1.4	2.62	.81			
	3	1319	7.1	32.7	52.4	6.4	1.4	2.62	.77			
Mathematics	1	819	9.9	29.9	48.8	9.9	1.5	2.63	.85	1.884	.15	.001
	2	814	10.7	26.0	46.9	13.5	2.8	2.72	.93			
	3	1316	9.9	31.2	44.0	11.9	3.0	2.67	.92			
Spoken Irish	1	807	7.2	21.2	43.6	20.9	7.1	3.00	1.00	4.725	.01	.003
	2	806	6.1	18.7	45.0	21.3	8.8	3.08	1.00			
	3	1306	5.6	19.1	41.3	24.2	9.7	3.13	1.01			
Irish reading	1	810	8.9	32.3	42.6	11.7	4.4	2.70	.94	6.177	.00	.004
	2	805	7.0	34.5	40.5	12.5	5.5	2.75	.95			
	3	1306	7.4	27.7	43.6	15.0	6.2	2.85	.97			
Written Irish	1	803	7.2	26.2	45.3	16.4	4.9	2.86	.94	10.494	.00	.007
	2	800	6.6	29.1	46.2	13.7	4.2	2.80	.91			
	3	1297	5.0	25.3	42.5	20.9	6.3	2.98	.96			
English reading	1	815	22.6	47.5	26.4	3.2	.4	2.11	.80	1.034	.36	.001
	2	816	20.5	51.3	23.9	3.9	.4	2.12	.79			
	3	1318	22.5	43.9	29.1	3.7	.7	2.16	.84			

Table 5.4. (Continued)

Rating	Treatment	N	Percentages					M	S.D.	F	p	R^2
			Top (1)	Well Up (2)	Middle (3)	Well Down (4)	Bottom (5)					
English composition	1	814	14.4	41.9	38.5	4.7	.6	2.35	.80	3.436	.03	.002
	2	811	15.9	41.6	35.8	5.9	.9	2.34	.85			
	3	1311	14.0	37.7	41.2	5.9	1.3	2.43	.85			
Interest in school	1	810	24.1	37.4	31.7	5.2	1.6	2.23	.93	3.79	.02	.003
	2	809	20.9	37.6	32.6	5.3	3.6	2.33	.98			
	3	1308	23.3	32.6	33.9	6.6	3.6	2.34	1.02			

the post-hoc comparisons indicated that Treatment 1 pupils differed significantly from Treatment 3 pupils, with the former group manifesting more positive self-perceptions than the latter. On one variable (written Irish), the Treatment 1 mean differed significantly from both Treatment 2 and 3 means. On the remaining two variables, English composition and keenness to do well in school, the post-hoc analyses revealed no significant differences between groups. In light of the small mean treatment differences and the inconsistent pattern of the post-hoc comparisons, obtaining a clear and meaningful interpretation of the differences between treatment groups in students' self-perceptions is difficult.

If testing or test results have an impact on pupils who have experience of testing, one area in which one might expect that impact to manifest itself is in the relationship between pupils' self-perceptions and other measures of student characteristics, particularly teachers' ratings and pupils' own test scores. As we have just seen, sixth-grade pupils in our study were asked to rate themselves relative to their classmates on fourteen characteristics, and these ratings were coded from 1 (a high rating) to 5 (a low rating). Around the same time teachers were asked to rate their pupils on a number of the same variables. Teachers rated each pupil's general intelligence on a 5-point scale: "well above average" (coded 1), "above average" (coded 2), "average" (coded 3), "below average" (coded 4), and "well below average" (coded 5). They also rated each pupil's achievement in English reading, Irish reading, and mathematics by indicating in which fifth of the class a pupil belonged: "top fifth" (coded 1), "second fifth" (coded 2), "third fifth" (coded 3), "fourth fifth" (coded 4), and "bottom fifth" (coded 5). Two ratings were requested in mathematics, one for computation and one for problem solving. The correlation between the two ratings was high, around .9, and so the mathematics computation rating was selected to represent teachers' ratings of pupils' standing in mathematics.

By subtracting the pupil's self-rating from the teacher's rating, we obtained an index of agreement between the ratings. The index could range in value from −4 to +4. If a teacher rated a pupil "well above average" (scored 1) in an area and the pupil rated himself or herself "at the bottom" (coded 5), the discrepancy between the pair of ratings would be $1 - 5 = -4$. On the other hand, if a pupil rated himself or herself "at the top" (scored 1) and the teacher rated the pupil in the bottom fifth (coded 5), the discrepancy would be $5 - 1 = +4$. Since our primary interest in the analysis was a comparison of the magnitude of the mean discrepancy for the three treatments, the absolute value of the discrepancy for each pupil within a treatment was taken and treatment means were computed.

We have already seen that the distributions of the pupil ratings were negatively skewed. Teacher ratings, particularly in the three achievement areas, tended to be distributed in a rectangular manner, since teachers were asked to divide the pupils in their classes into fifths. Thus, the differences in the shapes of the pupil- and teacher-rating distributions tend to accentuate the magnitude of the discrepancies observed. However, the issue addressed in the analyses is whether or not the three treatment groups differ in the magnitude of their mean discrepancies. Differences in the shapes of the distributions should not preclude these comparisons.

Mean discrepancies across treatments in the three achievement areas are all around 1.0, with relatively large standard deviations (Table 5.5). Means and standard deviations for the intelligence ratings are considerably lower. This difference is most likely a function of the rating scales used, rather than of any substantive difference between perceptions of intelligence and achievement. We found no statistically significant differences between treatments in the mean discrepancies in Irish reading, English reading, or mathematics. There was, however, a statistically significant difference on the ability ratings. Scheffé post-hoc comparisons showed that pupils and teachers in Treatment 2, in which testing was carried out but no test results were provided, manifested significantly more agreement in their ratings than did pupils and teachers in either the no-information group (Treatment 1) or the test-information group (Treatment 3). This is, to say the least, a strange finding.

The final topic to be considered is the correspondence between the pupils' perceptions and pupils' actual test performance. Ratings and test scores in four areas were examined: intelligence (ability), English reading, Irish reading, and mathematics. Pupils had rated themselves on these variables and had also taken standardized tests in the four areas toward the end of sixth grade. To compare the correspondence between pupil self-ratings and test scores, we had to rescale the test score data. Since pupil self-ratings were distributed on a 5-point scale, we decided to convert the test scores into a comparable metric. Moreover, since the self-ratings were provided in the context of a pupil's perceived standing within his or her own classroom, the converted test score metric also had to be referenced to the pupil's standing within the classroom. To do this we converted test scores to percentile class on the basis of ranks, which were then divided into five categories to correspond to the five categories of pupils' self-ratings. Percentiles 1 to 20 were coded 1; 21 to 40 were coded 2; 41 to 60 were coded 3; 61 to 80 were coded 4; and 81 to 100 were coded 5. This procedure was performed separately for each of the four test scores. For each pupil in each class on each test, a rating—test performance discrepancy was calculated by subtracting the scaled test score from the scaled self-rating score. The absolute value of this discrepancy was obtained to prevent positive and negative discrepancies from canceling one another when the data were aggregated across pupils. The discrepancy indices for all pupils in a treatment were aggregated and a mean treatment discrepancy was calculated.

Table 5.5. Discrepancies between Teacher Rating of Pupils and Pupils' Self-Ratings, by Treatment

Area Rated	Treatment	N	Mean Discrepancy	S.D.	F	p	R^2
Intelligence	1	696	.668	.749	6.714	.001	.007
	2	465	.551	.655			
	3	862	.701	.733			
Irish reading	1	742	1.034	.862	.483	.617	.000
	2	570	.988	.856			
	3	860	1.023	.883			
English reading	1	751	1.021	.916	.893	.410	.001
	2	580	1.090	.969			
	3	880	1.044	.921			
Mathematics	1	750	.937	.830	.866	.421	.001
	2	575	.988	.856			
	3	864	.932	.813			

The mean rating—test score discrepancy in each treatment on each variable was found to be quite large, considering that both ratings and test scores were limited to 5-point scales (Table 5.6). The largest mean discrepancies for each treatment were in the area of intelligence, although on all variables the treatment means were about 2.0. There was also substantial variance around means. This is not to be unexpected; when discrepancies are calculated between a distribution that is skewed and another that is uniform, we would expect them to be large. Our interest, however, is not in the absolute magnitude of the discrepancies, but in their relative magnitude across treatment groups.

The only variable for which the magnitude of the mean discrepancies differed significantly across treatments was English reading. The mean English reading discrepancy for pupils in the test-information group (Treatment 3) was found to be significantly larger than the mean discrepancies in the two control groups. In other words, pupils whose teachers had received test information were more discrepant in their self-perceptions relative to their test performance than were the pupils whose teachers had not received test information. This is quite the opposite of the effect one would anticipate if test information were influential in providing pupils with data to judge their own standing relative to their classmates. Statistically significant differences between treatment groups were not found for intelligence, Irish reading, or mathematics. On the basis of these findings, we cannot conclude that being in a class in which the teacher has test information about pupil test performance has the effect of aligning pupils' self-perceptions of their academic standing with their test performance.

PUPILS' SELF-CONCEPTS

In this section we examine the effect of information derived from standardized ability and achievement tests on pupils' self-concepts. Our measure of self-concept is derived from measures of pupils' perceptions of their own scholastic ability and performance, as described in the preceding section, together with measures of pupils' attitudes toward themselves as learners.

Two sections of the Pupil Questionnaire contained items relevant to a self-concept scale. On one item each pupil was asked to compare him- or herself to other pupils in the class on eleven variables. For each variable the pupil was asked to indicate whether, compared to classmates, he or she was "at the top" (coded 5), "well up" (coded 4), "around the middle" (coded 3), "well down" (coded 2), or "at the bottom" (coded 1). The eleven variables were: intelligence, mathematics, spoken Irish, Irish reading, written Irish, English reading, English composition, exam results, memory, originality, and keenness to do well in school. Since responses to items were scored from 1 to 5, a total

Table 5.6. Discrepancies between Pupils' Test Scores and Pupils' Self-Ratings, by Treatment

Area Rated and Tested	Treatment	N	Mean Discrepancy	S.D.	F	p	R^2
Intelligence	1	819	2.209	1.557	.790	.454	.001
	2	818	2.300	1.606			
	3	1328	2.830	1.598			
English reading	1	816	2.142	1.559	4.665	.010	.003
	2	813	2.135	1.529			
	3	1322	2.319	1.646			
Irish reading	1	768	1.889	1.390	1.522	.219	.001
	2	757	1.884	1.348			
	3	1139	1.794	1.349			
Mathematics	1	777	1.920	1.397	.674	.510	.001
	2	764	1.914	1.360			
	3	1152	1.855	1.366			

score on the eleven items could range from 11 to 55. A student who rated himself or herself "at the bottom" on all items would score 11, and one who rated him- or herself "at the top" on all items would score 55.

These variables were supplemented by ten attitudinal variables from another item on the Pupil Questionnaire. Pupils were asked to indicate whether they agreed (coded 1), were not sure (coded 2), or disagreed (coded 3) with ten statements pertaining to examinations, success in school and life, and pupils' own ability and achievement: (1) "I often doubt that I will get on well in school"; (2) "There is no connection between how hard I study and my exam marks"; (3) "I always do better than my classmates in school"; (4) "Getting a high grade or mark in exams is very important to me"; (5) "I sometimes feel I just can't learn"; (6) "I am good at learning things off by heart"; (7) "I am able to do many things well"; (8) "If I try hard enough, I will succeed in life"; (9) "It is important to get the Intermediate Certificate"; (10) "It is important to get the Leaving Certificate." Pupils' responses to items 3, 6, and 7 were recoded to reflect the positive aspects of the statements. Total score on the ten items could range from a low of 10 to a high of 30.

Since the responses to the first eleven items were on a 5-point scale and those to the last ten on a 3-point scale, we converted all responses to a common metric so each item would receive equal weight in the scale. To do this and to permit summing scores across items to calculate treatment means, we converted pupil responses to each item in the self-concept scale to z-scores based on the mean and standard deviation of the entire sample's responses.

Before using the self-concept scale in our analyses, we carried out a number of investigations to supplement the logical selection of the items (Mostue, 1979). First, we examined the intercorrelations among the twenty-one items and found them to be uniformly high and significantly different from zero. Second, we computed Cronbach's coefficient alpha to assess the internal consistency of the scale; the obtained value of alpha was .85, indicating high homogeneity among the twenty-one items. Third, we examined the construct validity of the scale by correlating total score on the scale with pupil's actual test scores and with teachers' ratings of pupils. The expectation was that pupils' self-concept scores would correlate positively and significantly with their test performance scores and with teachers' ratings of pupils' ability. Correlations of the order of .4 or higher were in fact found.

A comparison of the mean self-concept scores of pupils in the test-information and two control groups revealed no statistically significant difference (Table 5.7). Thus, we may conclude that whether or not pupils had taken tests and whether or not their teachers had received results did not affect their self-concepts.

Table 5.7. Self-Concept Scores, by Treatment

Treatment	N	M	S.D.	F	p	R^2
1	609	.031	.458	.487	.61	.000
2	417	.006	.501			
3	602	.006	.509			

CONCLUSION

In this chapter we have examined a range of possible effects of norm-referenced standardized testing on sixth-grade pupils whose schools had been involved in a standardized testing program for four years. We found that students generally reacted positively to taking the tests. A large majority actually enjoyed sitting for them, found them interesting, thought they were fair, and tried to do their best. However, the prospect of receiving test results seemed to reduce the pupils' enjoyment somewhat. Pupils in the test-information group were less likely to enjoy sitting for the tests and more likely to feel afraid than were pupils in the no-information groups. The differences between treatments, while significant, were small. We may assume that the differences originated somewhere in the history of the pupils' experiences with tests. Perhaps some teachers who had received test results had used them in ways that made the test situation and the anticipation of results anxious and stressful for some pupils.

When we considered factors that had changed pupils' ideas about how well they were doing in school, we found no differences between treatment groups for a number of factors; however, we found that the role of exam results and of test results were perceived differently by treatment groups. In the case of both factors, responses indicating improved self-perceptions were fewer in the group that had received test information than in the groups that had not received such information.

Students in the treatment that received test information did not differ from students in other treatment groups in their self-ratings in a number of scholastic areas for which test measures were available—intelligence, mathematics, and English reading. However, they did record lower self-ratings in a number of other areas—spoken Irish, Irish reading, written Irish, interest in school, and originality. One might have expected an effect in the areas for which test scores were available rather than for nontested areas, but the only tested area for which a significant difference was found was Irish reading. On an overall composite measure of self-concept, we found no significant differences between treatment groups.

Given that pupils' ratings in general tended to be markedly skewed, exhibiting a tendency for them to rate themselves highly, the above findings might suggest that pupils in the treatment that received test information tended to "correct" these ratings more than did other pupils. If this were so, then we might expect the ratings of pupils in the information group to align more with other indices of pupils' ability and achievement than would be the case in the groups without information. However, this was not found to be so. In fact, in comparisons of students' ratings with teachers' ratings of ability, and of students' ratings of English reading with their test scores in the same area, we found the opposite tendency. Thus, the availability of test information was not found to have the effect of aligning pupils' self-perceptions of their academic standing with other indices.

These findings lead us to conclude that the availability of test information did not have a major impact on pupils. For many of the variables we investigated, we found no significant differences between treatment groups. For other variables we found significant, though small, differences, which generally suggested that the availability of test information had a negative rather than a positive impact on pupils. These conclusions must be tempered by the fact that differences between groups were very small and that our findings were based on quasi-experimental rather than experimental analyses.

6 EXPECTANCY EFFECTS:
The Role of Test Information

An initial impetus for carrying out the present study was the opportunity it presented to examine the expectancy or "Pygmalion" effect, which was described by Rosenthal and Jacobson (1968). They concluded that the provision of false test information to teachers had led to an improvement in pupils' measured scholastic ability. Their study led to many attempted examinations of the role of induced expectancies based on test scores as well as to several studies that examined naturally occurring expectancies, most of which, however, did not consider the role of test information.

We can postulate four basic steps in the expectancy process (Brophy and Good, 1974; Good and Brophy, 1973) whether or not information from tests is involved. First, teachers form differential expectations on the basis of their perceptions of pupils' personal characteristics (e.g., gender, socioeconomic background, dress, appearance), past educational history, behavior in class (e.g., attention, interest, ability to work with other children), and perhaps test results. Second, teachers treat pupils in line with the expectations they form. Third, pupils react in accordance with those expectations, reinforcing the teacher's judgment. And fourth, teachers' expectations and pupils' adaptations to them are eventually reflected in the pupils' measured ability and achievement. In the Rosenthal and Jacobson type of study, test information that is discrepant

159

from the teacher's expectation is interposed to alter initial expectations, and its eventual influence on pupils' measured scholastic ability is assessed.

The design of our study possessed a number of advantages for examining the role of tests in the expectancy process. First, we were able to simulate a school testing program in which standardized tests were routinely administered to pupils at the beginning of the year and norm-referenced information on pupils' performance was given to teachers. The information supplied in our study was, as it is in the normal school setting, the pupil's actual test score, not a false score, as in the Rosenthal and Jacobson study. Second, our experimental design and the availability of a control group permitted a comparison between the situation in which test information was available to teachers and one in which such information was not available.

The basic question as far as tests are concerned is how information derived from them might affect teachers' perceptions of pupils. This question may be broken down into a number of more specific questions. First, how are teachers' perceptions, in the absence of test information, related to pupils' test performance? Second, when teachers receive test information that does not agree with their perceptions, does this lead to a change in their perceptions? And third, after a period of time in which teachers' perceptions and test information have had an opportunity to affect pupils, is there evidence that the pupils' test performance is influenced by the teachers' initial perceptions or by the test information?

It will be noted that we use the term "teacher perception" rather than "teacher expectation," even though we are speaking in the context of expectancy. This is because we do not have a direct measure of teacher expectation, which would have involved asking teachers to predict a future event (Finn, 1972). Rather, teachers were asked to rate pupils' current status on intelligence and in a number of scholastic areas. Likewise, the information supplied to teachers was limited to norm-referenced scores based on pupils' current performance on ability and achievement tests; it did not include predictions about the child's future performance. Thus, the teacher was left to form or not to form expectations for pupils on the basis of his or her own perceptions or on the basis of the test information that was made available. This would seem to be a more normal situation for the teacher than one in which information is elicited about expectations for pupils or one in which explicit expectations are posited for them.

Before considering the results of analyses, we may consider briefly how a self-fulfilling prophecy might operate in situations in which teachers either have or do not have test information. In Figure 6.1 initial teacher perception or rating of a pupil and the pupil's initial test performance have been dichotomized to simplify discussion. In cells 1 and 4, the test performance and the teacher's assessment of the pupil are similar; in this case, test information should not cause a change in the teacher's initial perception of the pupil. If the initial

Pupil's Initial Ability or Achievement Test Performance

	High	Low
High	1 No Effect	2 No Information Provided: Expectancy "Advantage" Test Information Provided: Expectancy "Disadvantage"
Low	3 No Information Provided: Expectancy "Disadvantage" Test Information Provided: Expectancy "Advantage"	4 No Effect

Teacher's Initial Perception of a Student's Ability or Achievement

Figure 6.1. Predicted Impact of Test Information on the Self-Fulfilling Prophecy Mechanism

perception remains undisturbed by the test information, the teacher should behave toward the pupil in accordance with it, and thus the pupil's subsequent test performance should continue to agree with the teacher's assessment. Similarly, if the teacher does not receive test information, his or her initial perception should continue to influence his or her behavior and ultimately the pupil's test performance, in which case test performance should again continue to agree with the teacher's assessment. In line with this reasoning, we have labeled cells 1 and 4 "no effect" cells. In cells 2 and 3, on the other hand, expectancy could work either to the "advantage" or "disadvantage" of a pupil, depending on whether or not the teacher receives information about test performance. In cell 2 the teacher's assessment of the pupil's ability or achievement is high but the pupil's test performance is low. In this situation, if test information is effective, it will alter the teacher's perception, and the pupil's performance on subsequent tests should remain low. From the pupil's point of view, this could be called an "expectancy disadvantage"—the pupil would have been "better off" if the teacher's perceptions had not been altered. Pupils in cell 2 whose teachers do not receive test information would be treated according to the teacher's initial, more favorable perception, and therefore we would expect their subsequent test performance to improve. Such a pupil can be regarded as having an "expectancy advantage" in the absence of test information. Cell 3, where teacher perception is low and test performance high, is the mirror image of cell 2. A pupil in this cell whose teacher does not receive test information should be at an expectancy "disadvantage," while one whose teacher receives such information should be at an expectancy "advantage."

In this chapter we are concerned with Treatments 1, 2, and 3, particularly with Treatments 2 and 3, since only in these latter groups was testing carried out throughout the life of the study. In Treatment 2 tests of ability and achievement were administered to pupils over a period of four years, but the results of the testing were not returned to teachers. In Treatment 3 tests of ability and achievement were also administered to pupils over the four-year period, but in this case norm-referenced information (standard scores and percentile ranks) on each pupil's performance was returned to teachers.

Our analyses (with one exception) are confined to pupils who were in grades 2, 4, and 6 in the final year of the study. The grade 2 pupils entered the study in its final year. In addition to the final end-of-year testing in which all treatment groups participated, grade 2 pupils in Treatments 2 and 3 were also tested at the beginning of the final year. Pupils in grade 4 participated in the study for three years. As well as being tested at the end of the study, these pupils were also tested at the beginning of each year when they were in grades 2, 3, and 4. Grade 6 pupils participated in the study for the longest time (four years). In addition to being tested at the end of the study, those pupils who were in

Treatment 2 were tested at the beginning of each year in grades 3, 5, and 6; pupils who were in Treatment 3 were tested at the beginning of each year in grades 3, 4, 5, and 6.

We focus on pupil performance in four test areas: ability or intelligence, as measured by the Otis-Lennon Mental Ability Test, Elementary 1 level, at grade 2 and the Drumcondra Verbal Reasoning Test at grades 4 and 6; English reading as measured by the Drumcondra English Tests, Levels I, II, and III for grades 2, 4, and 6, respectively; mathematics computation as measured by the Drumcondra Mathematics Test, Levels I, II, and III for grades 2, 4, and 6, respectively; and, in some analyses, Irish reading as measured by the Drumcondra Irish Tests, Levels II and III for grades 4 and 6, respectively. Teachers' ratings of pupils on intelligence, English reading, mathematics computation, and Irish reading were also available. Each pupil was rated by his or her teacher on a Pupil Evaluation Form on a 5-point scale as being, in comparison with pupils generally at the same grade level, "well below average," "below average," "average," "above average," or "well above average."

We are concerned primarily with relationships between teacher perceptions or ratings and pupil test scores. In the first section we examine discrepancies between initial teacher perceptions and test scores for intelligence, English reading, and mathematical computation (but not Irish reading) in order to establish the potential for change in perceptions under the impact of discrepant test information. In this examination we are limited to data from the two treatment groups, Treatments 2 and 3, in which test scores were available from the beginning of the school year. We then examine discrepancies between teacher perceptions of the same pupils recorded at two points in time (at the beginning of the school year and at its end). In these analyses data from the three treatment groups are compared. In the second section we examine relationships between teacher perceptions and test scores, using a correlational approach, for intelligence, English reading, mathematical computation, and Irish reading. We are particularly interested in correlations between measures obtained at different points in time (i.e., the correlation between test scores at the beginning of the year and teacher perceptions at the end of the year, and the correlation between beginning-of-year teacher perceptions and end-of-year test scores). Data both within and across Treatment 2 (testing–no-information group) and Treatment 3 (testing-information group) can be used to determine the extent to which initial test performance influences subsequent teacher perceptions as well as the extent to which initial teacher perceptions influence subsequent pupil test performance. In both the discrepancy and correlational analyses, we focus on differences between the initial test score and the initial teacher perception since, recalling our model in Figure 6.1, if no such difference exists, we have no reason to expect a change in a later measure of either test performance or teacher perception.

TEACHERS' PERCEPTIONS: STABILITY AND CHANGE

The impact of test information will to some extent be a function of the strength of the relationship that exists between a pupil's performance on a standardized test of ability or achievement and the teacher's judgment of that ability or achievement, made without knowledge of the test performance of the pupil. Obviously, if a pupil's test score and a teacher's rating are closely related, there can be little room for test information to exert an influence on any later judgment that the teacher might make of a pupil, except to confirm the original perception.

In this section we look first of all at the extent of discrepancies between teachers' perceptions of pupils and pupils' test scores, measures for both of which were obtained at the beginning of the school year for pupils in Treatment 2 and 3 schools. We then examine changes that occurred in teachers' perceptions over the course of the school year. Specifically, we consider the magnitude of changes in ratings, the stability of ratings (the proportion of pupils for whom ratings did not change), the proportion of pupils for whom the final rating was higher than the initial one, and the proportion for whom the final rating was lower than the initial one. Finally, we consider the net proportion of pupils for whom ratings increased or decreased. For the latter analyses we make comparisons between our three treatment groups.

Discrepancies between Teachers' Ratings and Pupils' Test Scores

One simple way to portray relationships between teacher ratings and test scores is in terms of discrepancy scores. However, since the ratings and scores were on different scales, before computing discrepancy scores between the two measures, we needed to collapse the raw test scores to a 5-point scale corresponding to the teacher ratings. This was accomplished in the following way:

Values of 1 and 5, respectively, were assigned to scores corresponding to the lowest and highest 3 percent of the test-score distribution.

Values of 2 and 4, respectively, were assigned to scores corresponding to the next highest or lowest 13 percent of test-score distribution.

A value of 3 was assigned to the remaining 68 percent of cases.

Discrepancies were calculated by subtracting a collapsed test score from the corresponding teacher rating and range from -4 through $+4$. A negative discrepancy would indicate that a teacher's initial rating of the pupil was lower than the collapsed test score; a positive one that the rating was higher.

Before considering the results of analyses based on collapsed test scores, we should acknowledge that a number of weaknesses are associated with the use of such scores. In our study test information was given to teachers in the form of standard scores and percentile ranks; we cannot assume that in processing the scores, teachers collapsed them in any way. Further, the number of discrepancies one finds could be a function of differences in the distributions of the two measures being compared—teacher ratings and collapsed test scores. Because of these disadvantages we use the original uncollapsed test scores later in this chapter in correlational analyses to examine relationships between teachers' ratings and test performance.

When we examined mean discrepancy scores for each subject area, a strong congruence between initial test scores and teachers' initial perceptions of their pupils' ability and achievement was obvious. Over grade level and treatment, the two assessments were in perfect agreement for 46 to 60 percent of all pupils. Close to 40 percent of the ratings diverged from the collapsed test score by plus or minus a single unit, while discrepancies of more than one unit occurred for 4 to 11 percent of pupils (Table 6.1).

Differences between the percentages of ratings that were lower than test scores and the percentages that were higher than test scores were not very great. On average, teachers tended to rate pupils higher than their test performance in intelligence. In English reading, too, teachers rated pupils higher than their test performance; here the difference was greater than in the case of intelligence. In the case of mathematics, however, ratings were more often lower than the test score than higher. Since the average item difficulties of the three tests are about equal, it would seem that teachers have higher standards for numerical than for verbal skills. Archer (1979), Kellaghan, Macnamara, and Neuman (1969), and Pedulla (1976) reached similar conclusions about Irish teachers.

Shifts in Teachers' Perceptions of Pupils

If test information affects teachers' perceptions of their pupils, this effect should be detectable when we compare changes in the perceptions of teachers who receive test information with changes in the perceptions of teachers who do not receive such information. Whether or not teachers receive test information, they may, of course, change their perceptions of a pupil for a variety of reasons over time. Besides, error is involved in our measurement, and changes in ratings may simply reflect it. However, these conditions are common to both treatment groups and should be reflected in changes in the two groups. Our expectation

Table 6.1. Discrepancies between Initial Teacher Perception and Initial Test Score, by Magnitude of Discrepancy, Treatment, and Grade, in Percentages

Treatment	Grade	Rating Lower than Test Score by		Rating Equals Test Score (3)	Rating Greater than Test Score by		Total Discrepancies >1 in Either Direction (6)	Number of Pupils (7)
		>1 Unit (1)	1 Unit (2)		1 Unit (4)	>1 Unit (5)		
Intelligence 2*	2	1.5	17.6	49.7	26.9	4.3	5.8	670
3†	2	4.3	18.1	46.5	25.8	5.4	9.7	796
2	4	2.4	16.6	60.1	19.6	1.2	3.6	572
3	4	2.2	13.8	55.5	25.0	3.5	5.7	1010
2	6	3.1	19.5	57.5	18.8	1.0	4.1	605
3	6	2.1	22.2	49.8	22.9	2.9	5.0	951
English reading 2	2	3.8	16.5	45.5	27.5	6.7	10.5	705
3	2	4.2	15.3	49.0	26.4	5.0	9.2	836
2	4	1.7	17.2	52.4	24.9	3.8	5.5	638
3	4	1.8	14.5	52.4	25.5	5.9	7.7	1072
2	6	2.9	15.6	54.7	24.0	2.9	5.8	629
3	6	2.8	19.5	47.0	25.1	5.7	8.5	1069

Table 6.1. (Continued)

Treatment	Grade	Rating Lower than Test Score by		Rating Equals Test Score (3)	Rating Greater than Test Score by		Total Discrepancies >1 in Either Direction (6)	Number of Pupils (7)
		>1 Unit (1)	1 Unit (2)		1 Unit (4)	>1 Unit (5)		
Math computation								
2	2	3.6	22.8	51.1	18.4	4.1	7.7	705
3	2	4.4	22.4	47.6	20.3	5.3	9.7	843
2	4	4.5	24.4	50.5	17.3	3.4	7.9	620
3	4	3.0	20.1	50.5	21.8	4.6	7.6	1097
2	6	6.5	24.2	50.6	16.5	2.3	8.8	624
3	6	6.1	25.9	46.4	18.4	3.2	9.3	1070

*Treatment 2 = Ability and achievement testing—no information (control).
†Treatment 3 = Ability and achievement testing—norm-referenced information.

is that additional changes, which can be attributed to the availability of test information, will be found in the test-information group. To examine this issue, we consider across treatments (1) the magnitude of change in ratings from the beginning to the end of the year; (2) the percentage of pupils for whom the teacher's rating did not change over the year; (3) the percentage of pupils for whom the final ratings were higher than the initial ratings; and (4) the percentage of pupils for whom the final ratings were lower than the initial ones; and (5) the net proportion of pupils for whom ratings became higher or lower.

Magnitude of Change in Teachers' Perceptions of Pupils

Here we investigate whether the teachers who received norm-referenced test information make more or larger changes in their ratings over the course of a year than do teachers who are unaware of their pupils' test scores. We calculated an index of the magnitude of change in teacher perceptions for each pupil for intelligence, English reading, and mathematics computation by taking the absolute value of the difference between the beginning-of-year and end-of-year ratings. Since the ratings were made on a 5-point scale, the resultant index can range between 0 and 4 for each construct. To test for differences in the magnitude of rating change between the no-testing group (Treatment 1), the ability and achievement testing—no-information group (Treatment 2), and the ability and achievement testing—norm-referenced information group (Treatment 3), we employed a 3(treatment) by 3(grade) analysis of variance. Separate ANOVAs were carried out for each of three cognitive measures—intelligence, English reading, and math computation. A belief that test information affects teachers' perceptions of pupils would lead us to expect that the absolute value of the magnitude of any shifts in teacher ratings should be largest for teachers who had received norm-referenced test information.

Actually, we found a high degree of stability of teachers' perceptions of their pupils in all treatment groups over the course of the academic year. The average change in perception, on a scale from 0 to 4, never reached .5; magnitude of change ranged between .26 and .46 over all constructs, grades, and treatments. The standard deviations were larger than the means, but still relatively small, indicating substantial homogeneity in the size of the shifts (Table 6.2). Significant treatment, grade, and interaction effects for intelligence ratings, a significant treatment effect for English reading ratings, and significant treatment and inter-action effects for mathematics computation ratings were found. Differences in the magnitude of shifts in teacher perceptions of English reading could be attributed to differences between treatments. As predicted, the effect for the test-information group had the highest positive value. While the differences

Table 6.2. Magnitude of Change in Teachers' Perceptions from Beginning to End of Year, by Treatment and Grade

Intelligence

Grade	T1: No Testing			T2: Testing–No Information			T3: Testing–Information			Total		
	M	S.D.	N	M	S.D.	N	M	S.D.	N	M	S.D.	N
2	.28	.46	457	.30	.48	508	.35	.52	516	.31	.49	1481
4	.26	.47	405	.33	.60	481	.28	.46	657	.29	.51	1543
6	.32	.55	773	.26	.46	482	.38	.55	841	.33	.53	2096
Total	.30	.51	1635	.30	.51	1471	.34	.52	2014	.32	.51	5120

English Reading

Grade	T1: No Testing			T2: Testing–No Information			T3: Testing–Information			Total		
	M	S.D.	N	M	S.D.	N	M	S.D.	N	M	S.D.	N
2	.32	.59	477	.42	.56	549	.40	.55	572	.42	.57	1598
4	.35	.50	420	.35	.53	560	.43	.57	707	.38	.54	1687
6	.35	.50	832	.35	.54	602	.42	.57	995	.38	.54	2429
Total	.37	.53	1729	.37	.54	1711	.41	.56	2274	.39	.55	5714

Math Computation

Grade	T1: No Testing			T2: Testing–No Information			T3: Testing–Information			Total		
	M	S.D.	N	M	S.D.	N	M	S.D.	N	M	S.D.	N
2	.40	.59	499	.39	.55	547	.46	.59	558	.42	.58	1604
4	.36	.52	417	.36	.53	555	.45	.62	688	.40	.57	1660
6	.46	.58	826	.38	.55	594	.42	.58	989	.42	.57	2409
Total	.42	.57	1742	.38	.55	1696	.44	.60	2235	.42	.57	5673

were significant, the amount of explained variance was very small —less than two-tenths of one percent. In the case of intelligence rating changes, the overall positive treatment effect for the test-information group was not consistent across grades, while in the case of mathematics rating changes, the interaction effects are not consistent with a significant main effect of treatment. The R^2 values associated with both intelligence and mathematics computation are extremely small; less than three-tenths of one percent of the variance in the size of the shifts from beginning to end of year in teacher perceptions of their pupils' intelligence and mathematics computation was explained by treatment, grade, or interaction effects.

Thus, our prediction that teachers' ratings of pupils would exhibit greater change in the presence of test information was confirmed for English reading across all three grade levels, but was not consistent for intelligence or mathematics computation. Confirmation of any impact of test information on teacher perceptions must be tempered by the fact that the amount of variance in the magnitude of the rating shifts that we were able to explain was very small. Thus the practical or educational significance of the findings would appear to be slight. Similar analyses by Airasian et al. (1977), using data obtained in the second year of our study, reinforce this conclusion. The analyses confirm that teachers' ratings of their pupils' intelligence, reading, and mathematics progress are highly stable over the course of the academic year and that norm-referenced information about pupils' test performance has at most a minor impact on their subsequent ratings of pupils.

Stability of Teacher Ratings

Another way to gauge the impact of test information on teachers' perception of their pupils is to compare the stability of the two teacher ratings across our three treatment groups. If test information influences the way in which teachers perceive their pupils, this should be reflected in a larger proportion of changes in the perceptions of pupils in the test-information group (Treatment 3) than in either control group (Treatments 1 and 2). In other words, teachers' ratings should be significantly *less* stable in the presence of test information than in its absence.

To test this prediction, we calculated an index of rating stability by assigning a pupil a "1" whenever the pair of ratings (beginning and end of year) were identical. A "0" was assigned when the pair of ratings differed. Since the variable was coded as either a "1" or a "0," the means are directly interpretable as the proportion of pupils for whom there was *no* change in the teachers' ratings. The higher the mean, the larger the proportion of pupils for whom the teacher ratings did not change. Consequently, if our prediction about the influence of test information on teacher perceptions is correct, the information group (Treatment 3) should score significantly lower on our stability index than either of the treatments that did not have information.

The proportions of pupils for whom ratings did not change further underline the stability of teacher ratings that preceding analyses revealed. For about two-thirds of all pupils, across grade, treatment, and construct, teachers' beginning and end-of-year ratings were identical (Table 6.3). However, there were significant treatment and grade effects for the stability of ratings of intelligence, a significant treatment effect for the stability of ratings of English reading, and significant treatment and interaction effects for the stability of ratings of mathematics computation. For all three analyses the R^2 values were again small; less than four-tenths of 1 percent of the variance in the stability index was accounted for by the treatment, grade, and interaction factors.

Teachers who were given norm-referenced test information were on average less stable in their ratings of pupils' intelligence and progress in English reading than were teachers in either control group. For mathematical computation this pattern was not consistent over grade levels.

Ratings That Become More Favorable over Time

Next we consider whether there are treatment differences in the proportions of pupils for whom teachers' end-of-year ratings were higher than their beginning-of-year ratings. When a pupil's rating at the end of the year was higher than his or her rating at the beginning of the year, a score of "1" was entered for the pupil; otherwise, a score of "0" was entered. The mean for this index of higher ratings is directly interpretable as a proportion; it represents the proportion of pupils for whom the final end-of-year rating was higher than the initial beginning-of-year rating.

Predictions based on the expectancy model are not as straightforward for this index as for the indices examined in the previous two sections. In the groups that did not receive information (Treatments 1 and 2), a rise in teacher ratings over time could be attributed to factors other than test information, including error. On the other hand, a rise in the information group (Treatment 3) could be attributed to knowledge of test results as well as to factors similar to those operating in the other groups. However, the provision of test information could also result in a drop in teachers' ratings. This presumably would happen in cases where the information convinced the teacher that he or she had overrated the pupil. Since this cannot happen in the groups that did not receive information, predictions about mean differences on our index are less clear than they are for the magnitude and stability indices.

Table 6.3. Stability of Teachers' Perceptions from Beginning to End of Year, by Treatment and Grade

Intelligence

Grade	T1: No Testing			T2: Testing–No Information			T3: Testing–Information			Total		
	M*	S.D.	N	M	S.D.	N	M	S.D.	N	M	S.D.	N
2	.72	.45	457	.70	.46	508	.67	.47	516	.70	.46	1481
4	.75	.43	405	.72	.45	481	.72	.45	657	.73	.44	1543
6	.71	.45	773	.74	.44	482	.65	.48	841	.69	.46	2096
Total	.73	.45	1635	.72	.45	1471	.68	.47	2014	.71	.46	5120

English Reading

Grade	T1: No Testing			T2: Testing–No Information			T3: Testing–Information			Total		
	M	S.D.	N	M	S.D.	N	M	S.D.	N	M	S.D.	N
2	.62	.49	447	.62	.49	549	.63	.48	572	.62	.48	1598
4	.65	.48	420	.67	.47	560	.61	.49	707	.64	.48	1687
6	.66	.47	832	.68	.47	602	.62	.49	995	.65	.48	2429
Total	.65	.49	1729	.66	.48	1711	.62	.49	2274	.64	.48	5714

Math Computation

Grade	T1: No Testing			T2: Testing–No Information			T3: Testing–Information			Total		
	M	S.D.	N	M	S.D.	N	M	S.D.	N	M	S.D.	N
2	.65	.48	499	.65	.48	547	.59	.49	558	.63	.48	1604
4	.66	.47	417	.67	.47	555	.60	.49	688	.64	.48	1660
6	.58	.49	826	.65	.48	594	.62	.48	989	.61	.49	2409
Total	.62	.49	1742	.65	.48	1696	.61	.49	2235	.63	.48	5673

* Means can be interpreted as proportion of pupils for whom there was no change in teacher perceptions.

The proportions of pupils in each treatment for whom teacher ratings of their intelligence, English reading, and mathematics computation became more favorable over the year ranged between .12 and .25, with most in the mid- to high-teens range (Table 6.4). Thus, for close to one out of five pupils across grades, treatment, and variables rated, teachers' final perceptions of pupils were more favorable than their beginning-of-year ratings. The results of analyses of variance indicated a significant treatment effect. The provision of test information resulted in significantly higher proportions of pupils in Treatment 3 at the end of the year for whom teachers had more favorable perceptions of progress in mathematical computation than they had at the beginning of the year across all grade levels. There was no such consistent treatment effect across grades for intelligence or English reading. Once again, the very small amounts of variance associated with the differences (never exceeding three-tenths of 1 percent) must temper the practical or educational significance of these conclusions.

Ratings That Become Less Favorable over Time

The final index of change in teachers' ratings that we consider concerns the proportion of pupils for whom teachers' perceptions in the areas of intelligence, English reading, and mathematics computation were less favorable at the end of the year than they were at the beginning. Such a variable was created by assigning a "1" to a pupil when the final rating was lower than the initial one; otherwise a "0" was assigned.

The proportion of pupils seen in a less favorable light by teachers at the end relative to the beginning of the year ranges from .09 to .24, with most proportions in the mid-teen range (Table 6.5). In the case of all three variables, neither the treatment nor grade effect was statistically significant. However, the interaction between treatment and grade level was significant for all three variables. Again, the amount of explained variance involved was very small—less than two-tenths of 1 percent. The wide variation in the pattern of effects across treatments and grades makes it impossible to reach any conclusion about the role of test information in causing teachers to revise downward their estimates of pupils.

Net Proportion of Pupils for Whom Ratings Increased or Decreased

Up to this point we have examined the impact of test information on rating shifts in terms of the amount of variance accounted for. While several of our findings were statistically significant, and more often than not in the direction we had predicted, the amounts of variance accounted for were quite small.

Table 6.4. Teachers' Perceptions That Became More Favorable from the Beginning to the End of the Year, by Treatment and Grade

Intelligence

Grade	T1: No Testing M*	S.D.	T2: Testing–No Information M	S.D.	T3: Testing–Information M	S.D.	Total M	S.D.
2	.14	.35	.17	.37	.21	.41	.17	.38
4	.16	.36	.14	.34	.12	.33	.14	.34
6	.13	.34	.15	.35	.19	.39	.16	.37
Total	.14	.35	.15	.36	.17	.38	.15	.36

English Reading

Grade	T1: No Testing M	S.D.	T2: Testing–No Information M	S.D.	T3: Testing–Information M	S.D.	Total M	S.D.
2	.23	.42	.21	.41	.23	.42	.22	.42
4	.24	.43	.19	.39	.23	.42	.22	.41
6	.14	.35	.21	.41	.25	.43	.21	.40
Total	.19	.39	.20	.40	.24	.43	.21	.41

Math Computation

Grade	T1: No Testing M	S.D.	T2: Testing–No Information M	S.D.	T3: Testing–Information M	S.D.	Total M	S.D.
2	.17	.38	.19	.40	.24	.43	.20	.40
4	.21	.41	.20	.40	.20	.40	.20	.40
6	.18	.38	.17	.38	.22	.41	.19	.40
Total	.18	.39	.19	.39	.22	.41	.20	.40

*Means can be interpreted as proportion of pupils for whom the end-of-year rating was higher than the beginning-of-year rating.

Table 6.5. Teachers' Perceptions That Became Less Favorable from the Beginning to the End of the Year, by Treatment and Grade

Intelligence

Grade	T1: No Testing		T2: Testing–No Information		T3: Testing–Information		Total	
	M*	S.D.	M	S.D.	M	S.D.	M	S.D.
2	.14	.34	.13	.33	.12	.33	.13	.34
4	.09	.24	.14	.35	.15	.36	.13	.34
6	.15	.36	.11	.31	.16	.37	.14	.35
Total	.13	.34	.13	.33	.15	.35	.14	.34

English Reading

Grade	T1: No Testing		T2: Testing–No Information		T3: Testing–Information		Total	
	M	S.D.	M	S.D.	M	S.D.	M	S.D.
2	.15	.36	.17	.37	.14	.35	.15	.36
4	.11	.31	.14	.35	.16	.37	.15	.35
6	.20	.40	.11	.32	.13	.34	.15	.36
Total	.16	.37	.14	.35	.14	.35	.15	.36

Math Computation

Grade	T1: No Testing		T2: Testing–No Information		T3: Testing–Information		Total	
	M	S.D.	M	S.D.	M	S.D.	M	S.D.
2	.18	.38	.16	.36	.17	.38	.17	.37
4	.13	.34	.14	.34	.20	.40	.16	.37
6	.24	.43	.18	.38	.15	.36	.19	.39
Total	.20	.39	.16	.36	.17	.38	.18	.38

*Means can be interpreted as proportion of pupils for whom the end-of-year rating was lower than the beginning-of-year rating.

Before leaving the question of shifts in teacher ratings, we will try to estimate the impact of test information on rating shifts in a more descriptive way. This we may do by looking at the net proportions of pupils for whom ratings increased or decreased, using our control groups as a baseline from which to estimate the impact of test information.

Overall, net change was positive (i.e., the proportion of positive shifts was larger than the proportion of negative shifts). This was so for all areas rated at all grade levels for the group that had test information (Treatment 3), with one exception—intelligence at grade 4. Similarly, for the group that tested but did not receive information (Treatment 2), there was only one instance of negative net change (mathematics computation at grade 6). For the group that did not test (Treatment 1), however, there were four negative net changes: mathematics computation at grade 2 and intelligence, English reading, and mathematical computation at grade 6 (Table 6.6). Thus, shifts in teacher perceptions appear to be, on net, positive in Treatments 2 and 3, while they are as likely to be negative as positive in Treatment 1. This speaks for a net "advantage" for pupils in the groups in which tests were administered.

We can obtain a rough descriptive estimate of how much of this net "advantage" can be attributed to the teachers' receipt of norm-referenced test information by using either control group (Treatments 1 and 2) as a baseline; we can then compare the proportions of net positive rating shifts in Treatment 3 with the proportions in the baseline group. If we use Treatment 1 as the baseline, we have an estimate of changes in teacher perceptions that naturally occur when teachers do not administer tests or receive test information. Subtracting the Treatment 1 proportion from the relevant proportion in Treatment 3 gives us an estimate of the changes in perception attributable to administering tests and receiving information. Limiting our discussion to those favorable shifts that were statistically significant, we find that the estimated maximum effect attributable to administering tests and receiving information was .07 for intelligence at grade 2, .11 for reading at grade 6, .06 for intelligence at grade 6, and .04 for mathematics computation across the three grades. Testing and receipt of test information was associated with between 4 and 11 percent more favorable shifts. If we use Treatment 2 as the baseline group, we find that changes in teachers' perceptions attributable to receiving information about pupil perform-ance were less—on the order of about 4 percent.

TEACHERS' PERCEPTIONS AND PUPILS' TEST SCORES: CORRELATIONAL ANALYSES

In this section we examine partial cross-lagged correlational data based on measures of teacher perceptions and of pupil test performances obtained at the

Table 6.6. Summary of Proportion of Pupils for Whom Teachers Change Their Perceptions from the Beginning to the End of the Year, by Treatment and Grade

Grade	No Change (1)			More Favorable (2)			Less Favorable (3)			Net Change (4) (2 − 3)		
	T1	T2	T3	T1	T2	T3	T1	T2	T3	T1 (a)	T2 (b)	T3 (c)
Intelligence												
2	.72	.70	.67	.14	.17	.21	.14	.13	.12	.00	.04	.09
4	.75	.72	.72	.16	.14	.12	.09	.14	.15	.07	.00	−.03
6	.71	.74	.65	.13	.15	.19	.15	.11	.16	−.02	.04	.03
Total	.73	.72	.68	.14	.15	.17	.13	.13	.15	.01	.02	.02
English Reading												
2	.62	.62	.63	.23	.21	.23	.15	.17	.14	.08	.04	.09
4	.65	.67	.61	.24	.19	.23	.11	.14	.16	.13	.05	.07
6	.66	.68	.62	.14	.21	.25	.20	.11	.13	−.06	.10	.12
Total	.65	.66	.62	.19	.20	.24	.16	.14	.14	.03	.06	.10
Math Computation												
2	.65	.65	.59	.17	.19	.24	.18	.16	.17	−.01	.03	.07
4	.66	.67	.60	.21	.20	.20	.13	.14	.20	.08	.06	.00
6	.58	.65	.62	.18	.17	.22	.24	.18	.15	−.06	−.01	.07
Total	.62	.65	.61	.18	.19	.22	.20	.16	.17	−.02	.03	.05

beginning and end of the final year of the study. In our analyses we address two basic questions: First, does the provision of test information about pupils to teachers affect the teachers' subsequent perceptions of the pupils? And second, does the provision of test information about pupils to teachers affect the pupils' subsequent test performance? Data obtained in Treatment 2 (testing–no information) and Treatment 3 (testing-information) are used in the analyses.

In Figure 6.2 we present a schema of all possible correlations between test performance and teacher ratings, measures of which were obtained at two points in time (at the beginning and at the end of the final year of the study). The relationship between test scores and teacher ratings obtained at the same time are represented in the schema (the unlagged synchronous correlations), as are the relationships between performance on a test taken on two occasions and between teacher ratings obtained on two occasions (the lagged auto-correlations). Finally, the correlations that are crossed and lagged provide information on the relationship between a test taken on one occasion and a teacher rating obtained at another time. For these relationships we used partial rather than simple correlations, since if initial test score and teacher rating do not differ, a subsequent change in a measure of one of these variables could not be attributed to information derived from the other. If there is no initial discrepancy between test score and teacher rating, we would expect subsequent measures of these variables to be similar to the earlier ones. By using the partial correlation, we restrict our analyses to an examination of initial discrepancies between scores and ratings and how these relate to later changes.

Before considering how partial cross-lagged correlations might be used to throw light on the interaction of test information and teacher perception, we consider the initial relationships between test scores and teacher perceptions. This procedure, like the discrepancy analyses in the last section, is a way of estimating the extent to which the possibility that test information influences subsequent teacher perception is limited by the initial relationship between the variables. Correlations by treatment group and grade level between teachers' ratings of pupils' intelligence, English reading, and mathematics computation and corresponding pupil test performance in these areas were found to range between .46 and .67. This indicates substantial, if far from perfect, agreement between teacher ratings and tests; the figures agree reasonably well with reports in the literature (Scanlon, 1973).

The magnitude of the correlations indicates that there is some room for test information to alter teacher perceptions. For example, the largest correlation (.67) between a beginning-of-year rating and the comparable beginning-of-year test score is that for English reading at grade 6. If one were to obtain a correlation of 1.00, then of course 100 percent of the variance shared by the two estimates of reading achievement would be explained. The amount of variance

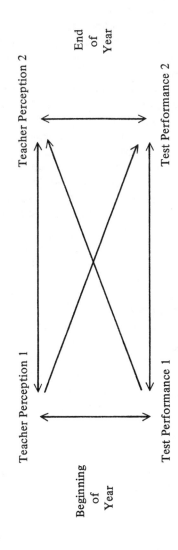

Figure 6.2. Schema of Cross-Lagged Correlations between Teachers' Perceptions and Test Performance at Beginning (Fall) and End (Spring) of School Year

actually shared, however, was 45 percent (i.e., $.67^2$); thus 55 percent of the variance was not common to the two English reading measures. However, this conclusion is somewhat misleading; the upper limit of shared variance cannot be 100 percent because of the unreliability associated with each measure. We can correct for attenuation by using the correlation between the initial and final test as the reliability index for the test (.89) and the correlation between the initial and final ratings as an estimate of the reliability of the ratings (.79). While using reliability estimates based on a shorter time interval or internal consistency would be preferable, these were not available for the teacher ratings. Those available for the tests indicate that reliability measures based on test administrations over a short time period (usually two weeks) (see Educational Research Centre, 1977, 1978a, 1978b) do not differ greatly from the measures based on administration at the beginning and end of the school year. Thus, the use of the latter measures in estimating attenuation does not seem unreasonable. On the basis of this method, the maximum correlation we could expect between the rating and test is .80. If the maximum possible correlation were in fact obtained, then 64 percent of the variance ($.80^2$) would be shared by the rating and the test. However, as we saw, the correlation obtained indicated that the percentage of variance common to both estimates of English reading is actually 45 percent. Subtracting 45 percent from 64 percent (the maximum variance that could be shared), we see that only 19 percent of the variance—as opposed to 55 percent—is *not* common to the two estimates.

The lowest obtained correlation (.46) was between the two beginning-of-year estimates of intelligence at grade 2. If we use a perfect correlation of 1.00 as a base, 79 percent of the variance will not be common to the two measures. Correcting for the unreliability of the two measures by using the corresponding beginning to end-of-year correlations as the indices of reliability, the maximum correlation we could expect would be .61. After this correction for unreliability, 37 percent of the variance is the maximum that could be shared between the two measures. Given our obtained correlation of .46, 16 percent of the variance (37 percent − 21 percent) is not common to the two initial estimates of intelligence.

Thus, after correction for unreliability in our estimates, the amount of unexplained variance drops from a range of 35 percent to 79 percent to one of 16 percent to 19 percent. These figures indicate that while there is a potential for the provision of test information to influence teacher perceptions, it is not as large as at first it seemed. Nonetheless, we can say that while the test and teacher ratings both tap common aspects of the constructs of intelligence and achievement, both estimates also capture aspects of the constructs that are unique to the mode of assessment. Consequently, knowledge of test performance can provide teachers with information about some pupils that is discrepant from their assessment of the pupils' ability or achievement.

Some other correlations between teachers' ratings and test scores are worthy of note. First, the correlations between the initial and final tests are uniformly high—all but two in the .70 to .85 range—indicating both the stability of the constructs measured and the reliability of the measures. Second, the correlations between initial and final ratings are also high, ranging from .66 to .84, with most in the mid-.70 range. These correlations are very similar in magnitude to the corresponding correlations between test scores, indicating that the construct assessed by the teacher ratings is also quite stable. The correlations between the final ratings and final test scores range from .41 to .72; overall these correlations tend to be slightly higher than those between the initial ratings and initial test scores, indicating that there has been some realignment over time.

We may now turn to the cross-lagged links of Figure 6.2, since we hope in examining these to be able to throw light on the expectancy process. These, as we indicated, are partial correlations; one portrays the relationship between initial test score and final teacher perception, from which the influence of initial teacher perception has been partialed out, and the other, the relationship between initial teacher perception and final test score, from which the contribution in initial test score has been eliminated.

In the context of our original questions—whether test information affects teachers' subsequent perceptions and pupils' subsequent test performance—we may make predictions about the relative magnitude of partial correlations both between and within treatment groups. The predictions are based on the reasoning that only if teachers receive information about the test performance of their pupils can their subsequent perceptions alter in line with that information. Thus, we would expect differences between treatments in patterns of partial correlations. Specifically, we would predict that the correlation between initial test score (T_1) and subsequent teacher perception (P_2), with the effect of initial teacher perception (P_1) partialed out, would be significantly larger for the group that received information (Treatment 3) than for the group without such information (Treatment 2). A further possible consequence of providing test information is that the future test performance of pupils is influenced by it as well as by teachers' initial perceptions. In the absence of test information, on the other hand, future test performance can be influenced by initial teacher perception, but not by test information. Relevant data on this issue will be obtained by determining if the effect of initial teacher perception on subsequent test performance is reduced in the presence of test information. Thus, we would expect that the correlation between initial teacher perception (P_1) and subsequent test performance (T_2), when the effect of initial test score (T_1) has been partialed out, would be significantly higher for the group without test information (Treatment 2) than it would be for the group with such information (Treatment 3).

On the basis of the same reasoning, we would expect to find differences in partial correlations *within* treatments. In the treatment that did not receive test information (Treatment 2), the influence of initial teacher perception on subsequent test performance must, if it operates at all, be stronger than the influence of initial test scores. Thus, the partial correlation between initial teacher perception and subsequent test performance should be larger than the partial correlation between initial test performance and subsequent teacher perception. In the group that received test information (Treatment 3), we would expect that the effect of such information being available would be reflected in a reversal of the relative magnitude of these correlations within the treatment (i.e., the partial correlation between initial test performance and subsequent teacher perception should be larger than the partial correlation between initial teacher perception and subsequent test performance).

Tables 6.7 to 6.10 present the cross-lagged partial correlations between teacher perceptions of intelligence and of achievement in English reading, mathematics computation, and Irish reading and the corresponding test performance of pupils at three grade levels—2, 4, and 6. The number of cases on which each correlation is based is also shown in the tables.

Differences between Treatments

We first consider the influence of test information on teachers' perceptions. This involves looking at differences between treatments in correlations between initial test performance and subsequent teacher perceptions, having partialed out initial teacher perception (column r_1 in Tables 6.7 to 6.10). All are positive, indicating that initial test performance and final teacher perception shared variance that was not shared with the initial teacher perception. The comparisons between the eleven partials are found in the first column (r_1) of the tables. Our prediction that the partial correlations would be higher in Treatment 3 than in Treatment 2 is supported in eight of the eleven comparisons. Furthermore, the difference, using a one-tailed test, is statistically significant in four of them: intelligence at grades 4 and 6 and English reading and Irish reading at grade 6.

Patterns across grades or scholastic areas are not very obvious. However, significant differences tended to be found at senior rather than at junior grade levels. Thus, test results would seem to have a greater impact on teachers of older children. As far as ability and achievement areas are concerned, the most persistent influence of test scores seems to be on teachers' perceptions of general ability or intelligence, the least persistent on perceptions of progress in mathematics. This is not unreasonable when one recalls that teachers had many formal indices of a pupil's achievement in mathematics (such as examinations,

Table 6.7. Cross-Lagged Partial Correlations between Test Performance and Teacher Perception of Intelligence, by Treatment, for Grades 2, 4, and 6

	$r_{T_1P_2 \cdot P_1}$		$r_{P_1T_2 \cdot T_1}$		Relationship of Partials within Treatment Is in the Predicted Direction?	
	r_1	N	r_2	N		
Grade 2						
Testing—no information (T2)	.17	475	.16	465	$r_2 > r_1$	No
Testing—norm-referenced information (T3)	.19	483	.24	675	$r_1 > r_2$	No
Relationship of partials between treatments is in the predicted direction?	T3>T2 Yes N.S.		T2>T3 No			
Grade 4						
Testing—no information (T2)	.11	415	.29	473	$r_2 > r_1$ Yes	Sig.
Testing—norm-referenced information (T3)	.36	613	.23	751	$r_1 > r_2$ Yes	Sig.
Relationship of partials between treatments is in the predicted direction?	T3>T2 Yes Sig.		T2>T3 Yes N.S.			
Grade 6						
Testing—no information (T2)	.23	461	.24	486	$r_2 > r_1$ Yes	N.S.
Testing—norm-referenced information (T3)	.35	794	.14	836	$r_1 > r_2$ Yes	Sig.
Relationship of partials between treatments is in the predicted direction?	T3>T2 Yes Sig.		T2>T3 Yes Sig.			

Table 6.8. Cross-Lagged Partial Correlations between Test Performance and Teacher Perception of Mathematics, by Treatment, for Grades 2, 4, and 6

	$r_{T_1P_2 \cdot P_1}$		$r_{P_1T_2 \cdot T_1}$		Relationship of Partials within Treatment Is in the Predicted Direction?	
	r_1	N	r_2	N		
Grade 2						
Testing—no information (T2)	.25	520	.36	489	$r_2 > r_1$	Yes Sig.
Testing—norm-referenced information (T3)	.28	527	.26	695	$r_1 > r_2$	Yes N.S.
Relationship of partials between treatments is in the predicted direction?	T3>T2 Yes N.S.		T2>T3 Yes Sig.			
Grade 4						
Testing—no information (T2)	.22	492	.27	516	$r_2 > r_1$	Yes N.S.
Testing—norm-referenced information (T3)	.30	655	.17	861	$r_1 > r_2$	Yes Sig.
Relationship of partials between treatments is in the predicted direction?	T3>T2 Yes N.S.		T2>T3 Yes Sig.			
Grade 6						
Testing—no information (T2)	.27	559	.24	557	$r_2 > r_1$	No
Testing—norm-referenced information (T3)	.26	926	.29	936	$r_1 > r_2$	No
Relationship of partials between treatments is in the predicted direction?	T3>T2 No		T2>T3 No			

Table 6.9. Cross-Lagged Partial Correlations between Test Performance and Teacher Perception of English Reading, by Treatment, for Grades 2, 4, and 6

	$r_{T_1P_2 \cdot P_1}$		$r_{P_1T_2 \cdot T_1}$		Relationship of Partials within Treatment Is in the Predicted Direction?		
	r_1	N	r_2	N			
Grade 2							
Testing—no information (T2)	.30	516	.46	480	$r_2 > r_1$	Yes	Sig.
Testing—norm-referenced information (T3)	.28	532	.39	677	$r_1 > r_2$	No	
Relationship of partials between treatments is in the predicted direction?	T3>T2 No		T2>T3 Yes N.S.				
Grade 4							
Testing—no information (T2)	.27	497	.36	533	$r_2 > r_1$	Yes	Sig.
Testing—norm-referenced information (T3)	.34	652	.27	821	$r_1 > r_2$	Yes	Sig.
Relationship of partials between treatments is in the predicted direction?	T3>T2 Yes N.S.		T2>T3 Yes Sig.				
Grade 6							
Testing—no information (T2)	.19	565	.18	544	$r_2 > r_1$	No	
Testing—norm-referenced information (T3)	.38	927	.16	924	$r_1 > r_2$	Yes	Sig.
Relationship of partials between treatments is in the predicted direction?	T3>T2 Yes Sig.		T2>T3 Yes N.S.				

Table 6.10. Cross-Lagged Partial Correlations between Test Performance and Teacher Perception of Irish Reading, by Treatment, for Grades 4 and 6

	$r_{T_1P_2 \cdot P_1}$		$r_{P_1T_2 \cdot T_1}$		*Relationship of Partials within Treatment Is in the Predicted Direction?*	
	r_1	N	r_2	N		
Grade 4						
Testing—no information (T2)	.36	492	.39	518	$r_2 > r_1$	Yes N.S.
Testing—norm-referenced information (T3)	.28	650	.21	829	$r_1 > r_2$	Yes N.S.
Relationship of partials between treatments is in the predicted direction?	T3 > T2 No		T2 > T3 Yes Sig.			
Grade 6						
Testing—no information (T2)	.23	545	.26	530	$r_2 > r_1$	Yes N.S.
Testing—norm-referenced information (T3)	.31	897	.26	928	$r_1 > r_2$	Yes N.S.
Relationship of partials between treatments is in the predicted direction?	T3 > T2 Yes Sig.		T2 > T3 No			

tests, and questions in class) available to them, while they had no formal measure of intelligence or general ability as such.

Coefficients of determination (r^2) were calculated for the cross-lagged partial correlations. The coefficient provides an index of the amount of variance in the final teacher perceptions that is accounted for by initial test performance, after the effect of initial perceptions has been excluded. The difference between the coefficient associated with Treatment 2 correlations and that associated with Treatment 3 correlations can be interpreted as the variance attributable to the impact of test information on teachers' perceptions. An inspection of the differences for pairs of correlations that differed significantly indicates that the provision of test information accounted for between 5 and 12 percent of the final teacher perceptions of their pupils.

The second set of treatment differences (shown in column r_2 of Tables 6.7 to 6.10) are relevant to a consideration of the impact of test information on subsequent test performance. Here we are interested in differences between the two treatment groups in the correlations between initial teacher perception and subsequent pupil test performance. If providing teachers with test information affects subsequent pupil test performance, then the partial correlations for the information group (Treatment 3) should be significantly smaller than those for the no-information group (Treatment 2). All the cross-lagged correlations are again positive. Support for our prediction that the partial correlations would be smaller for the information group was found in eight of the eleven comparisons; of these, five are statistically significant: intelligence at grade 6, mathematics at grades 2 and 4, and English reading and Irish reading at grade 4. Support for our prediction was somewhat more frequent at the intermediate level (grade 4) than at grade 2 or grade 6. However, the pattern of significant differences across the ability and achievement variables does not indicate a stronger or a more persistent impact for any particular variable.

We saw in the previous set of correlations that at both grades 4 and 6, information about pupils' intelligence test performance had a significant impact on teachers' subsequent perceptions of pupils' intelligence. Inspection of column r_2 in Table 6.10, which relates to data from the present analysis, shows that, at grade 6, providing teachers with information about their pupils' performance on an intelligence test also significantly influenced pupil performance on a subsequent test of intelligence. While the direction of the effect was also as predicted at grade 4, the difference between treatment groups was not significant. At grade 2 the direction of the effect ran counter to our prediction, but again the difference between treatment groups was not significant.

A consideration of differences between coefficients of determination associated with the pairs of correlations for which significant treatment differences were found indicates that from 4 to 11 percent more variance in subsequent test performance can be accounted for by initial teacher rating when teachers were *not* given norm-referenced test information. The import of this finding is perhaps clearer when put in terms of the group that received test information. In the information group the intrusion of test information seems to have disrupted teachers' initial perceptions of pupils, so that the subsequent test performance of pupils was less influenced by those perceptions than was the case in the group without information, in which teachers' initial perceptions were not disturbed.

Differences within Treatments

Up to this point in considering the influence of test information on test scores, we have examined the partial correlations in terms of differences between treatments. Let us now consider the same correlations within each treatment group. In light of our earlier reasoning, we would expect in the no-information treatment (Treatment 2) that the partial correlation between initial teacher perception and subsequent pupil test performance (column r_2 in Tables 6.7 to 6.10) would be greater than the partial correlation between the initial test performance and subsequent teacher perception (column r_1 in tables 6.7 to 6.10). Because teachers in Treatment 3 did receive information, we would expect the opposite tendency (i.e., the partial correlation between initial test performance and subsequent teacher perception [column r_1, Tables 6.7 to 6.10] should be greater than the partial correlation between initial teacher perception and subsequent pupil test performance [column r_2 in Tables 6.7 to 6.10]).

Within the no-information group (Treatment 2), the difference between the partial correlations was in the predicted direction in eight of the eleven comparisons; of these, four were statistically significant: intelligence at grade 4, mathematics computation at grade 2, and English reading at grades 2 and 4. There was a slight tendency for the significant differences to occur at the lower and intermediate grades (2 and 4) rather than at higher (grade 6) ones. No tendency was in evidence for a significant effect to be associated with a particular construct.

In the case of the group that had received test information (Treatment 3), eight of the differences between partial correlations were in the expected direction, and five of these were statistically significant: intelligence and English reading at grades 4 and 6 and mathematics computation at grade 4. Thus, the effect of test information was more strongly manifested in the case of intelligence and English reading at the intermediate and higher grade levels.

Overall, the comparison of partial correlations within treatment groups provides further evidence that an expectancy process operates whether or not teachers have information about their pupils' test performance. When test information was available, the effect of that information is in evidence in the later test performance of pupils. When teachers did not have test information, on the other hand, the influence of their already established perceptions can be seen.

PUPIL CHARACTERISTICS AND EXPECTANCY

In this section we again use cross-lagged partial correlational analysis to examine the effect that the provision of test information has for different types of pupils. Specifically, we shall examine the expectancy effect for boys and for girls; for pupils from urban, town, and rural schools; and for pupils from different socioeconomic backgrounds.

The Effect of Test Information on Teachers' Perceptions and Pupil Test Performance by Gender

Although we had no reason to expect that the provision of test information would have different effects for boys and girls, we did examine this possibility, since teacher expectancy effects have been shown to be gender-specific in some cases (see Garner and Bing, 1973). Our total sample in each treatment group was divided by gender and we calculated cross-lagged partial correlation coefficients for boys and girls separately within each treatment. There were 1,828 boys and 1,881 girls spread over three grades. The partial coefficients calculated were the same as in the preceding analyses: one for initial test performance and subsequent teacher perception (with initial teacher perception held constant) and one for initial teacher perception and subsequent test performance (with initial test performance held constant). Differences between treatments—one that had received test information (Treatment 3) and one that had not received information (Treatment 2)—in the magnitude of the cross-lagged correlations were examined. In these comparisons we follow the same logic and procedure as we did when we compared the total group partial correlations in the last section. In the case of both boys and girls, we would expect the availability of test information to affect teachers' subsequent perceptions of pupils. The correlation between initial test scores and subsequent teacher perceptions (with the effect of initial perceptions partialed out) should, if test information is effective, be higher in the group that received test information (Treatment 3) than in the one that did not (Treatment 2). We should also expect the availability of test information to affect pupils' subsequent test performance. If it does, the correlations between initial teacher perceptions and subsequent test scores (with the effect of initial test scores partialed out) should be higher in the group that did not receive test information than in the group that did. In examining differences between treatments in patterns of partial correlations, we use one-tailed tests to assess the significance of the differences.

As in the preceding section, we compared the magnitude of the cross-lagged correlations within treatments for each gender separately to see to what extent these comparisons supported the inferences made on the basis of between-treatment comparisons. We also compared the partial correlations obtained for boys with those obtained for girls. If test information is more effective in altering teachers' perceptions for one gender than for another, we would expect that difference to be reflected in the test-information group in the relative values of the partial correlations between initial test scores and subsequent teacher perceptions. For example, if we find a lower correlation for boys than for girls, this would indicate that teachers paid less attention to test information in the case of boys than in the case of girls. The effect of test information on subsequent test performance would be reflected in the magnitude of the partial correlation between initial teacher perceptions and subsequent test scores also in the test-information group. For example, if teachers pay more attention to the test results of girls than of boys, the partial correlation coefficient for girls will be lower than that for boys. Thus, in the test-information group, a relatively high partial correlation between initial test scores and subsequent perceptions and a relatively low partial correlation between initial perceptions and subsequent test scores both indicate the influence of test information.

An examination of the partial correlations between initial test scores and subsequent teacher perceptions for boys indicated that differences between treatments were in the predicted direction for nine of the eleven correlations. Further, in five instances, the differences were statistically significant: intelligence in grade 4 (Treatment 3, $r = .33$; Treatment 2, $r = .08$), intelligence in grade 6 (Treatment 3, $r = .34$; Treatment 2, $r = .21$), mathematics computation in grade 2 (Treatment 3, $r = .49$; Treatment 2, $r = .29$), mathematics computation in grade 6 (Treatment 3, $r = .36$; Treatment 2, $r = .24$), and English reading in grade 6 (Treatment 3, $r = .35$; Treatment 2, $r = .14$). The most consistent evidence relating to the effect of test information on teachers' perceptions of boys was found in the final year of primary school, when the predicted effect was significant for all subject areas except Irish reading.

The effects of test information on teachers' perceptions of girls were less clear. Eight of the eleven partial correlations were larger in the information group (Treatment 3) than in the group without information (Treatment 2). This is in line with our prediction. However, the differences were statistically significant in only two cases. As it happened, the two scholastic areas for which significant differences were found for girls had also had significant differences associated with them for boys: intelligence at grade 4 (Treatment 3, r = .40; Treatment 2, r = .09) and English reading at grade 6 (Treatment 3, r = .39; Treatment 2, r = .23).

When we found significant differences between treatments, we subtracted the coefficient of determination (r^2) for Treatment 2 from that for Treatment 3 to obtain an index of the magnitude of the observed effect of the test information in terms of the amount of variance attributable to it. For the five significant differences found for boys, 7 to 16 percent of explained variance could be attributed to the provision of norm-referenced test information; in the case of the two significant differences found for girls, the amounts of explained variance were 10 percent and 15 percent.

In considering partial correlations between initial teacher perceptions and subsequent test performance, we predicted that the test performance of pupils whose teachers did not receive test information (Treatment 2) would relate more closely to initial perceptions than would be the case for pupils whose teachers had access to test information (Treatment 3). Thus, if test information is effective, the partial correlation between initial teacher perceptions and subsequent test performance should be larger in the group without test information than in the group with test information.

For boys we found that all the partial correlations were positive and that five of the differences between treatments were in the expected direction. Only one of these, mathematics computation at grade 2 (Treatment 2, r = .53; Treatment 3, r = .37), however, was significant. The differences between the coefficients of determination for the two treatments indicated that the provision of test information accounted for 14 percent of the explained variance in the relationship between initial teacher perception and subsequent test performance for grade 2 mathematics computation.

For girls, eight of the eleven pairs of partial correlations between initial perception and subsequent test performance were in the predicted direction and four differed significantly—English reading at grade 2 (Treatment 2, r = .46; Treatment 3, r = .29), mathematics computation at grade 4 (Treatment 2, r = .47; Treatment 3, r = .26), Irish reading at grade 4 (Treatment 2, r = .45; Treatment 3, r = .20), and intelligence at grade 6 (Treatment 2, r = .31; Treatment 3, r = .14). Between 8 and 16 percent of variance in the correlation was attributable to the provision of test information.

An examination of the relative magnitude of the partial correlations within the information group carried out separately for boys and girls produced results not dissimilar to those obtained for the total sample. In the case of boys, there was some evidence of a trend for the correlation between initial test score and subsequent teacher perception to be greater than the correlation between initial teacher perception and subsequent test score, supporting the view that the impact of test information on teachers' perceptions is stronger for boys. However, in terms of actual statistically significant differences, the results for boys were the same as those for girls and for the total sample.

In considering differences within treatments in the magnitude of partial correlations obtained for boys and girls, we had no basis for predicting the direction of any differences which we might find. Thus, we used two-tailed tests in testing for statistical significance. When we compared the magnitude of the correlations between initial test score and subsequent teacher perception for boys and girls in the test-information group, five of the eleven differences were significant; in each case, the partial correlation for boys was greater than the one for girls. The significant differences occurred for mathematical computation at grade 2 (boys' r = .49; girls' r = .18), at grade 4 (boys' r = .38; girls' r = .20), and at grade 6 (boys' r = .36; girls' r = .15), for English reading at grade 4 (boys' r = .40; girls' r = .26), and for Irish reading also at grade 4 (boys' r = .36; girls' r = .18). The amount of variance accounted for by the partial correlations on the variables was found to be between 9 percent and 21 percent greater in the case of boys. This provides further evidence that the impact of test information on teachers' perceptions was greater for boys than for girls.

We found no significant difference between boys and girls in the partial correlations between initial perception and subsequent test performance in the test-information group. Thus, the finding from our between-treatment analyses that girls are more frequently affected by test information in their test performance than are boys is not supported in the within-treatment analyses.

One further finding from our within-treatment analyses is perhaps worth mentioning even though, since it refers to the no-information group, it cannot speak directly to the effects of test information. It is, however, of interest that in four cases, the partial correlations between initial teacher perception and subsequent test performance were significantly higher for girls than for boys; in only one case was the boys' correlation significantly higher than the girls' one. Thus, in the absence of test information, the influence of teachers' perceptions on pupils' test performance seems to be greater for girls than for boys.

Our findings on gender differences serve to elucidate our earlier findings on the effects of test information when our sample was not divided by gender. Variables for which significant differences occurred in the combined analyses tend to occur again in the analyses for separate genders. For example, the combined analyses produced evidence that teachers' perceptions of intelligence at grade 4 and of English reading at grade 6 were affected by test information; our gender analyses indicate that that is true for both boys and girls. Some of the significant findings in the combined analyses, however, relate to only one gender. In some cases in which the finding in the combined analysis was not significant, the findings in the separate gender analyses were significant.

The implication of these findings is that the impact of test information differs somewhat for boys and girls. While differences were not found uniformly across grade levels or subject areas, there are indications that teachers react differently to information about boys and girls and that boys and girls react differently to teachers. While on the one hand we found teachers' perceptions to be more amenable to alteration in the case of boys than in the case of girls, we also obtained evidence which indicated that the effect of teachers' perceptions was greater for girls than for boys. Whether or not teachers' perceptions are informed by test information, it would appear that girls are more responsive to such perceptions (and expectations) than are boys. In the absence of test information, teachers' perceptions were found to be more closely related to subsequent test performance for girls than for boys, while when test information was available, the impact of such information, mediated through teachers, was again more in evidence in the test performance of girls than in the test performance of boys.

The Effect of Test Information on Teachers' Perceptions and Pupil Test Performance by School Location

Hypothesizing that the provision of test information would differentially affect urban, town, and rural teachers would seem reasonable. For one thing, teachers in rural schools are likely to know their children better than do teachers in urban schools. The rural teacher, in contrast with the urban one, is likely to teach in a smaller class and to stay with pupils through multiple grades, as well as to know and interact with pupils and their families in the community. Because of the greater knowledge of pupils that the rural teacher is likely to have, we could argue that he or she would be less susceptible to the influence of test information than would a city teacher. The influence of test information on teachers in towns might fall somewhere between that for rural and urban teachers.

In this section we again use cross-lagged partial correlations to examine differences between urban, town, and rural school settings in the impact of test information on teachers' subsequent perceptions of pupils and on pupils' subsequent test performance. Pupils were first stratified according to the location of the school they attended: urban (if located in one of five cities), town (if located in a town with a population of 1,500 or more, but not in a city), and rural (if located in an area with a population of less than 1,500). There were 1,307 city pupils, 1,681 town pupils, and 744 rural pupils. We carried out separate correlational analyses for pupils in each category.

Our expectation in examining differences between the group with information (Treatment 3) and the group without information (Treatment 2) in the magnitude of partial correlations between initial test performance and subsequent teacher perception was that the correlations would be larger in the test-information group than in the group without information. We also expected that this relationship would be more common in city schools than in rural ones. We did, in fact, find stronger evidence in urban schools than in schools in other locations that test information affected teacher perceptions. For the urban sample, eight of the eleven differences between partial correlations were in the predicted direction, and of these, four were significantly different: at grade 4, mathematics computation (Treatment 3, $r = .38$; Treatment 2, $r = .17$), and at grade 6, intelligence (Treatment 3, $r = .40$; Treatment 2, $r = .05$), English reading (Treatment 3, $r = .35$; Treatment 2, $r = .10$), and Irish reading (Treatment 3, $r = .30$; Treatment 2, $r = .12$). In the case of the town sample, six of the differences between partial correlations were in the predicted direction, but only two of these were significant: mathematics computation at grade 4 (Treatment 3, $r = .34$; Treatment 2, $r = .21$) and English reading at grade 6 (Treatment 3, $r = .36$; Treatment 2, $r = .24$). For rural schools, while eight of the differences between partial correlations were in the expected direction, only two differed significantly: intelligence at grade 4 (Treatment 3, $r = .55$; Treatment 2, $r = -.34$) and English reading at grade 6 (Treatment 3, $r = .51$; Treatment 2, $r = .12$). The amounts of variance attributable to test information—7 to 25 percent—are similar to those reported in earlier analyses.

In examining data within treatments, we compared the magnitude of the partial correlations between initial test performance and subsequent teacher perceptions for each location in the treatment that received test information. No consistency was apparent in the pattern of results. Thus, we found no evidence in the within-treatment analyses that test information had a differential impact on teachers' perceptions in different locations.

In examining the partial correlations between initial teacher perception and subsequent pupil test performance, our expectation was that these would be higher in the group without information than in the information group and further, that this would be more common in city than in rural schools. In city schools we found differences between treatments to be in the predicted direction in eight of eleven comparisons. In three of these, all at grade 4, the differences were statistically significant: mathematics computation (Treatment 2, $r = .39$; Treatment 3, $r = .12$), English reading (Treatment 2, $r = .47$; Treatment 3, $r = .26$), and Irish reading (Treatment 2, $r = .42$; Treatment 3, $r = .22$). In town schools seven of the eleven comparisons were in the predicted direction, three of them significantly so: at grade 4, English reading (Treatment 2, $r = .36$; Treatment 3, $r = .23$) and Irish reading (Treatment 2, $r = .35$; Treatment 3, $r = .22$), and at grade 6, intelligence (Treatment 2, $r = .31$; Treatment 3, $r = .13$). In rural schools five of the eleven comparisons were in the predicted direction, and in two cases the differences were significant: at grade 4, Irish reading (Treatment 2, r = .37; Treatment 3, r = .19) and at grade 6, Irish reading again (Treatment 2, r = .51; Treatment 3, r =.28). Examination of the differences between associated coefficients of determination indicated that the availability of test information reduced the variance in the relationship between teacher perception and pupil test performance by 2 to 15 percent. Inspection of differences between correlations for different locations within treatments did not reveal any striking patterns. Some significant location differences relating to the effects of test information on teachers' perceptions and on pupil test performance were found. However, these differed from variable to variable and between locations without a consistent pattern. While in general these analyses provide slight support for the view that test information has a stronger impact in larger, city schools than in smaller, rural schools, differences were slight.

The Effect of Test Information on Teachers' Perceptions and Pupil Test Performance by Socioeconomic Status

There is a popular belief that teacher expectations are more likely to operate to the detriment of children of low socioeconomic status than of children of higher status. To examine whether test information, insofar as it might influence teachers' perceptions, has a differential impact on pupils from differing socio-economic backgrounds, the pupils in our sample were assigned to one of three socioeconomic categories on the basis of father's occupation: professional/ white-collar (high) (N = 655); skilled worker and farmer with over 50 acres (medium) (N = 1,250); and unskilled worker and farmer with less than 50 acres (low) (N = 664).

Correlations between initial test scores and subsequent teacher perceptions (after controlling for initial teacher ratings) stratified by the socioeconomic status of pupils are relevant to a consideration of the effect of test information on teachers' perceptions. At grade 2 we found no significant differences between treatments within any of the SES categories for any of the three social classes. At grade 4 we found only one significant difference between treatment groups for any of the SES categories: in the middle SES group, there was a significant difference between treatments in the partial correlations for mathematics (Treatment 3, r = .39; Treatment 2, r = .26). At grade 6 we found no treatment differences for either the high- or middle-social-class groups. However, in the lowest SES group, three of the four correlations differed in the predicted direction, and two of these were statistically significant: English reading (Treatment 3, r = .42; Treatment 2, r = .22) and Irish reading (Treatment 3, r = .34; Treatment 2, r = −.01). Thus, test information has a stronger impact on teachers' perceptions at grade 4 for middle SES pupils and at grade 6 for lower SES pupils.

Within the test-information group we found no significant differences between social classes for any of the pairs of partial correlations, except in the case of English reading at grade 4. Here we found a significantly higher correlation for the middle SES group (r = .38) than for the high SES group (r = .11). Thus, the within-treatment analyses revealed no effect for the low SES group.

To investigate influences associated with socioeconomic status on test performance, we examined the partial correlations between initial teacher perceptions and subsequent pupil test performance stratified by socioeconomic status. An examination of differences between the partial correlations of the group that had test information and the group that had not within each socio-economic stratum revealed that at grade 2 there was a significant difference between correlations for the middle SES group in mathematics computation (Treatment 2, r = .34; Treatment 3, r = .16) and for the low SES group in English reading (Treatment 2, r = .52; Treatment 3, r =.34). At grade 4 there were no differences between treatments within the high or low groups; two of the treatment comparisons, however, were significant in the middle SES group: intelligence (Treatment 2, r = .38; Treatment 3, r = .26) and Irish reading (Treatment 2, r = .41; Treatment 3, r = .22). At grade 6 there were no treatment differences within the lowest socioeconomic class group. In the middle SES group, significant differences between treatment correlations were found for English reading (Treatment 2, r = .38; Treatment 3, r = .15) and intelligence (Treatment 2, r = .32; Treatment 3, r = .12). In the high SES group, there was a significant difference for English reading (Treatment 2, r = .24; Treatment 3, r = −.03) in addition to one for Irish reading (Treatment 2, r = .26; Treatment 3, r = .04). Thus, the effects of teachers' perceptions on pupils' test performance were limited to the high and middle SES groups.

A comparison of correlations across socioeconomic categories within the treatment group that had received test information provided somewhat inconsistent results. Differences between only three pairs were significant. The low SES group had a higher correlation than the middle SES group for mathematics computation at grade 2 (low SES, r = .36; middle SES, r = .16) and than the high SES group for English reading at grade 6 (low SES, r = .25; high SES, r = −.03). However, at grade 4 the correlation for the middle SES group was higher than that for the low SES group for English reading (middle SES, r = .33; low SES, r = .08). Thus, at grades 2 and 6 we found some evidence that teachers attend less to the test results of low SES students than they do to the test results of other groups. At grade 4, however, test results had a relatively greater impact on low SES students than on middle SES ones.

Correlations from the group that did not receive test information should provide further evidence on the strength of the influence of teachers' perceptions on pupils' test performance. When we examined partial correlations within this group for the three socioeconomic strata, we found two cases of significant differences between socioeconomic groups. Both related to Irish reading and, as far as the low socioeconomic group is concerned, they are inconsistent. At grade 4 the influence of teachers' perceptions on pupil performance was most evident in the case of the high and middle SES groups (middle SES, $r = .41$; high SES, $r = .40$; low SES, $r = -.11$). At grade 6 it was more evident in the case of the low SES group (low SES group, $r = .41$; high SES group, $r = .26$; middle SES group, $r = .15$).

In these findings we find little evidence that test information has a different impact on pupils from low socioeconomic background than it does on pupils from any other socioeconomic group. In our examination of the correlations between initial test performance and later teachers' perceptions, we found evidence that test information was affecting teachers' perceptions of pupils in only four instances. Two of these related to middle SES children and two to low SES children.

The influence of test information was more in evidence in the correlations between initial teachers' perceptions and subsequent test performance. In eight comparisons between the group that had received test information and the one that had not, we found evidence of such influence. However, it concerned middle SES children more frequently (six comparisons), high SES children (two comparisons) to a lesser extent, and low SES children not at all. In comparisons of the correlations between initial teacher perceptions and subsequent test performance across SES categories in the group that received test information, the differences between the correlations of the socioeconomic groups achieved significance in three cases. Two of these related to the low SES group and one to the middle SES group, and the magnitude of the correlations indicated a low impact on the part of test information on these groups. In similar comparisons in the group that did not receive test information, the impact of teachers' perceptions on pupils' subsequent test performance was indicated in one case for each of the three socioeconomic groups.

CONCLUSION

In this chapter we described the results of analyses that were designed to examine the role of testing in the expectancy process in classrooms. We posited four steps in the process. Teachers form differential expectations for pupils, they then treat pupils in line with those expectations, pupils react accordingly, and eventually their scholastic achievement comes to reflect the expectations.

We were primarily interested in how the availability of test information might change the expectations that teachers form for their pupils. We obtained measures of teachers' perceptions of pupils early in the school year. We also tested pupils on standardized, norm-referenced tests of ability and attainment and provided teachers with information on the performance of pupils on the tests. Toward the end of the school year, teachers' perceptions were again elicited and pupils tested. In a control group of schools, information on teachers' perceptions was also obtained and pupils were tested in a similar fashion, but no information was given to teachers on the pupils' performance. Our expectation was that, if test information influenced teachers' perceptions, this would be reflected in differences between the test-information group and the group without test information in end-of-year teachers' perceptions as well as in the end-of-year test performance of the pupils.

We adopted two analytic procedures to examine this issue. First, we calculated changes in teachers' perceptions of pupils over the course of the school year and hypothesized that teachers who received test information would show more change than teachers who did not receive information. Second, we calculated cross-lagged correlation coefficients between beginning-of-year measures and end-of-year measures. For the cross-lagged correlation between teachers' beginning-of-year perceptions of pupils and the pupils' end-of-year test performance (partialing out the beginning-of-year test scores of pupils), we hypothesized that the correlation in the test-information group would be lower than that in the group without information. For the cross-lagged correlation between pupils' beginning-of-year test scores and teachers' end-of-year perceptions of pupils (partialing out the beginning-of-year teachers' perceptions), we hypothesized that correlations in the test-information group would be higher than correlations in the group without information. Both hypotheses were based on the assumption that test information would influence teachers who received such information, but obviously could not influence teachers who did not have access to it. On the basis of similar reasoning, we also formed a number of hypotheses relating to the relationship of partial correlations within treatments.

Before considering the results of these analyses, we may note that initial test scores and teachers' perceptions showed considerable congruence. This was so whether one used a discrepancy model or a correlational model to examine the relationship. However, lack of agreement between initial test scores and initial teachers' perceptions was sufficient to allow room for test information to affect teachers' later perceptions of their pupils.

A consideration of two related indices of discrepancies between teachers' perceptions obtained at the beginning and end of the school year—magnitude of change and stability of perception—provided considerable support for the hypothesis that, overall, teachers who received test information were less stable in their ratings, making more and larger changes in them, than were teachers without information. This was most clear in teachers' ratings of English reading but appeared also, though less strongly, in ratings of mathematics and intelligence.

With respect to the index of shift in ratings in a more favorable direction, we found only one clear significant treatment effect, that for mathematics ratings. No clear relationship was found between ratings in a less favorable direction and the presence or absence of test information. When we compare shifts in the group that received information with shifts in the two groups that did not, we find that more favorable shifts occurred in the test-information group.

The cross-lagged partial correlational analyses provided further evidence for an interaction between availability of test information on the one hand and teachers' perceptions of pupils and pupils' subsequent test performance on the other. When test information was made available to teachers, their subsequent ratings of their pupils' intelligence and scholastic achievement tended to move into line with that information. In the cases in which that movement was found to be statistically significant, the provision of test information was found to account for 5 to 12 percent more variance in the relationship between the test scores and subsequent teacher perceptions in the group that had test information than in the group that had not. This effect was consistent in grade 6, where all of the results except those for mathematical computation were statistically significant. If, on the other hand, test information was not available to teachers, pupils' subsequent test performance tended to move into line with initial teacher perceptions of their intelligence and achievement, in comparison with the group that received test information. We can infer that test information "disrupts" teacher perceptions and that this disruption is reflected in the differential relationship between initial teacher perception and subsequent pupil test performance in the two groups. The effect was most consistent at grade 4, where all of the differences between correlations, except those for intelligence, were statistically significant. The size of the effect for subsequent test performance was similar to that for subsequent teacher perceptions; 4 to 11 percent less variance in the relationship between initial ratings and subsequent test scores was accounted for in the treatment group that had information than in the group that had not.

These conclusions are based on differences that were statistically significant between and within treatments. While we indicated the number of times the comparisons between pairs of partial correlations differed in the predicted direction, most of our discussion was limited to differences that were statistically significant. Looking back over our results, however, one cannot help but be struck by a clear trend for the differences to be in the expected direction—that is, our predictions about direction, based on the operation of an expectancy process, were supported more often than not, both between and within our two treatments. Thus, an expectancy process seems to have been operating in classrooms, regardless of whether or not standardized norm-referenced test information was provided to teachers.

Our results relating to gender were equally consistent, if not so readily interpretable. They indicate that test information has a differential impact on boys and girls. Differences did not occur uniformly across grade levels or subject areas; however, they did occur frequently enough to indicate that test information and teachers' perceptions do not interact in the same way for boys as for girls. While we had no way beforehand of predicting precisely how test information and teachers' perceptions interact for boys and girls, there is some evidence in the literature with which our findings seem compatible. Such evidence relates to findings that interactions between teachers and pupils differ for the two genders. Furthermore, some of these differences relate specifically to evaluation. For example, teachers have been observed to direct more criticism toward boys and to evaluate them less positively on scholastic tasks (Dweck, 1976; Dweck and Bush, 1976; Morrison, McIntyre and Sutherland, 1965) as well as on nonscholastic behavior (Coopersmith, 1967; Digman, 1963). Teacher evaluations of boys are also more frequent and indiscriminate than their evaluations of girls (Brophy and Good, 1970; Meyer and Thompson, 1956).

If teachers' evaluations of boys are more unfocussed, they may also be more uncertain and so more amenable to change in the light of new information. Boys, however, precisely because of this uncertainty and also because of the lack of discrimination which they might have experienced in being evaluated by teachers in the past, may not place a high premium on the informational cues they receive from teachers. Thus, we would not expect to find major changes in their test performance corresponding to changes in teachers' perceptions induced by test information.

When we looked at school location, we found that the impact of test information differed by school setting at grades 4 and 6 but not at grade 2. City teachers were more likely to be influenced by test information than were town or rural teachers. At grade 6 test information influenced the subsequent perceptions of city teachers more often than it did those of town or rural teachers. At grade 4 test information had a more pervasive effect on the subsequent test performance of pupils in city schools than of pupils in town or rural schools.

The impact of test information on the teachers' subsequent perceptions of the progress of pupils from different social class backgrounds was confined to grades 4 and 6. At grade 4 the effect was associated with pupils from all three social classes; at grade 6 the effect on teacher perceptions was confined to pupils from the lowest socioeconomic group. The impact of test information on subsequent test performance was most often associated with middle-class children. We found little support for the claim that test information is especially likely to have a detrimental effect in the expectancy process in the case of children from low socioeconomic backgrounds.

7 EFFECTS OF
TESTING ON PARENTS

We developed an interview schedule for parents whose children had been involved in the study. Our purpose was to ascertain if the testing program in schools had any effect on them. We sought information relating to four areas: the familiarity of parents with changes in assessment procedures in schools; communication between school and parents; parents' perceptions of their children's school progress; and parents' knowledge of the standardized testing program that had been initiated in schools. Some of the information we hoped to obtain was very specific and concrete, such as, for example, the number of parents who were aware that their children had been tested. We also wished to learn if parent-teacher contacts had increased as a result of the testing program. Less tangible areas of interest were whether knowledge of children's performance on standardized tests had altered parents' perceptions of children's scholastic ability and progress and whether experience with standardized tests had affected parents' attitudes toward such tests.

The population to be sampled was made up of parents of pupils attending school in three treatment groups: the nontesting group (Treatment 1), the testing–no-information group (Treatment 2), and the test-information group (Treatment 3). Parents of all pupils in the lower grades (2, 3, and 4) were eligible for selection, but in the higher grades (5 and 6), the population was restricted to parents who had been interviewed at the beginning of the study. This was to ensure that we would have a group of parents whose children had been exposed to the testing program in its entirety and should have served to maximize the possibility of demonstrating effects.

In the sample-selection procedure, pupils were stratified by treatment and grade, and 416 parents were selected for interview. We could, however, interview only 395 of them. Interviews were carried out in parents' homes in the month of March following the termination of the testing program in schools. Actually, by this time testing had been carried out in the schools that had not tested during the course of the study (Treatment 1) to obtain dependent variable information. This testing may have tended to reduce possible differences between treatment groups in the responses of parents.

In analyses presented in this chapter, we compare the responses of parents in the norm-referenced, test-information group (Treatment 3) and the two control groups (Treatments 1 and 2). Separate analyses were carried out for parents of children in grades 2, 3, and 4 and parents of children in grades 5 and 6.

FAMILIARITY OF PARENTS WITH CHANGES IN EVALUATION

Parents were asked if they had heard or read about any efforts over the last few years to make changes in school examinations. Thirty percent replied that they had. At grades 2, 3, and 4, actually fewer of Treatment 3 parents (24 percent) than Treatment 1 (26 percent) or Treatment 2 (43 percent) parents gave this reply. The chi-square value for this difference was significant at the .02 level ($\chi^2 = 11.56$; df = 4). At the fifth- and sixth-grade levels, the treatment groups did not differ significantly. When parents who had indicated they had heard about changes were asked in an open-ended question what kinds of changes those were, most referred to public examinations (68.4 percent of parents of children in grades 2, 3, and 4; 75.0 percent of parents of children in grades 5 and 6). At grades 2, 3, and 4, only five parents reported that they had heard about standardized intelligence tests and four that they had heard about standardized attainment tests. The figures for grades 5 and 6 were even lower; one parent reported having heard about intelligence tests and one having heard about attainment tests.

The parents were then told of three proposed changes relating to assessment procedures and were asked in the case of each to indicate whether they thought it was "for the better," "made no difference," or "for the worse." The three changes were: giving tests that permit the comparison of a pupil's attainment with that of pupils nationwide, giving tests that permit the comparison of a pupil's intelligence with that of pupils nationwide, and changing the system of examinations. Approximately half the parents of pupils at both higher and lower grade levels saw the provision of tests that permit the comparison of pupils' attainment and intelligence with national norms as a change for the better. The numbers who perceived the change as being for the worse in all cases were small (always less than 10 percent). A sizable number of parents (between 23 percent and 32 percent) said that they did not know whether the change was for the better or the worse. These replies, one suspects, indicate a lack of familiarity with the tests on the part of many parents. There were no significant differences between treatment groups in their responses to these issues. Neither were there significant differences between treatments in their views on changing the system of examinations. Again, the largest number of parents of pupils at both junior (38 percent) and senior (46 percent) grade levels saw the change as for the better. At each level also, however, a sizable number (around 30 percent) professed not to know.

COMMUNICATION BETWEEN SCHOOL AND PARENTS

Parents were asked a number of questions relating to communication with the school. These questions related specifically to talking with teachers and to schools' methods of reporting on a pupil's progress. Parents were first asked what they thought of school arrangements to see a teacher and whether they were "completely satisfied," "somewhat satisfied," or "not satisfied." The vast majority expressed complete satisfaction. Differences between treatment groups were not significant.

While parents may have been satisfied with communication arrangements, not all of them had talked about their child to a teacher during the preceding year. Approximately 20 percent, at both grade levels, had no such contact. However, the remainder of parents did talk to their child's teacher on at least one occasion, and approximately 28 percent of parents, at both grade levels, talked with teachers at least three times. The treatment groups did not differ in frequency of parental contact with teachers.

A more frequent form of communication from teachers and schools would seem to be the school report. Asked if they had received a report about their child's progress in the preceding year, 84 percent of parents of children in junior grades and 94 percent of parents of children in senior grades reported that they had. Furthermore, parents who received reports practically all expressed satisfaction with the kind of information contained in them (82 percent at the junior level and 93 percent at the senior level). There were no differences between treatment groups in the reception of reports or in satisfaction with them.

Parents were asked a specific question about the provision in the school report of information about their child's performance on a test of intelligence or attainment. This was intended as a very direct question to find out if information regarding pupils' performance on standardized tests had been provided to parents. A relatively large number of parents (30 percent of parents of children in junior grades and 27 percent of parents of children in senior grades) reported that the school report had contained such information. However, we have reason to suspect these figures, since there were no significant differences between groups. Thirty-four percent of junior-grade parents and 24 percent of senior-grade parents in Treatment 1 claimed to have received information on standardized test performance. Children in this treatment had taken part in the final testing for the study, and results from it were available to schools at the time the parental questionnaire was carried out. However, some parents may have interpreted a test of attainment in a general sense rather than as a standardized test.

PARENTS' PERCEPTIONS OF THEIR CHILDREN'S SCHOOL PROGRESS

A number of questions relating to the child's school progress were asked. We were particularly interested in determining whether information based on the standardized test performance of children had reached parents and perhaps changed their views of their child's ability and progress in school. Parents were first asked to rate the education their children were receiving as "excellent," "pretty good," "only fair," or "poor." A large majority of parents of children at both grade levels (83 percent of junior grade parents and 90 percent of senior grade parents) rated their children's education as either "pretty good" or "excellent." There were no significant differences between treatments.

Parents were then asked to indicate their degree of satisfaction with their child's school progress in general. Most parents were either "satisfied" or "very satisfied" (84 percent of junior-grade parents and 89 percent of senior-grade parents). Again, there were no significant differences between treatment groups. Likewise, parents were on the whole optimistic about their child's ability to do school work. Among parents of children in junior grades, 89 percent perceived their children's ability as average or better; among parents of children in senior grades, the figure was 94 percent. Differences between treatment groups were again not significant.

Parents were asked directly whether anything had happened over the past few years to change their opinion about their child's school progress or ability to do school work. On the question of school progress, a large majority (85 percent of parents of children in junior grades and 90 percent of parents of children in senior grades) had not changed their opinions. Numbers relating to change of opinion regarding children's ability to do school work were similar; 90 percent of parents of children in junior grades and 91 percent of parents of children in senior grades had not changed their opinions. Those parents who had changed their opinions about their children's ability to do school work were asked what had happened to bring about that change. No parent mentioned information from standardized tests.

PARENTS' KNOWLEDGE ABOUT AND ATTITUDES TOWARD STANDARDIZED TESTING

A final set of questions asked of parents related specifically to attainment and intelligence tests. They were asked if their children had ever taken either kind of test and, if so, if they had received information about their child's performance. Fourteen percent of parents of junior-grade pupils and 25 percent of parents of senior-grade pupils indicated that their child had taken an attainment test, one that would tell "how well your child is doing in school subjects (English, Irish, and mathematics) compared to other children in school." A slightly higher percentage of junior-grade parents in Treatment 3 (17 percent) than in Treatments 2 or 3 (13 percent) reported this; among parents of children in higher grades, more parents in Treatments 1 (26 percent) and 2 (33 percent) than in Treatment 3 (18 percent) reported their child had taken such a test. However, differences between treatment groups were not significant. Those parents who said their child had taken an attainment test were asked if they had received any information on the child's test performance; 68 percent of junior-grade parents and 48 percent of senior-grade parents said they had. In most cases this information was conveyed in a written report of the child's school progress. All but one parent, who "did not know," said the information was helpful. Finally, parents were asked whether, if teachers had information on attainment tests, they would want the teachers to pass the information on to them. The vast majority (87 percent of junior-grade parents and 88 percent of senior-grade parents) said yes. There were no significant differences between treatment groups in their responses to any of these questions.

Parents' responses regarding intelligence tests were not very dissimilar to their responses regarding attainment tests. A slightly lower proportion (12 percent of parents of junior-grade pupils and 20 percent of parents of senior-grade pupils) indicated that their child had taken an intelligence test than had reported that their child had taken an attainment test. Of those reporting that their child had taken an intelligence test, a slightly higher percentage came from Treatment 3 than from the other treatments. Differences between treatments, however, were not significant. Of the thirty parents of pupils in junior grades who said their child had taken an intelligence test, twenty-three (77 percent) said they received information about the child's test performance; at the senior-grade level, seventeen (71 percent) of the twenty-four parents who said their child had taken a test said they received information on the child's performance. The information for most parents came in the form of a written report. All parents at both junior and senior levels, with two exceptions, said the information was helpful. The two exceptions were parents of junior class pupils, one of whom said it was unhelpful and one of whom said she "did not know."

An even larger number of parents (95 percent of junior-grade and 92 percent of senior-grade parents) expressed an interest in receiving information about the intelligence test performance of their children than had expressed an interest in the attainment test performance of their children. Differences between treatment groups in reply to any of the items relating to intelligence tests were not significant.

CONCLUSION

Our survey of parents revealed a number of interesting findings. A majority were satisfied with the education their child was receiving and with their child's school progress. A large majority were also satisfied with school arrangements to see a teacher and with the kind of information provided on school progress report forms.

However, as far as detecting the effects of a standardized testing program on parents was concerned, our survey revealed very little. With one sole and odd exception, we found no statistically significant differences between parents of children who had participated in the testing program and parents of children who had not in their responses to any questions in the interview. This was true for parents of children at both junior (second, third, and fourth) and senior (fifth and sixth) grade levels, even though in the case of the latter, we are sure that children had participated in the testing program over all the four years in which it had been in operation. Our findings should not come as a surprise, perhaps, in the case of the rather general question that asked about satisfaction with the education that children were receiving. However, it does seem surprising that differences between treatment groups were not detected in the case of responses to questions that asked specifically about parents' knowledge of the use of standardized tests in schools attended by their children. Indeed, information among parents about the testing program that we had initiated in schools was very sparse, despite a reasonable amount of contact between parents and schools. A relatively small number of parents (between 12 and 25 percent) indicated that they knew their child had taken an intelligence or attainment test. Because of the similarity of responses of parents of children in the nontested group and those of parents of children in the test groups, however, this may be an overestimation. We cannot be sure that parents in any of the treatment groups correctly understood the terms *intelligence test* and *attainment test*. This, of course, in itself is interesting. If the tests did not achieve saliency among the parents of tested children, then we must assume the participants did not regard the testing program in a very important light.

Despite all this, parents' attitudes toward standardized tests were very positive. The relatively small number who received test results for their children said these were helpful. About half the parents thought the provision of norm-referenced attainment and intelligence tests would be a change for the better in Irish education; more than a quarter admitted they did not know, but the number who saw it as a change for the worse was small. Further, a large majority of parents said they would be interested in receiving information on the performance of their children on tests of intelligence and attainment if such information were available. In evaluating such positive attitudes, one must bear in mind that parents seemed poorly informed about standardized tests. And perhaps that is the most significant finding to emerge from the parental interviews.

8 ALTERNATIVE TREATMENTS

Shortly after the commencement of the study, we found that some changes would have to be made in the original design. In particular, the planned provision of test results to parents no longer seemed feasible. We took the opportunity to introduce a number of new treatments into the altered design. In one of them ability testing only was carried out (Treatment 4B). In a second, achievement testing only was carried out (Treatment 5B). In both treatments results on pupil performance were given to teachers. In a third group, a criterion-referenced test in mathematics was administered to pupils and results returned to teachers (Treatment 5A). In a fourth group, teachers were provided with diagnostic information in addition to norm-referenced information (Treatment 4A). This treatment was envisaged in the original design; however, implementing it was possible only at grade levels for which machine-scorable answer sheets were used (grades 4 to 6).

In the "ability" treatment (Treatment 4B), children took ability tests at the beginning of second, third, and fourth grades, and their teachers received norm-referenced results. In the "achievement" treatment children took tests of achievement at the beginning of second, third, and fourth grades, and their teachers received norm-referenced results. In the second grade, tests of English and mathematics were taken; in the other two years, tests of English, mathematics, and Irish were taken.

In Treatment 4A, in addition to norm-referenced information, diagnostic information on achievement test performance was provided to teachers of pupils in grades 5 and 6 in each year of the study. The information related to performance on tests in English, mathematics, and Irish.

The criterion-referenced test-information group (Treatment 5A) actually comprises a number of treatments. The conditions in those treatments are described later in the chapter.

In this chapter we examine the effects of these alternative treatments. As in preceding chapters, effects are examined at the level of the school, at the level of teachers, and at the pupil level.

In examining school-level effects our analyses are confined to the test performance of pupils aggregated to the school level. We compare the performance of the "ability" group (Treatment 4B), the "achievement" group (Treatment 5B), and the diagnostic information group (Treatment 4A) with the performances of the norm-referenced group (Treatment 3) and of the two control groups (Treatment 1, in which no testing was carried out and Treatment 2, in which norm-referenced testing was carried out but information on test performance was not provided). Some information on school-level effects on organizational and evaluative practices may be gleaned from the analyses described in Chapter 3. However, for the analyses in that chapter, we were not able to differentiate the A and B versions of Treatments 4 and 5 in school-level analyses based on responses to the School Questionnaire since these subtreatments were not uniquely identified with schools over the whole four years of the study.

The teacher-level analyses in this chapter parallel closely those described for Treatments 1, 2, and 3 in Chapter 4. Data are based on responses to the same teacher questionnaire items, and the same statistical procedures were used. As in the school-level analyses, responses of teachers in the "ability" group (Treatment 4B), the "achievement" group (Treatment 5B), and the diagnostic information group (Treatment 4A) are compared with the performance of the norm-referenced information group (Treatment 3) and the two control groups. We are interested in ascertaining whether the addition of three other treatment groups to our analyses alters substantially the findings reported in Chapter 4. For example, does the availability of only norm-referenced ability test information lead teachers to perceive and report using this information in a way that differs in some consistent manner from teachers who had both norm-referenced ability and attainment information available? A similar question may be posed for Treatment 5B teachers, who received only norm-referenced attainment information about their pupils. It is also of interest to examine whether teachers who received diagnostic information about their pupils' performance differed from teachers who did not receive such information as regards their perceptions of tests and test use, particularly in areas concerned with the relationship between tests, test results, and instruction.

The pupil-level analyses also follow the pattern of earlier chapters. Many of the analyses pertaining to pupil effects, however, are limited to comparisons between the diagnostic information group (Treatment 4A) and the three main treatments (Treatments 1, 2, and 3). Since the "ability" (Treatment 4B) and "achievement" (Treatment 5B) groups were composed of pupils below the level of sixth grade, Pupil Questionnaire data were not available for them. In examining expectancy effects, we will be able to look at the "ability" and "achievement" groups. The criterion-referenced information group (Treatment 5A) is dealt with in a separate section because of the nature of the treatment and criterion variable used as well as because our information on the group is more limited than in the case of other treatments.

SCHOOL-LEVEL EFFECTS

Ability and Achievement Tests

We carried out an examination of the differences between the effects of ability and achievement testing in the second, third, and fourth years of the study. It was confined to pupils who had entered the second grade in the second year of the study.

At the end of the study's final year, children in the "ability" group (who were still in fourth grade at the time) sat for an ability test, while those in the "achievement" group (also in the fourth grade) sat for achievement tests in English, mathematics, and Irish. Clearly, comparisons cannot be made directly between these two groups since the criterion measures obtained differ for the groups. Comparisons are therefore made with other groups (Treatments 1, 2, and 3) that had taken the same final tests. School-level comparisons between Treatments 1, 2, and 3, which were the main treatments of the study, were described in Chapter 3. In the analyses that follow, the school-level performance of pupils on the ability test in Treatment 4B (the ability-only group) is compared with the performance of pupils in Treatments 1, 2, and 3. Similarly, the performance of pupils on the achievement tests in Treatment 5B (the achievement-only group) is compared with the performance of pupils in Treatments 1, 2, and 3. Thus, the questions addressed are whether children with a history of either only ability testing or only achievement testing perform differently on an ability test or on an achievement test, respectively, from children with a history of either no testing (control) or a combination of ability and achievement testing (in one case with results, in the other without).

Univariate analyses of variance revealed no significant differences between treatment groups (Table 8.1). Thus there was no difference in end-of-study test

Table 8.1. Final School Test Performance, by Treatment, Fourth Grade

Test	Treatment 1			Treatment 2			Treatment 3			Treatment 4B			Treatment 5B			F	df	p
	N	M	S.D.	N	M	S.D.	N	M	S.D.	N	M	S.D.	N	M	S.D.			
Drumcondra Verbal Reasoning	31	55.41	9.04	23	55.20	7.88	32	55.93	6.86	28	57.73	7.10				.60	3,110	NS
Mathematics	32	86.20	7.47	23	81.84	9.19	32	81.09	8.88				27	85.87	11.90	2.36	3,110	NS
Irish reading	32	47.85	8.91	23	44.56	9.55	32	43.36	8.91				27	46.85	11.51	1.38	3,110	NS
Irish usage	32	18.18	2.35	23	17.23	2.30	32	17.15	2.12				27	17.82	2.81	1.27	3,110	NS
Irish spelling	32	23.30	3.90	23	21.53	4.55	32	21.24	3.89				27	22.21	4.30	1.52	3,110	NS
English reading	32	55.53	4.80	23	53.32	6.70	32	53.72	4.72				27	54.03	6.53	.86	3,110	NS
English capitalization/ punctuation	32	22.04	2.76	23	22.42	2.74	32	21.81	2.59				27	22.59	2.97	.46	3,110	NS
English grammar	32	16.18	1.15	23	16.06	1.28	32	16.11	1.04				27	16.52	1.51	.75	3,110	NS
English spelling	32	34.29	2.76	23	33.79	3.00	32	32.90	2.68				27	33.94	3.61	1.22	3,110	NS
Age (in months)	32	118.21	2.76	27	118.24	2.29	35	118.45	2.50	31	118.41	2.45	30	118.02	2.33	.15	4,150	NS

scores on the *ability* test between fourth grades in schools where children had experience of ability testing only and whose teachers had received results (Treatment 4B) and fourth grades in other treatments. Nor was there any difference in the end-of-study *achievement* test scores of fourth grades in schools where the children had experience of achievement testing only and whose teachers had received results (Treatment 5B) and fourth grades in other treatments.

In Chapter 3 we noted the absence of significant differences at the univariate level of analysis between the fourth-grade test performance of pupils in the three major treatments (Treatments 1, 2, and 3). The addition of Treatment 4B to the comparison for ability test scores and of Treatment 5B to the comparison for achievement test scores brought about no change in the situation. Apparently, whatever the effects of practice or of information may be, the restriction of such practice or such information to only one kind of test—ability or achievement—does not lead to differences in performance on that kind of test. Pupils who have had experience of only one kind of test and whose teachers have received information about their performance do not differ in their test performance from pupils with no experience of either kind of test; nor do they differ from pupils who have had experience with both kinds of test, whether or not their teachers received information about pupil test performance.

At the multivariate level of analysis in the three-treatment situation, we were able to derive a function that distinguished significantly between the three groups. Since pupils in Treatment 4B had taken only ability tests and those in Treatment 5B only achievement tests, multivariate analysis could not be carried out for the four (or five) treatment comparisons.

Diagnostic Information from Achievement Tests

The performance of children in grades 5 and 6 of the diagnostic information treatment (Treatment 4A) was compared at the end of the study with the performance of children in Treatments 1, 2, and 3. Comparisons were made for performance on ability and achievement (English, mathematics, and Irish) tests. The question of interest was whether the additional kind of information that was made available to teachers in the diagnostic group would affect pupil performance. Since the diagnostic categories were more closely related to typical units of classroom instruction (e.g., use of the correct form, tense, and number of a verb in English usage; reading and analysis of simple graphs and bar charts in mathematics) than were the overall subtest scores reported in norm-referenced form (e.g., mathematics computation, Irish vocabulary), we hypothesized that teachers would find the diagnostic information more useful in the instructional process, with possible beneficial results for students.

Table 8.2. Final School Test Performance, by Treatment, Fifth Grade (df = 3,110)

Test	Treatment 1 (N = 32)		Treatment 2 (N = 23)		Treatment 3 (N = 32)		Treatment 4A (N = 27)		F	p
	M	S.D.	M	S.D.	M	S.D.	M	S.D.		
Drumcondra Verbal										
Reasoning	61.76	8.82	67.92	10.47	68.75	8.65	70.19	5.27	5.93	<.001*
Mathematics	65.83	9.33	66.91	10.39	65.13	9.13	68.16	6.85	.63	NS
Irish reading	41.57	10.13	41.98	8.44	41.00	9.54	41.30	7.46	.06	NS
Irish usage	22.57	2.79	22.62	2.41	22.41	3.30	22.55	2.52	.03	NS
Irish spelling	20.45	3.29	20.00	3.59	19.36	3.76	20.25	3.39	.57	NS
English reading	57.61	7.31	57.43	8.04	58.03	6.38	59.75	3.80	.70	NS
English capitalization/ punctuation	23.18	2.65	23.90	3.17	24.27	2.59	24.82	2.17	2.02	NS
English grammar	24.45	2.66	24.51	2.84	24.94	2.67	24.93	2.24	.30	NS
English spelling	37.35	3.73	37.90	3.29	37.09	2.87	38.43	2.50	1.02	NS

Note: Lambda value of MANOVA = .576 (p < .001; df = 18).

*In Scheffé contrasts, Treatment 1 schools inferior to Treatments 3 and 4.

Table 8.3. Discriminant Function Coefficients for Treatments 1, 2, 3, and 4A: Loadings for Grade 5

Variable	Weight
English reading	− .96
English usage	− .49
Mathematics	− .39
Irish reading	− .20
Irish spelling	− .15
Irish usage	.10
English spelling	.17
English capitalization/punctuation	.77
Drumcondra Verbal Reasoning	1.58
Group	Centroid*
Treatment 1	−1.09
Treatment 2	.27
Treatment 3	.45
Treatment 4A	.53

Note: One significant discriminant function accounts for 34.30 percent of total variance.
*The centroid for Treatment 1 differs significantly from the centroids for Treatments 3 and 4A.

Multivariate analyses of variance were carried out to test the hypothesis of overall differences between groups at fifth and sixth grades separately. At grade 5 there was one significant difference between pairs of treatments; the performance of Treatment 1 was significantly inferior to the performance of Treatments 3 and 4 on the ability measure (Table 8.2). In a discriminant function analysis, the diagnostic information group (Treatment 4A) was found to differ significantly from the control group (Treatment 1) but not from the other tested groups (Treatment 2, which had no information, and Treatment 3, which had norm-referenced information) (Table 8.3). An examination of the weights derived from this analysis shows that the difference between groups is largely attributable to the ability test. The weights in fact are very similar to those derived in the three-treatment discriminant-function analysis reported earlier. At grade 6 a significant difference between pairs of treatments was not found for performance on any of the individual tests (Table 8.4). In a discriminant-function analysis, however, the overall performance of Treatment 1 schools was found to differ from the overall performance of schools in all the other treatments, which did not differ among themselves (Table 8.5). As at grade 5, the main difference that

Table 8.4. Final School Test Performance, by Treatment, Sixth Grade (df = 3,111)

Test	Treatment 1 (N = 31)		Treatment 2 (N = 24)		Treatment 3 (N = 33)		Treatment 4A (N = 27)		F	p
	M	S.D.	M	S.D.	M	S.D.	M	S.D.		
Drumcondra Verbal										
Reasoning	74.01	7.37	79.16	7.65	76.22	8.08	78.67	7.41	2.73	<.05*
Mathematics	77.78	8.56	76.43	10.26	75.41	11.46	77.02	9.57	.31	NS
Irish reading	48.72	9.44	48.84	9.09	45.11	10.12	48.31	7.48	1.17	NS
Irish usage	24.81	2.66	24.33	2.69	23.45	3.07	24.60	2.29	1.56	NS
Irish spelling	21.95	3.39	22.26	3.69	20.88	4.25	22.86	3.24	1.53	NS
English reading	64.82	4.97	64.44	5.60	62.89	6.27	65.76	5.82	1.35	NS
English capitalization/ punctuation	25.18	2.24	25.70	2.62	25.75	2.54	26.65	2.88	1.62	NS
English grammar	27.07	2.85	27.14	2.86	26.67	2.95	27.35	2.86	.29	NS
English spelling	40.13	3.17	40.04	3.03	39.16	2.84	41.10	2.86	2.11	NS

Note: Lambda value of MANOVA = .491 (p < .001; df = 27).

*In Scheffé contrasts, no significant differences between pairs of groups.

Table 8.5. Discriminant Function Coefficients for Treatments 1, 2, 3, and 4A: Loadings for Grade 6

Variable	Weight
English reading	2.00
Irish usage	.70
English spelling	.35
Irish reading	.16
Mathematics	.00
Irish spelling	.00
Drumcondra Verbal Reasoning	− .79
English usage	− .92
English capitalization/punctuation	−1.13

Group	Centroid*
Treatment 1	.86
Treatment 2	− .19
Treatment 3	− .70
Treatment 4A	.03

Note: One significant discriminant function accounts for 38.62 percent of total variance.
*The centroid for Treatment 1 differs significantly from the centroids for Treatments 2, 3, and 4A.

emerged at the sixth grade was between the nontested control group and the tested groups. While the diagnostic information group (Treatment 4A), in common with the other tested groups, differed from the nontested group, it did not differ from the other groups.

The similarity of the results for the four-treatment comparisons with those for the three-treatment comparisons reported in Chapter 3, both at the multivariate and univariate levels of analysis, is striking. Performance of pupils in the diagnostic information group never differed significantly from that of pupils who had sat for norm-referenced tests of ability and achievement, whether or not their teachers received results. Whenever the performance of pupils in the norm-referenced information group differed from that of pupils who had not been tested, the performance of pupils in the diagnostic information group differed also. Therefore, while no significant differences were found between the norm-referenced information group and the nontested group, this apparently cannot be ascribed to the "weakness" of the norm-referenced information provided, at least in comparison with the provision of diagnostic information. Overall, experience with testing, rather than the provision of any kind of information, seems to be the factor that most affects performance.

TEACHER-LEVEL EFFECTS

In this section we examine a range of teachers' attitudes toward beliefs about uses of standardized tests. We compare teachers in the "ability" group (Treatment 4B), the "achievement" group (Treatment 5B), the diagnostic information group (Treatment 4A), and in the three main treatments of the study—the norm-referenced information group (Treatment 3) and the two control groups (Treatments 1 and 2).

Since the three additional treatments were not implemented in all grades or by all teachers in a school, we had to identify the teachers in each school who were affiliated with the treatments. When this was done, those who had responded to Teacher Questionnaires both at the start and at the end of the study were selected. Altogether, there were 122 such teachers (thirty-five in Treatment 4A, forty-five in Treatment 4B, and forty-two in Treatment 5B) who had responded to Teacher Questionnaire I in year 1 and Teacher Questionnaire I-Revised in year 4. A total of 107 teachers (thirty-seven in Treatment 4A, thirty-two in Treatment 4B, and thirty-eight in Treatment 5B) had responded to Teacher Questionnaire II in year 2 and its revision, Teacher Questionnaire V, in year 4. The responses of these samples of teachers to the two sets of parallel questionnaires administered at the start and at the conclusion of the study form the basis for the analyses presented in this section. One additional sample of teachers, which satisfied the first three selection criteria, was also identified. These teachers, thirty-five in Treatment 4A, thirty-eight in Treatment 4B, and fifty-four in Treatment 5B, responded to Teacher Questionnaire IV, which was administered in year 4 of the study. The numbers in Treatments 1, 2, and 3 were reported in Chapter 4.

The analyses that were carried out parallel those described in Chapter 4 and are based on responses to the same Teacher Questionnaire items. The same statistical procedures were used. Within a year, data on any particular questionnaire item were analyzed by means of a one-way analysis of variance; when statistically significant differences at the .05 level were found, post-hoc comparisons were carried out to identify the source of the differences. When statistically significant treatment differences were found in responses early in the study, analysis of covariance was used to examine end-of-study differences. Most of the analyses in this section report on comparisons of the responses of teachers in six treatments, the three main treatments described in Chapter 4 and the three additional treatments described above. Some analyses, however, are confined to treatment groups that tested and/or received test information. Because of the comparatively small sample sizes in Treatment 4A, 4B, and 5B, we did not perform analyses stratified by teacher sex or school location.

We do not report on all the analyses that were carried out. In general, we report the results of analyses only if statistically significant differences were found between treatments. However, nonsignificant results, if they seem of particular interest, are also included.

Teachers' Perceptions of the Accuracy of Standardized Tests

At the start of the study and again at its end, teachers were asked to judge the accuracy in assessing a pupil's scholastic ability of (1) intelligence tests, (2) standardized attainment tests, (3) Irish public examinations, and (4) classroom exams. Judgments for each type of information were made on a 5-point rating scale that ranged from "very accurate" (coded 5) to "very inaccurate" (coded 1). At the end of the study, statistically significant treatment differences were observed on the items dealing with intelligence and standardized attainment tests. In general, teachers who had administered tests throughout the study, regardless of whether or not they had received results of the tests, perceived standardized tests to be more accurate indicators of pupils' scholastic ability than did teachers who had not tested. Post-hoc comparisons indicated that Treatment 3 teachers perceived intelligence tests to be significantly more accurate than did Treatment 1 teachers, but there were no significant differences between treatments for the item dealing with the accuracy of standardized attainment tests. The responses of teachers in the alternative treatments (Treatments 4A, 4B, and 5B), we should add, were very similar to the responses of teachers in Treatments 2 and 3.

Teachers' Perceptions of the Constructs Measured by
Intelligence Tests

Teachers were asked their opinion about the degree to which they perceived intelligence as measured by tests to correspond to the type of intelligence needed to succeed at various educational and occupational levels. Overall, across treatments, teachers perceived a greater similarity between tested intelligence and the type of intelligence needed for school success than between tested intelligence and the kind of intelligence needed for success in the world of work. Significant treatment differences were found in the responses to items dealing with primary and postprimary schools. On both items Treatment 3 teachers perceived more similarity between the kind of intelligence measured by tests and the kind of intelligence necessary for school success than did teachers in the other treatments. Treatment differences accounted for about 3 percent of the variance. The responses of teachers in Treatments 1, 2, 4A, and 5B did not differ.

Our analyses in Chapter 4, based on the three major treatment groups, would give considerably greater weight to teacher recommendations than to other forms of evidence in making a series of instructional and selection decisions about pupils. A similar result was found when analyses were performed on the six treatments. One statistically significant treatment difference explained 3 percent of the total variance in the six-treatment analyses. Teachers in Treatment 5B, who received only norm-referenced attainment test information, reported that they would give teacher recommendations significantly less weight in making instructional decisions than did teachers in the other five treatments.

Further corroboration of the fact that teachers in the six treatments reported that they would rely most heavily on teacher recommendations in making decisions about pupils is provided in teachers' rankings of the accuracy of five judges of a pupil's intelligence and attainment. Across all treatments the pupil's teacher was perceived to be the most accurate judge. Standardized tests and classroom exams were perceived to be moderately accurate indicators. Standardized tests were judged as slightly more accurate indicators of a pupil's intelligence than classroom exams, while the reverse was true as regards a pupil's attainment. The pupil and the pupil's parents were uniformly perceived to be the least accurate judges. Interestingly, we found no statistically significant treatment differences on any of the rankings. Thus, teachers who had access to a particular type of test information did not necessarily perceive that information to be more or less accurate. For example, the means for Treatment 4B and Treatment 5B teachers, who received only ability or only attainment test results, respectively, are quite similar as regards the perceived accuracy of standardized tests in judging a pupil's intelligence and attainment. By the same token, the means for Treatment 3 and 4A teachers, who received both ability and attainment test results, are often disparate, particularly as regards the perceived accuracy of standardized tests in providing an index of a pupil's intelligence.

Teachers' Grouping Practices

Teachers were asked whether or not they grouped pupils within their classes for instructional purposes. Teachers who reported that they did group within the classroom were then asked to indicate which of nine criteria (e.g., teacher recommendations, intelligence tests, observation, age) they used in forming groups.

There were no differences between treatment groups in the numbers of teachers who reported that they grouped pupils. Thus, we find further confirmation of our findings in the three-treatment analyses that the availability of test information did not lead to a significantly higher incidence of within-class grouping. The findings of the present six-treatment analyses, however, did diverge from the findings of the three-treatment analyses on the reported use of teacher recommendations, standardized intelligence tests, and standardized attainment tests as grouping criteria. The significant treatment differences found for teacher recommendations and intelligence tests in the three-treatment analyses were not confirmed in the six-treatment analyses. In the six-treatment analyses, however, a statistically significant treatment difference was observed in the reported use of standardized attainment tests as a grouping criterion. Treatment 4A teachers, who had received both norm-referenced and diagnostic information about pupil performance, were significantly different from the remaining treatments in that in grouping pupils for instruction in their classes, they relied on standardized attainment tests to a significantly greater extent than did teachers in other treatments. Indeed, about two-thirds of the Treatment 4A teachers who grouped reported using standardized attainment tests, as compared with one-third or fewer of teachers in most other treatment groups.

Teachers' Perceptions of the Relevance of Standardized Tests

In the final year of the study, teachers in the six treatments were asked to indicate the extent of their agreement with thirteen statements about standardized, multiple-choice tests. Responses to the items formed two factors, a *test-relevance factor*, which contained statements regarding the relevance of standardized, multiple-choice tests in the classroom (e.g., aid in the diagnosis of individual pupil needs, are generally unrelated to the objectives teachers consider important), and *an expectation factor*, which contained statements related to the degree to which the tests influence teachers' actions and perceptions (e.g., lead teachers to expect more or less of pupils than they had previously, attach labels to pupils, lead teachers to teach low-scoring pupils less).

No significant difference was found among the six treatments on the test-relevance factor. However, as in the prior three-treatment analysis, a statistically significant treatment difference was observed on the teacher-expectation factor. Teachers in Treatments 3 and 4A, who had received both ability and attainment test information throughout the study, were significantly less likely to view standardized, multiple-choice tests as influencing the way in which teachers perceive or act toward pupils than were teachers in the other treatments. Teachers in Treatments 4B and 5B, who respectively received norm-referenced ability information only and norm-referenced attainment information only, were somewhat more likely to perceive tests as having a smaller impact on teacher expectations than were teachers in Treatments 1 and 2, who had received no test results at all. The amount of variance associated with treatment differences in this analysis was 5.7 percent.

Teachers' Perceptions of Pupil Characteristics That Affect Test Performance

Teachers were asked if testing of the type carried out in this study favored higher performance by boys compared to girls, urban compared to rural children, creative compared to noncreative children, and so forth. Two items produced statistically significant treatment differences. In both cases, teachers in Treatment 4A, who had received norm-referenced ability and attainment test results as well as diagnostic information about pupils' performance on the attainment tests, differed from teachers in the remaining treatments in their responses. While the majority of teachers in Treatments 2, 3, 4B, and 5B perceived a distinct advantage for good readers as opposed to poor readers on the tests, Treatment 4A teachers were less certain of this presumed advantage. Similarly, while the majority of teachers in the other treatments felt that standardized tests did not favor superficial, glib children in comparison to reflective, thoughtful children, Treatment 4A teachers were less certain of this fact. Perhaps the insights obtained from having both norm-referenced and diagnostic data available on pupils led teachers in Treatment 4A to perceive less of a relationship between reading ability or glibness and test performance. If, for example, inspection of the diagnostic data for poor readers and children perceived to be glib and superficial revealed that reading ability or glibness was not always related to performance on sets of items, Treatment 4A teachers might indeed be less certain of the relation between these characteristics and test performance. Of course, the anomaly or question that arises from these data is that if diagnostic data led Treatment 4A teachers to perceive reading ability and glibness to be less related to test performance than did other teachers, why was this relationship not evidenced for other characteristics?

Practices with Tests and Test Results

A number of questions were asked of teachers who had received test results (Treatments 3, 4A, 4B and 5B) about their reactions to and use of tests. Although most questions revealed nonsignificant differences between treatment groups, a number did exhibit statistically significant differences, most of which involved a difference between Treatment 4A teachers and teachers in one or more of the other treatments. Thus, the combination of norm-referenced and more descriptive diagnostic results appears to have had an effect on teachers that was different from the effect of other types of information. For example, Treatment 4A teachers were significantly more likely than other teachers to bring out and use test results during the course of the school year. Similarly, significantly more teachers in Treatment 4A than in other treatments reported that they had seen their present pupils' test results from prior years. About 70 percent of Treatment 4A teachers reported seeing their pupils' prior results, as compared with 30 percent in Treatment 4B, 40 percent in Treatment 5B, and 55 percent in Treatment 3.

When teachers in the four treatments were asked to how many children in their class and to how many parents they had told attainment test scores, teachers in the diagnostic information group reported passing on test results to significantly more pupils and parents than did teachers in the remaining three treatments. Many teachers in the diagnostic group indicated that they passed on test information to all pupils or parents of pupils in their class. Teachers in this treatment also perceived the Irish attainment tests to be more accurate than did teachers in the other treatments. Finally, teachers in the diagnostic information group, to a significantly greater extent than teachers in the achievement information group (but not teachers in the other groups), reported that the attainment tests had or would influence the material they planned to cover in class. We found a few other significant differences between groups in these analyses; teachers in the ability test information group reported passing on test results to other teachers to a significantly greater degree than did teachers in the other treatments, and teachers in the achievement test information group talked significantly less with other teachers about test results than did teachers in the three other groups.

From these findings, it would appear that the combination of norm-referenced test results and diagnostic data that was given to Treatment 4A teachers made them better able to understand, interpret, explain, and judge the accuracy of pupils' test scores. They referred to the results more, disseminated them more widely, and used them in planning instruction to a greater extent than did teachers who received only norm-referenced test results. The possibility for teachers to go beyond single-number, normative indices of pupil attainment and to use the more descriptive item data to add "flesh and blood" to the skeleton provided by the normed scores may have made teachers in the diagnostic information group more comfortable with using and better able to conceptualize what the results were telling them about their pupils. Any tendency to over-generalize this interpretation should be tempered by our findings that, in terms of the total number of items analyzed, teachers in the diagnostic information group were more like than unlike teachers in the other treatments. Nevertheless, in terms of at least some aspects of test score use and dissemination, they did differ from teachers in other treatments in an interpretable manner. Differences were most evident in the case of teachers' reported use of test results. It would seem reasonable to conclude on the basis of our findings that norm-referenced test information in conjunction with information that helps teachers conceptualize and understand the norm-referenced data is a more powerful spur to practical use of results than is norm-referenced information on its own.

PUPIL-LEVEL EFFECTS

The analyses reported in Chapter 5 examined the effects of testing on pupils in the three main treatments of our study: the norm-referenced information group (Treatment 3) and the two control groups, one in which no testing had been carried out (Treatment 1) and the other in which testing had been carried out but information on test performance had not been supplied to teachers (Treatment 2). In this section we examine the effects of providing an alternative form of test information to teachers to determine whether the conclusions based on the three-treatment analyses of Chapter 5 will be altered when an additional treatment is included in analyses. The additional treatment is the group that, in addition to norm-referenced information on ability and achievement, also received diagnostic information on achievement. The analyses had to be confined to this group since most of the data on which analyses are based came from the Pupil Questionnaire, which was administered only to pupils in the sixth grade; since the ability-testing treatment (Treatment 4B) and the achievement-testing treatment (Treatment 5B) were confined to grades 2, 3, and 4, pupils in these treatments did not respond to questionnaires.

The analyses described in this section parallel those of Chapter 5. Our results here, however, are presented in more summary form; results for a number of areas in which no significant differences were found between treatments are not reported.

Pupils' Test Performance

At the end of the final year of the study, sixth-grade pupils in Treatments 1, 2, 3, and 4A were administered standardized ability and achievement tests, and the performance of pupils in the different treatments was compared. An examination of the results indicates that on the three achievement tests, pupils in Treatment 4A (the diagnostic information group) tend to perform more like pupils in the two control groups (Treatments 1 and 2) than like pupils in the other test-information treatment (Treatment 3). The means for Treatments 1, 2, and 4A tend to be higher than the means for Treatment 3, particularly in Irish and English reading (Table 8.6). Second, in two of the achievement areas (mathematics and English reading), pupils in Treatment 4A attained the highest mean scores. Third, on the ability test pupils in Treatments 2, 3, and 4A, who had had previous exposure to the tests, evidenced higher mean performance

Table 8.6. Final Pupil Test Performance, by Treatment, Sixth Grade

Test Score	Treatment	N	M	S.D.	F	p	R^2
Ability	1	1134	74.58	18.24	28.190	.000	.017
	2	905	80.56	16.74			
	3	1390	78.63	18.62			
	4A	1455	80.45	17.30			
Mathematics	1	1176	78.37	18.44	4.038	.007	.002
	2	935	77.68	19.92			
	3	1349	77.16	19.83			
	4A	1474	79.57	18.93			
Irish reading	1	1176	48.12	15.40	19.242	.000	.011
	2	941	49.06	15.67			
	3	1352	44.97	15.33			
	4A	1515	48.72	15.11			
English reading	1	1175	65.67	13.12	7.336	.000	.004
	2	933	65.95	13.20			
	3	1357	64.68	14.75			
	4A	1507	67.08	13.74			

than pupils in Treatment 1. Fourth, there was a statistically significant treatment difference on each of the four test scores. Scheffé post-hoc analyses indicated that on two of the achievement tests (mathematics and English reading), pupils in Treatment 4A performed significantly better than pupils in the remaining three treatments. In Irish reading, Treatments 1, 2, and 4A evidenced significantly higher means than Treatment 3. Thus, on all three achievement measures, pupils whose teachers received a combination of norm-referenced and diagnostic test information scored significantly higher than did pupils whose teachers received only norm-referenced test information. Although the percentages of variance attributable to treatment differences were small, we must conclude that the availability of diagnostic test information significantly enhanced pupils' performance on achievement tests over the availability of norm-referenced test information alone. Fifth, as in the three-treatment analyses, ability test performance showed a definite practice effect; pupils in Treatments 2, 3, and 4A, all of whom had taken ability tests previously in the study, performed significantly better than pupils in Treatment 1, who had their first encounter with the ability test at the end of the study.

Pupils' Perceptions of and Reactions to Standardized Tests

Sixth-grade pupils in all treatment groups except Treatment 1 were asked to respond to a series of eighteen questions dealing with their perceptions of and reactions to the tests they took. The results of significance tests on these items for pupils in Treatments 2, 3, and 4A were virtually identical to the results obtained when the responses of pupils in Treatments 2 and 3 were analyzed. Four of the eighteen items evidenced statistically significant treatment differences in the two sets of analyses. On these four items pupils in Treatment 4A responded more like pupils in Treatment 3 than like pupils in Treatment 2. Significantly fewer pupils in Treatments 3 and 4A reported that they enjoyed sitting for the tests than did pupils in Treatment 2, while significantly more pupils in Treatments 3 and 4A reported that they felt afraid about the tests and expected to be told their marks on the test than did pupils in Treatment 2.

There were two items on which significant differences were not found when Treatments 2 and 3 were compared but that did evidence statistically significant treatment differences when Treatment 4A was included in the analyses. Significantly more Treatment 4A than Treatment 2 pupils reported that they felt nervous during testing and also that they told their parents about the tests.

Pupils' Perceptions of Factors That Affect Getting Along Well in
Class and in School

Pupils were asked whether each of fourteen factors (e.g., hard work, intelligence, memory) helps, hinders, or does not matter in getting on well in class. When the responses of pupils in Treatment 4A were added to those of pupils in Treatments 1, 2, and 3 and analyses were performed on the four treatments, the results obtained were identical to those obtained in the three-treatment analyses for thirteen of the fourteen factors. Only the items inquiring about the influence of luck in getting on well in class evidenced a different result. For the four-treatment analysis, a significant difference was observed: Treatment 4A pupils, to a greater extent (58.9 percent) than Treatment 1 (53.1 percent) or 3 (50.1 percent) pupils, felt that luck hindered their getting on well in class.

On items that asked about the influence of test or examination results on getting on well in class, Treatment 4A pupils responded more similarly to pupils in Treatment 3 than to pupils in Treatments 1 and 2. While 90 percent of pupils in Treatments 1 (90.2 percent) and 2 (90.3 percent) felt that intelligence helped in getting on well in class, 86.2 percent and 86.3 percent of the pupils in Treatments 3 and 4A, respectively, agreed with this statement. Similarly, while 89.1 percent and 90.0 percent of pupils in Treatments 1 and 2, respectively, felt that good exam results helped in class, 87.5 percent and 87.7 percent of the pupils in Treatments 3 and 4A felt similarly. There was a statistically significant treatment difference on both these items. However, on other nontest- or exam-related items that evidenced statistically significant treatment differences, Treatment 4A pupils responded more like pupils in Treatments 1 and 2 than like Treatment 3 pupils. On items concerned with the influence of taking part in class discussion, asking questions in class, and having a good memory, the observed statistically significant differences represented differences between Treatment 3 pupils on the one hand and pupils in Treatments 1, 2, and 4A on the other.

Pupils were asked to indicate whether any of seven factors had changed their idea of how they were doing in school: exam results, test results, what a teacher said, the class the pupil was put in, what classmates thought about the pupil, the place the pupil sat in class, and how well the pupil felt he could learn. Each factor was responded to by selecting one of three response options: "yes, made me feel I am doing better than I thought"; "yes, made me feel I was doing worse than I thought"; and "no, made no difference about what I thought." The pattern of statistical significance on these seven items was similar in the four-treatment analyses to that in the three-treatment analyses; three of the items evidenced statistically significant treatment differences in both sets of analyses: exam results, test results, and how well the pupil felt he could learn. On the item dealing with the impact of exam results on changed perceptions of how they were doing in school, Treatment 4A pupils responded like Treatment 3 pupils. When asked about the influence of test results on perceptions of how well they were doing in school, Treatment 4A and Treatment 3 pupils, to a significantly lesser extent than Treatment 1 and 2 pupils, reported that knowledge of test results made them feel they were doing better in school than they previously had thought. Finally, on the item that inquired about the extent to which their perceptions of how well they could learn something influenced their judgments about school progress, Treatment 1 pupils, to a significantly greater extent than pupils in Treatments 2, 3, or 4A, reported that their judgments about school progress were enhanced by this information.

Overall, the results of these analyses lead to a number of generalizations. First, on the majority of items, there were no statistically significant differences between the responses of pupils in Treatments 1, 2, 3, and 4A. Whether or not they were tested did not appear to influence pupils' perceptions of testing and test taking or their judgments about factors that help or hinder their getting on well in class or factors that affect how well they are doing in school. Second, on the comparatively few items that did reveal statistically significant treatment differences, pupils in Treatments 3 and 4A, the two test-information groups, tended to respond similarly to questions dealing with perceptions of tests and test taking. However, on items that did not relate specifically to tests or test taking, Treatment 4A pupils tended to respond more like Treatment 1 and 2 pupils than like Treatment 3 pupils. In all cases absolute differences between the treatments were small and accounted for quite small proportions of variance.

Pupils' Ratings of Their Scholastic Behavior and Abilities

Each pupil in the sixth grade in all treatment groups was asked to provide a self-rating of him- or herself relative to his or her classmates in fourteen cognitive and affective areas (e.g., intelligence, mathematics, English reading, interest in school). Pupils were asked to indicate whether they were "at the top," "well up," "around the middle," "well down," or "at the bottom" relative to their classmates in each of the areas. In the analyses of Treatments 1, 2, and 3, we found that self-ratings of pupils were negatively skewed in all areas except spoken Irish—that is, substantially smaller percentages of pupils in all treatments rated themselves "well down" or "at the bottom" relative to the percentage who rated themselves "well up" or "at the top."

When the self-ratings provided by pupils in Treatment 4A were included in analyses with ratings of pupils in the other treatments, a number of points emerged. First, each of the seven rating areas that was statistically significant in the three-treatment analyses was also statistically significant in the four-treatment analyses (spoken Irish, Irish reading, written Irish, English composition, interest in school, originality, and keenness to do well in school). Second, in each of these areas, the responses of pupils in Treatment 4A were most similar to those of pupils in Treatment 3—that is, pupils in the two test-information treatments tended to evidence self-ratings that were significantly lower than pupils in Treatment 1, the control treatment. Third, an additional five areas in which there were no statistically significant differences in the three-treatment analyses did evidence significant difference in the four-treatment analyses. These five areas were: English reading, interest in reading, exam results, sport, and memory. In each of these areas, pupils in Treatment 4A had the lowest self-ratings of any treatment. Overall, the differences in mean ratings were not large in either the three- or four-treatment analyses, being of the order of .2 on a 5-point scale. Undoubtedly, the large number of degrees of freedom in these analyses (3,000 in the three-treatment analyses and over 4,000 in the four-treatment analyses) contributed to the observed significance of the differences.

Three points are important to note, however. First, in the four-treatment analyses, two of the four areas actually tested as part of the study evidenced significant treatment differences (Irish and English reading), while two others (intelligence and mathematics) did not. Second, in every case in which a statistically significant treatment difference appeared, pupils in the test-information treatments (3 and 4A) rated themselves lower than did pupils in Treatment 1, the control treatment. For whatever reason and through whatever mechanism, test information appeared to have a slight negative impact on pupils' self-ratings. Third, the self-ratings of pupils in Treatment 3 did not differ significantly from those of pupils in Treatment 4A; whether norm-referenced information was or was not accompanied by diagnostic information did not affect pupils' self-ratings.

We examined pupils' self-ratings in two additional analyses to determine whether or not they were affected by the provision of test information. In the first set of these analyses, we calculated the discrepancy between teacher ratings of a pupil and the pupil's corresponding self-rating in each of four areas: intelligence, English reading, Irish reading, and mathematics. Mean treatment-level discrepancies were examined to determine whether the provision of test information led to greater correspondence between teacher and pupil ratings. In the second set of analyses, we calculated discrepancies between pupils' test scores (scaled to place them on the same metric as the ratings) and again compared mean treatment discrepancies to determine whether pupils in treatments that received test information manifested greater agreement between self-ratings and test scores than pupils in treatments that did not receive information.

The results of the analyses with the four treatments were very similar to those for the three treatments. We found no statistically significant treatment differences for the discrepancies between teacher and pupil ratings in Irish reading, English reading, or mathematics. There was a significant treatment difference for intelligence, for which, however, only 0.5 percent of the total variance was associated with differences between the four treatments. Post-hoc analysis indicated a significant difference between the means of Treatments 1 and 3 on the one hand and Treatment 2 on the other. Thus, for none of the areas rated did rating discrepancies in the norm-referenced information group (Treatment 3) differ from those in the diagnostic information group (Treatment 4A).

In the analyses of discrepancies between pupils' self-ratings and pupils' scaled test scores in the same four academic areas, we found one statistically significant difference in both the three-treatment and four-treatment analysis. That was for English reading. In the four-treatment analysis we found that the mean discrepancies in Treatments 3 and 4A were significantly greater than the mean discrepancies in Treatments 1 and 2. Only 0.2 percent of variance in the analysis was attributable to treatment differences.

Overall, our analyses indicate that there is little difference between pupils in different treatment groups in discrepancies between pupils' self-ratings and either teacher ratings or pupils' test performance. Further, we find no evidence to suggest that the provision of diagnostic test information in addition to norm-referenced information has a discernible impact on pupils' self-perceptions.

Pupils' Self-Concepts

A twenty-one-item self-concept scale was constructed from items in the Pupil Questionnaire, and differences between treatment groups on the scale were examined. In the three-group analyses we did not find a significant difference between treatments. When the diagnostic information group (Treatment 4A) was added to the analyses, the difference was still not statistically significant.

THE ROLE OF TEST INFORMATION IN THE EXPECTANCY PROCESS

In this section we seek an answer to the question: Does the type of test administered, or the type of information provided to teachers, have a differential impact on teachers' subsequent perceptions of pupils and on pupils' subsequent test performance? Before turning directly to this issue, we examined the correlations between our four key variables—test scores and teacher ratings of pupils, obtained at both the beginning and end of the final year of the study —for each of three additional treatments, the ability testing–information group (Treatment 4B), the achievement testing–information group (Treatment 5B), and the group in which achievement and ability tests were administered and diagnostic as well as norm-referenced information was returned to teachers (Treatment 4A). These correlations presented a very similar pattern to those obtained for Treatments 1, 2, and 3. Correlations between the initial perceptions and initial test scores for Treatments 4A, 4B, and 5B ranged between .50 and .68, while those for Treatments 1, 2, and 3 ranged between .46 and .67. Correlations between test scores obtained on two occasions and correlations between teacher perceptions obtained on two occasions were higher.

We now consider in turn the impact on teachers' perceptions and pupils' test scores of each of the three additional treatments (Treatments 4A, 4B, and 5B) by comparing the cross-lagged partial correlation coefficients for these treatments with those obtained for Treatments 2 and 3. Our prediction is that the correlation between initial pupil test scores and final teacher perceptions, when the effect of initial teacher perceptions has been removed, will be positive and significantly higher in each of our three new treatments than in Treatment 2. This prediction is based on the same reasoning that originally led us to predict that similar partial correlations would be greater for Treatment 3 than for Treatment 2. We would expect that the initial perceptions of pupils would change to align with test information only in the case of teachers who had received such information.

Similarly, we predicted that the partial correlations between initial teacher perceptions of their pupils and subsequent pupil test performance, when the effect of initial test performance has been removed, would be positive and significantly lower in our three new treatment groups than in Treatment 2. This prediction was based on the same reasoning that led us to predict that the corresponding partial correlations would be higher in Treatment 2 than in Treatment 3. Since in Treatment 2 teachers' original perceptions could not have been affected by test information, subsequent pupil test performance should align more closely with the original perceptions in that treatment group than in treatments which received test information.

We were unable to make predictions regarding the magnitude of partial correlations for Treatments 4A, 4B, and 5B relative to Treatment 3. Certainly nothing in the expectancy model would provide a basis for such predictions.

Diagnostic Information and the Expectancy Effect

In the examination of the cross-lagged partial correlation coefficients between test performance and teacher perceptions in the diagnostic information group, two comparisons were of interest. First, did the two information groups differ from one another? And second, did both information treatments differ significantly from Treatment 2? In comparing either Treatment 3 or 4A with Treatment

2, we predicted the direction of the difference and therefore used a one-tailed test of significance. However, we had no basis for predicting the direction of a difference between Treatments 3 and 4A; hence we employed two-tailed tests to test significance.

For intelligence, our prediction was confirmed; the partial correlations for both Treatments 3 and 4A were found to differ significantly from the partial correlation for Treatment 2. There was no difference, however, between the partial correlations of Treatments 3 and 4A. Thus, while the availability of test information affected teachers' subsequent perceptions of their pupils' intelligence, whether that information was simply norm-referenced or also included diagnostic material did not affect the perceptions. This result should not surprise us, since the diagnostic information referred to pupils' achievement, not to their intelligence. We would expect that any effect such information would have would be on perceptions of achievement rather than of intelligence.

However, there was no effect associated with diagnostic information, as distinct from norm-referenced information, for the achievement tests either. Indeed, in the case of mathematics, there were no significant differences between any of the partial correlations. In the case of English reading and Irish reading, as expected, the partial correlations for the information groups (Treatments 3 and 4A) differed significantly from the partial correlations for the noninformation group (Treatment 2), though they did not differ from each other.

In the case of the partial correlations between initial teacher perceptions of their pupils and subsequent pupil test performance, with the effect of initial test score partialed out, our prediction was that the partial correlation for Treatment 2 would be significantly greater than those for either Treatment 3 or Treatment 4A. For the three achievement tests, we found no effect. Thus, the absence of test information did not cause the subsequent performance of pupils to align more closely with teachers' initial perceptions of their achievement in English reading, Irish reading, or mathematics.

In the case of the ability test, as predicted, the partial correlation for Treatment 3 was significantly smaller than that for Treatment 2. However, the Treatment 3 correlation was significantly smaller than that for Treatment 4A, which did not differ significantly from that for Treatment 2. Thus our effect relates uniquely to the provision of norm-referenced information only.

We saw in Chapter 6 that the overall impact of norm-referenced information on subsequent teacher perceptions was significantly stronger in the case of boys than in the case of girls. On the other hand, the impact of test information on subsequent test performance was found to be stronger for girls than for boys. We stratified our data by gender and examined partial cross-lagged correlations to determine whether the addition of diagnostic information to norm-referenced information would in any way change this picture. In only one case were our findings for the diagnostic information group (Treatment 4A) different from those for the norm-referenced information group (Treatment 3). Teachers' perception of boys' Irish reading was found to be uniquely influenced by the availability of diagnostic information.

In the case of school location, we saw in Chapter 6 that the provision of norm-referenced information had an impact on subsequent teacher perceptions of their pupils and on pupils' subsequent test performance more consistently within city than within town or rural schools. We stratified our data by school location (city, town, and rural) and examined partial cross-lagged correlation coefficients to determine whether the addition of diagnostic information to norm-referenced information would change this picture.

Comparisons between the three treatments within each stratum revealed that the provision of diagnostic information in addition to the regular norm-referenced information had a unique impact only on subsequent teacher perceptions of Irish reading in city and rural schools, but not in town schools. Within the diagnostic information group itself, information had a larger impact on teachers' subsequent perceptions of their pupils' intelligence in city schools than in town or rural schools. We found no unique effect associated with the provision of additional diagnostic information within any of the three school locations for pupils' test performance.

Finally, we examined the relationship between the socioeconomic status of pupils and the provision of diagnostic information. In Chapter 6 we found limited evidence of some significant expectancy effects within particular SES strata in terms of the impact of test information on subsequent teacher perceptions of their pupils. We also saw from comparisons within each stratum that no consistent effect on subsequent pupil test performance could be associated with a particular social-class grouping. Here we explore whether the addition of diagnostic to norm-referenced information changes these conclusions.

Whether we looked between SES strata within the diagnostic information group, or within a particular stratum between the three treatments, we did not find that the provision of diagnostic information had a large, consistent, or uniform effect on either teacher perceptions of their pupils or on pupils' actual test performance. The only finding of note was that the sixth-grade teachers' perceptions of the Irish reading progress of middle-class pupils was uniquely influenced by the provision of the additional diagnostic information.

Ability Test Information and the Expectancy Effect

When we looked at the effect of providing teachers with norm-referenced information about their pupils' performance on both ability and achievement tests in Chapter 6, we concluded that a rather strong expectancy effect was associated with the provision of test information. In this section we are interested in determining whether the expectancy effect operates when the information given teachers is limited to norm-referenced scores about pupils' ability. Pupils in grades 2 through 4 were administered an ability test only each year, and teachers were given norm-referenced information about their pupils' performance on the test (Treatment 4B). We examined the expectancy effect by comparing partial correlation coefficients for Treatments 2 and 3 with those for Treatment 4B. In the case of partial correlations between the initial ability test scores and teachers' subsequent perceptions of their pupils' intelligence, we predicted that Treatments 3 and 4B would have significantly higher partial correlations than Treatment 2, since teachers in both Treatment 3 and Treatment 4B received information about pupil performance that could alter their perceptions in line with the information provided. In a second set of partial correlations, those between initial teacher perceptions of their pupils' intelligence and the pupils' final performance on an intelligence test, we predicted that the correlations for Treatment 2 would be significantly larger than those for either Treatment 3 or Treatment 4B.

Our analyses revealed no unique effect attributable to ability test information (Treatment 4B). When teachers received only ability test information, or when they received ability and achievement test information, the resulting partial correlation between initial test scores and subsequent teacher perceptions of their pupils' intelligence was, as predicted, significantly higher than the same partial correlation for Treatment 2. The partial correlation for Treatment 4B did not differ significantly from that for Treatment 3. Thus the effect on subsequent teacher perceptions of pupils' intelligence of providing teachers with norm-referenced information was similar when the information was limited to ability testing and when it included both ability and achievement test results. Similarly, we found no evidence that the type of information provided affected pupils' subsequent test performance. An analysis of the two sets of postulated relationships by gender, by school location, and by socioeconomic status failed to reveal any indication of a unique effect that could be attributed to the provision of ability test information.

Achievement Test Information and the Expectancy Effect

Finally, we carried out analyses to determine whether the effect of providing teachers with information about their pupils' test performance differed when the information referred to ability and achievement or was limited to achievement only. From grades 2 through 4, pupils were administered achievement tests only each year, and teachers were given norm-referenced information about their pupils' performance on the tests (Treatment 5B). Thus, teachers in this treatment did not have any standardized test information about their pupils' ability. We examined the effects of providing different types of information by comparing partial correlation coefficients for this treatment with partial correlation coefficients for Treatment 3 (which received norm-referenced information for both ability and achievement tests) and Treatment 2 (which received no information on test performance).

We found no case in which the partial correlations for the group that had achievement test information only (Treatment 5B) differed from those for the group that had both achievement and ability test information (Treatment 3). Further, there was no case in which a correlation for the no-information group (Treatment 2) differed from a correlation for the ability and achievement test–information group (Treatment 3) if it did not also differ from the correlation for the achievement test–information group (Treatment 5B).

Analyses by gender involving the achievement–test information group (Treatment 5B) yielded findings similar to those relating to the ability and achievement test–information group (Treatment 3) reported in Chapter 6. In school location analyses, we found some differences between Treatment 3 and 5B. Within city schools we found a combination of ability and achievement test information to be more powerful in affecting teachers' perceptions of pupils' mathematical achievement than achievement test information alone. Further, when comparisons were made within Treatment 5B schools, test information was found to be more powerful in influencing teachers' perceptions in town schools than in urban ones. No effects on pupils' subsequent test performance were unique to Treatment 5B within any of the location strata. Rather, in two cases effects were found for the combination of ability and achievement test information (Treatment 3) but not for the achievement test information only (Treatment 5B). In town schools the combined ability and achievement test information affected pupils' performances in English and Irish reading to a significantly greater extent than did achievement test information alone (Treatment 5B) or no information at all (Treatment 2).

In the analyses stratified by socioeconomic status of pupils, we found a few effects that were unique to the achievement test information group (Treatment 5B). In terms of effects on teachers' perceptions, an effect relating to Irish reading attributable to Treatment 5B was found within the lowest socioeconomic group, while for pupils' test performance, effects relating to mathematics and English reading, which were attributable to Treatment 5B, were found for the middle socioeconomic group.

CRITERION-REFERENCED TEST INFORMATION

The final alternative treatment in our study involved the provision to teachers of criterion-referenced information on mathematical attainments. The information was derived from a test that had been designed to assess pupils' "mastery" of fifty-five objectives of the curriculum for fifth and sixth grades in primary schools. The objectives covered operations with whole numbers, whole number structure, fractional number structure, operations with fractions, decimals, and percentages, algebra, geometry, charts and graphs, and arithmetic problems (cf. Close et al., 1978; Educational Research Centre, 1980b; Kellaghan et al., 1976). Information was provided to teachers on the performance of each pupil in their classes on each objective (whether or not the pupil had "mastered" the objective).

The implementation of the criterion-referenced treatment was limited to sixth grades in the second and third years of the study. Thirty-two schools drawn from Treatment 5A (see Chapter 2) and nineteen further schools recruited to act as controls took part. The thirty-two schools were assigned at random to one of two treatments in the two years in which the criterion-referenced study was carried out. Altogether there were four treatment conditions. In one condition, criterion-referenced information was presented on its own. In the other conditions, criterion-referenced information was supplemented by information derived from norm-referenced tests: in one condition, a norm-referenced mathematics attainment test only; in another condition, an ability test only; and in a final condition, a combination of the norm-referenced mathematics and ability tests. In a control treatment the criterion-referenced test was administered at the beginning of the year, but no results were returned to teachers. Dependent-variable information was obtained from administration of the same criterion-referenced test that at the beginning of the year had served as the source of the test information that was given to teachers.

We calculated separate statistics for boys and girls in each treatment group since we thought it likely that differences associated with gender would exist in test performance. We found, in fact, that boys scored higher than girls on almost all sections of the test when they took the test for the first time. We also found differences in initial test performance between treatment groups as well as a number of treatment-by-gender interactions. To take account of such differences, initial test scores were covaried in the analyses of the test data obtained at the end of the treatment period.

The results of these analyses did not clearly indicate the superiority of any kind of test information. Among the test-information groups, there was a tendency, in the case of both boys and girls, for the group that had received most information on pupil performance (criterion-referenced and norm-referenced information on mathematical attainments and ability test information) to perform best on the end-of-year, criterion-referenced test. This conclusion, however, has to be qualified by the findings that the superiority of the groups was not consistent across all objectives, and the performance of the group that had not received any formal test information was not significantly inferior to the performance of the groups that had received information.

In considering these findings, we should recognize that the control-group teachers were not completely without information. True, they did not have information on individual pupils' performance. However, they had administered the test and no doubt had familiarized themselves to some extent with the range of objectives that it covered. The information they had derived from the test administration may have influenced their teaching throughout the year.

In considering our finding that test information did not clearly affect the performance of pupils, two further points may be relevant. The first concerns our failure to constitute groups that were equivalent in mathematical achievement for the experiment. As we saw, there were differences between groups on the first administration of the test at the beginning of the year. The groups that achieved the highest initial mean scores were the groups that also performed best in the final testing. Despite our efforts to equate the groups by covarying initial scores, we may not have been entirely successful. Second, our information model for the criterion-referenced test followed that used for the norm-referenced tests—that is, the test was administered in its entirety to a group of pupils at the beginning of the school year and results of the pupils' test performance were given to teachers. However, perhaps criterion-referenced testing should have been spread over time and pupils should have taken tests close to their point of existing "mastery." Under these conditions information on test performance might have a more formative and immediate impact (cf. Smith, 1976).

CONCLUSION

In this chapter we considered the effects of a number of alternative treatments—the provision of diagnostic in addition to norm-referenced information on attainment, the provison of norm-referenced ability test information only, the provision of norm-referenced achievement test information only, and the provision of criterion-referenced information on mathematical achievement, alone or in combination with norm-referenced information on ability and achievement. In general, we compared the effects of the alternative treatments with the effects of providing no information at all and with the effects of our main treatment, which involved the provision of norm-referenced information on ability and achievement. Our alternative treatments, it should be noted, were of shorter duration and implemented over a more limited range of grades than was our main treatment. Since a great many of the analyses involving comparisons of the main treatment group with groups that received no information did not reveal statistically significant differences, it is not surprising that the inclusion of the alternative treatments did not reveal a great many differences either.

In general, our examination of the effects of the alternative treatments leads us to conclude that while the provision of information on test performance does have a number of effects at both the teacher and pupil level, the precise type of information that is provided is not usually of significance. In most of the analyses in which differences were found between control and treatment groups (i.e., groups with information), the latter groups tended to respond very much like each other. A number of exceptions to this pattern, however, are worthy of note. Most of them relate to the treatment group that was provided with diagnostic information on pupils' performance in addition to norm-referenced information.

While the results of our school-level analyses of pupil test performance that included the alternative treatments were very similar to those in which the norm-referenced information group was compared with the control groups, analyses at the pupil level did reveal some additional differences. Pupils in the diagnostic information group were found to perform significantly better on all achievement tests than pupils in the group that received only norm-referenced information on achievement and ability. This is perhaps not surprising, since the diagnostic information was more detailed and related to classroom instruction; hence, we might expect it would be of more practical value to teachers than simple normative scores. Having said that, we have to acknowledge the fact that, given our experimental design, the school rather than the pupil was the more appropriate level for our analyses. Inferences based on pupil-level analyses do not have the same force as inferences based on school-level analyses.

Teachers were also provided with very specific information in the criterion-referenced treatment, and again it would not have been unreasonable to expect that this would have proved beneficial in the day-to-day instructional process. In addition, in some treatments teachers were provided with information only on mathematical achievement, and this might have served to focus their attention and efforts in this area. So again, we should not have been too surprised if we had found specific achievement effects associated with the provision of criterion-referenced information. However, we found no clear evidence that the provision of such information, either on its own or in combination with other types of information, contributed significantly to the mathematical achievement of students, though the treatment group that had received most information about students—criterion-referenced information on achievement and norm-referenced information on ability and achievement—tended to perform best.

In considering our findings, it is well to recall that the criterion-referenced treatment groups were selected during the course of the study and that some students had prior experience of testing in lower grades. When we consider these facts in conjunction with the finding that the control group, which received no test information at all and which had entered the study specifically for the criterion-referenced treatment, did quite well, we are forced to ask if novelty and lack of information may not have been a factor in test performance. We are reminded here of the relatively high achievement-test performance of the control group in the main analyses reported in Chapter 3. There we saw that schools in which no testing had been carried out performed very well in comparison with schools in treatments that had had four years' experience when both were tested at the end of the study.

In the context of the expectancy process, the addition of diagnostic information to norm-referenced information, or the limitation of information to ability test performance only or achievement test performance only, did not have a unique impact on teachers' perceptions of pupils, with the possible exception of perceptions of pupils' Irish reading achievement, which was found in two cases—once for the diagnostic information group and once for the group that had received only achievement test information. Nor did the provision of alternative forms of information affect pupils' subsequent test performance in any way that was different from the way in which the provision of norm-referenced information affected it, again with the one exception of the group that had been limited to achievement test information. However, this exception referred only to a section of the treatment group (middle-socioeconomic students), not the total sample.

As far as other pupil responses to the various treatments were concerned, very little emerged from our analyses to suggest that the type of information given to teachers was an important factor in determining such matters as pupils' perceptions of the factors that affect scholastic progress or their perceptions of their own scholastic behavior and abilities. Where differences between treatments were found, the perceptions of pupils in all the groups that had received test information tended to be similar, though in a few cases the diagnostic information group did depart from this pattern, again providing evidence for the view that diagnostic information was in some ways different from simple, norm-referenced information in its effects on ability and achievement.

Just as the strongest effects associated with the provision of test information were found at the teacher level in the main treatment comparisons, so the strongest indications that type of information was differentially effective also appeared at the teacher level. While in many analyses involving teachers' responses, no differences associated with any kind of testing were found, and while in those in which differences were found, all treatments that had received test information responded in a more or less similar fashion, the type of information seemed to be relevant to teachers' responses in a number of cases. Most often the effect was associated with the provision of diagnostic information rather than with the provision of other kinds of information. For example, teachers in the diagnostic information group, compared with teachers in other treatment groups, were more likely to have brought out and used test results during the year, to have seen their present pupils' test results from previous years, and to have told pupils and parents the results of the tests. Further, they were more likely to have relied on standardized tests as a criterion for the within-class grouping of pupils. While they admitted to these practices, the diagnostic-group teachers, as well as the group that received norm-referenced information on ability and achievement, were less likely than teachers in the groups that received only ability-test information or only achievement-test information, who in turn were less likely than teachers in the control groups, to perceive standardized tests as influencing the way in which they perceived or acted toward pupils. Thus, the more information on test performance teachers received, the less influential they perceived tests to be in affecting their behavior toward pupils.

9 CONCLUSION

In this study we set out to examine the effects of standardized testing in typical school settings in which tests were administered at the beginning of the school year and results given to teachers sometime later. The questions to which we sought answers were, on one level, relatively simple and straightforward. In the light of controversies about the effects of standardized testing, one could take one of two basic positions. On the one hand, following a tradition of half a century of standardized testing in the United States and Britain, one might expect that such testing would be found to be useful to teachers in their classroom practice, providing information of a kind that was not otherwise readily available to them, and that this information would be of use in making decisions about methods of classroom organization, choice of curriculum materials, and teaching strategies. As a result of such decisions, one would expect that students would show higher levels of achievement in the long run. On the other hand, the severe criticisms of standardized tests, particularly over the last decade, might lead one to suspect that testing would have adverse effects on classroom practice and students. In the light of these criticisms, one might not be surprised to find a narrowing of curricula, rigid grouping practices, labeling of students, and, ultimately, greater pupil failure, particularly among children from low socio-economic backgrounds (see Kellaghan, Madaus, and Airasian, 1980a). In our study, we set out to collect evidence that might help to throw light on those contradictory positions regarding the effects of standardized testing. In particular, we set out to measure the effects—on schools, on teachers, on parents, and, of course, on students—of providing teachers with information derived from standardized testing.

While on one level these issues seem relatively simple and straightforward, even the briefest reflection on the evaluative nature and complexity of the classroom, into which test information is introduced, should cause us to pause at the suggestion that any questions, or answers, relating to these topics would be simple or straightforward. We had introduced standardized testing into typical classroom situations, in which we were aware there was an already highly developed formal and informal, teacher-based evaluation system. Thus, in obtaining data about the possible effects of standardized testing, we looked not only at teachers' reactions to such testing, but also at their attitudes toward and perceptions of other evaluative processes. The relevance of the role of teachers' already-existing evaluative systems was perhaps most strongly urged on us when we considered the possible effects of testing on pupils' scholastic achievement. Here we had to take account of the considerable volume of literature relating to teachers' expectations for pupils and the possible effects of such expectations on pupils' achievement. We recognized that test information could be considered as just one further item of information about pupils for the teacher, and that, in assessing its impact, we would have to view it as interacting with, and possibly reinforcing or competing with, teachers' assessment of pupils based on other sources of information. Predicting what precise effects the introduction of a new type of evaluation procedure might have on an already strongly established evaluation system is difficult, but one would expect that the impact of the procedure would be related to both its function and its perceived value in fulfilling that function.

In examining data relating to these issues, where possible we compared schools, teachers, pupils, and their parents in the experimental treatments with control subjects. Most of our analyses were based on data obtained at the end of the period of four years during which our testing program ran. Thus, differences between groups should be interpretable as the effect of having participated in a testing program. In some analyses, however, comparative data were not available. For example, certain questions relating to the use of standardized tests could be addressed only to teachers who had participated in the testing program. We report the responses of teachers to such questions, and they are, of course, of interest. However, they cannot be regarded as being based on the same kind of experimental evidence as findings for which comparative data were available.

In considering our findings, we should also bear in mind that analyses were
carried out at a number of levels.   Since the experimental unit in our study was
the school, only our school-level analyses are strictly experimental.   Examples
of such analyses are the comparisons between treatments of school-level test
performance and school assessment procedures described in Chapter 3.   For
several of our analyses, we had to operate on the basis of different units, since
many questions regarding the use of standardized testing relate not to the
school but to individuals within it.   Thus the school would not seem to be the
appropriate level of analysis in examining the role of standardized testing in the
expectancy process, since the process involves an interaction between individual
teachers and pupils.   We chose to use the pupil as the unit in these analyses, even
though one could readily make a case for using the teacher.   Our examination of
other effects on teachers and pupils, as well as effects on parents, also used units
of analyses other than the school.   Among the disadvantages of using analytic
units other than the school is the change from an experimental to a quasi-
experimental model and the consequent weakening of the inferences that can
be made; the increase in the number of degrees of freedom in analyses, which
increases the likelihood of obtaining statistically significant findings, is also a
problem.   Despite the disadvantages of quasi-experimental analyses, they can
often throw light on issues that are not amenable to examination within the
constraints of a classical experimental design.

MAIN FINDINGS

What did we find when standardized testing was introduced into schools?
Two preliminary sets of findings are of particular interest.   The first relates to
the general reactions of teachers and students to tests and the testing program
and the second to the congruence between the test results and teachers' already-
formed judgments of pupils.
     Reactions of both teachers and pupils to the test program were very
positive.   Teachers perceived standardized intelligence and achievement tests
as accurate measures of a pupil's scholastic ability—more accurate, in fact,
than public examinations, though less accurate than their own classroom
examinations.   Further, the majority of teachers reported that they had
covered most or all of the content of the achievement tests prior to testing,
which indicates the content validity of the tests in terms of their teaching.
Most teachers also thought that the tests provided intellectual stimulation
(88 percent) and did not see them as increasing anxiety (83 percent) or
competitiveness (70 percent) or as being too much like examinations (82
percent).

The reports of pupils as well as of teachers indicate that the pupils approached the tests seriously. About three-quarters of the pupils said they thought it important to do well on the tests, while over 90 percent tried to do their best. Despite these attitudes, a large majority of pupils enjoyed sitting for the tests (80 percent) and did not feel afraid (85 percent), nervous (70 percent), or bored (83 percent).

Testing thus was carried out in a basically hospitable environment. Further, the performance results that were supplied to teachers were such that we would expect them to do little to change this situation. When we consider the relationships between teachers' ratings of pupils' ability and achievement and pupils' test scores for the same variables, we find considerable agreement. Whether we carry out analyses in terms of discrepancies or correlations, we find that test scores, on the whole, serve to confirm teacher ratings. When teachers themselves were asked if the test scores that were reported to them closely corresponded to their own estimates of pupils' ability, 85 percent agreed that this was so.

Thus, we can conclude that the potential for testing and test information to upset the existing evaluative ecology of the classroom was quite limited. Indeed, we should not have been too surprised if we had found that the provision of test information had no impact at all on teachers or pupils. After all, teachers were operating on the basis of well-established evaluative systems, and the provision of test information largely confirmed the judgments they had already formed about pupils. Why should the addition of a limited amount of information, even where discrepant, alter those judgments or any behavior that might be based on them? Viewed in this context, some of our findings on the effects of testing on teachers and pupils would seem to indicate that test information can have a surprisingly strong impact indeed.

School-Level Effects

In analyzing the effects of our testing program on schools, we compared school principals' responses regarding the organization and practices of schools across the five treatment groups as they were constituted at the beginning of the study. Our findings were surprising in at least two respects. The first surprise related to the almost total lack of effects on school practices and organization as reported by school principals. The overall impact of the testing program on various aspects of school organization was slight. More directly relevant to our investigation, we found no significant differences between schools in the reported use of standardized tests. Tests, for example, were not used more frequently—indeed were hardly used at all—in the experimental schools to assign pupils to classes, nor did the availability of test information lead to a greater provision for remediation. Somewhat more evidence of test use was found in replies to questions directly relating to our testing program. Obviously, these questions were confined to principals in schools in which testing had been carried out. Thirteen percent of principals reported that tests had affected the content of curricula in their schools, while 23 percent reported a shift in curricular emphasis as an outcome of receiving test results. These figures, if they are a realistic estimate of curricular changes, are not insignificant, even though they do not convey any details on the real extent of the changes. They are much larger than any of the figures we obtained relating to the effect of testing on organizational factors. In general, the impact of testing, to the extent that it had any, seems to have been within the classroom rather than in the more general context of organization of the school. In retrospect, this perhaps was to be expected; our testing program was classroom based rather than school based, with results being returned directly to individual classroom teachers rather than to school principals.

The generally low level of impact of testing on school organization may indicate that principals perceived testing as peripheral to the formal working of the school. This, however, should not be taken to mean that test information was not attended to in schools. Making test results part of permanent records and the passing on of results from one teacher to another occurred in more than half our schools. Thus, even if the effects of testing on school organization and practice seem slight, we may still expect to find effects at the teacher and pupil levels.

The second major surprise in our findings relating to the effects of testing at the school level concerns the test performance of pupils at the end of the study. If testing and giving information about performance to teachers has a beneficial effect on the scholastic achievement of pupils, then we should expect that effect to be reflected in improved test performance over time by the group that had received test information. While our findings about the test performance of pupils were complex, they certainly cannot be interpreted as supporting the view that the provision of test information to teachers invariably leads to increases in mean performance on standardized tests.

The performance of the group that was tested and did not receive information usually fell somewhere between the performance of the group with no test experience and the group that had received norm-referenced information. This is perhaps as one would expect if one thinks of the treatment groups as representing a continuum from no testing experience through testing to testing with inform- ation. It would not be too surprising if that performance were found to increase with intensity of treatment. Our findings, however, do not fit this simple expectation. First, while the group that tested and received information tended to manifest the best performance on the ability test, the group with no prior test experience tended to perform best on the achievement tests. And second, the two tested groups (one with information, one without) never differ significantly from one another in their performance. An explanation of the relatively good showing of the group with no previous experience of testing on the achievement tests may be found in the reactivity of the group to the treatment. This group was taking tests for the first time; perhaps teachers and pupils approached the task with greater enthusiasm and effort than their counterparts, many of whom had several years of experience with testing. If this is so, then it is not without interest that novelty worked for achievement test performance but not for ability test performance. In looking for an explanation for this, we may note that while the ability test would have been strange to children taking the test for the first time in two respects—content and format—the achievement tests would have been strange in only one respect—format. Perhaps the additional enthusiasm and effort of both the teachers and pupils in the control group in the final testing could cope with the novel format but not with a novel format combined with novel content.

We also investigated at the school level whether testing students with only an ability test affected their later performance on an ability test and whether testing students with only an achievement test affected later performance on an achievement test. We found no difference between these two sets of students and students who had had experience of a combination of ability and achievement testing. A comparison between schools that had received diagnostic information as well as norm-referenced information, schools that had received only norm-referenced information, and control groups revealed that the diagnostic group performed very much like the norm-referenced group on standardized tests. Thus, we are led to conclude that the type of information that schools received was not a significant factor in determining school-level achievements. This finding, however, will have to be reconsidered when we consider the results of our pupil-level analyses.

In a final set of school-level analyses, we examined the distribution of ability, achievement, and socioeconomic background of students within and between classes in schools that had more than one class at a grade level. If test results were used to stratify pupils, then we would expect that classes in schools that had information would become, relative to classes in schools without such information, internally more homogeneous in terms of ability or achievement. Further, class means at a grade level should become more widely dispersed. These hypotheses were not substantiated. Schools that had test information did not exhibit in their classes greater homogeneity in ability, achievement, or socioeconomic background than did schools without such information. If anything, the trend of our findings, though not statistically significant, suggested that the opposite was happening.

Teacher-Level Effects

In considering school-level analyses, we noted that the school practices most likely to be affected by the availability of test information were those directly under the control of the classroom teachers. When we come to consider teacher-level effects, we obtain further evidence that the testing program had an impact on teachers.

At the end of the study, data were collected from teachers on their activities, beliefs, and opinions related to standardized tests and test results. They were also asked about their use of tests in making decisions about pupils. On most topics, information was obtained from teachers at two points in time, and we were thus able to examine changes in the teachers' perceptions of standardized testing that occurred during the study.

— In general, teachers in all treatments expressed positive attitudes toward the standardized tests used in the study. They liked the tests and perceived their pupils as liking them. They also perceived a number of advantageous outcomes as issuing from their use. Comparisons between teachers who had received test information and control-group teachers (one group had tested and not received information, the other group had not tested) indicated that teachers who had received test information were significantly more likely to perceive standardized tests as being an accurate measure of a pupil's scholastic ability. They were also significantly more likely to perceive a similarity between tested intelligence and the kind of intelligence needed for success in school. While the availability of test information was not associated with a greater amount of grouping of pupils in classes, among teachers who did group those who received test information used intelligence test results to a greater degree in making decisions about grouping than did teachers who had not received such information. Testing apparently was used to support an already-established policy decision rather than to determine a policy, with test results playing a supplementary or confirmatory role (see also Salmon-Cox, 1981). Finally, teachers who had received test information were less likely than other teachers to see standardized tests as influencing teachers' expectations for pupils, as being used for labeling pupils, or as being used as a rationale for paying less attention to low-scoring pupils. This may seem surprising; however, it confirms Salmon-Cox's finding that teachers in the United States report that they consciously take action to prevent the use of test results to label students.

Against these effects of standardized testing on teachers can be set a number of areas in which no effects were observed. Teachers who received test information did not differ from teachers who did not in the weight they would give tests in making decisions about pupils, in the criteria they reported using in assigning pupils to classes, in their perceived relevance of tests for classroom use, in the ways in which they structured their classroom for instruction (in incidence of grouping, in pupil seating arrangements), or in their beliefs about the stability of intelligence and achievement test scores over time.

While some changes in teachers' perceptions, beliefs, and reported practices were associated with the availability of standardized test results, and these were in a predictable direction, they cannot be regarded as being either extensive or radical. This conclusion is compatible with the finding that teachers, at the beginning of the study and at its end, in all treatment groups, perceived themselves as being the most accurate judges of a pupil's intelligence and achievement. The provision of one further piece of information would be unlikely to seriously disrupt this perception, even if it differed radically from already-formed judgments. When we consider that teachers had rated the accuracy of standardized tests very highly and that the results of such tests basically confirmed their judgments about and perceptions of pupils that were based on a multiplicity of cues and variety of information sources, then major changes in the perceptions and behavior of teachers would clearly be very improbable indeed.

While our results indicate that experience with standardized tests and norm-referenced information alters teachers' perceptions of some characteristics of tests, it is also apparent that the availability of test information did not substantially alter the evaluative criteria that teachers report they would most rely on in making a variety of decisions about their pupils. Rather than replacing teacher judgments and observation, classroom tests, and recommendations from other teachers, standardized test results seem to be integrated into the existing mass of information about pupils and probably are seen as basically confirming rather than as replacing other sources of information. Thus their impact does not become very apparent in terms of reported practice.

We might expect that teachers' attitudes toward, perceptions of, and uses of evaluation information would to some extent be a function of the type of information they received. Thus, teachers who received norm-referenced information on ability and achievement test performance might be expected to differ in some respects from teachers who had access to other kinds of information. In particular, we might expect teachers who had received diagnostic as well as norm-referenced information on pupil test performance to have found the information more useful, since the additional information would seem to be more appropriate to decisions about actual teaching than would the simple descriptive information contained in normative scores. An examination of the responses of teachers who had received such information indicates that this is indeed so. While, on the whole, teachers who received other kinds of information (ability test information only, achievement test information only, and diagnostic information on achievement test performance) were more like than unlike teachers who received norm-referenced information on ability and achievement test performance in their perception of and attitudes toward a variety of assessment procedures, including standardized testing, we found some notable differences. These differences most frequently involved the group that had received diagnostic information. Such teachers were more likely than teachers in other treatment groups to bring out and use test results, to have seen pupils' test results from previous years, and to have communicated test results to more pupils and parents. Further, while teachers who had only norm-referenced information on intelligence and achievement tended to group their pupils within their classes on the basis of the intelligence test scores, those teachers who had diagnostic-achievement information in addition to norm-referenced information tended to group on the basis of achievement test scores.

Some differences were associated with the group that received ability test information only and the group that received achievement test information only. In the former group, teachers engaged in greater preparation for testing, possibly because of the novelty of ability tests, and they also passed on test results more frequently than did other teachers. On the other hand, the group that received only achievement test results talked less with other teachers about the results than did teachers in other treatments. Are these findings to be taken as an indication that teachers found ability test results more useful than achievement test results in communicating with other teachers? Or do they indicate that teachers are more sensitive about their pupils' achievement test scores, unless they are presented in diagnostic form, than their pupils' ability test scores? Perhaps teachers believe that their pupils' achievement test scores reflect their effectiveness as teachers to a greater extent than their pupils' ability test scores, which they are likely to see as being less amenable to teacher influences (very few of our teachers believed performance on intelligence tests depends mainly on learning).

In a number of respects, male teachers showed more positive attitudes toward and made greater use of standardized tests than did female teachers. Compared with female teachers, they perceived standardized tests as more accurate measures of achievement, and they believed that the kind of intelligence measured by tests was important in life. They also gave greater weight to standardized tests in making decisions about pupils, and they used test results for within-class grouping to a greater extent than did female teachers.

Parent-Level Effects

If teachers were the group most immediately involved in our testing program, the group that was most remotely concerned was parents. Nevertheless, since we may assume a high level of interest in their children's schooling on the part of parents and since test information might be used in school-parent communications, we conducted a survey of parents of children who had participated in our study. Our analyses in this area were limited to comparisons between parents of children in three treatment groups: the no-testing group, the group that tested and did not receive information, and the group that tested and received norm-referenced information. Questions were asked of parents concerning their familiarity with changes and proposed changes relating to methods of evaluation in the educational system, communications between themselves and the school, their perceptions of their children's scholastic progress, and their knowledge about and attitudes toward intelligence and achievement testing in their children's school.

As far as detecting the effects of a standardized testing program on parents was concerned, our survey revealed very little. Perhaps the only finding of any note was a negative one—that parents, on the whole, reported they were unaware of any such program. This is surprising, given the fact that a large percentage of sixth-grade pupils (about 80 percent) said they had told their parents they had sat for standardized tests. Perhaps this did not happen or, if it did, was not effective, and either parents or children misunderstood what was involved in the test program or in the interviewers' questions. Again, parents may have forgotten about the information, perhaps because they did not perceive it as relating to anything very important in their children's education.

Despite lack of specific information about the testing program in this study, parents' attitudes toward standardized testing were positive; however, a question must be raised about their understanding of precisely what such tests involve. Even if they had some idea of the nature of standardized tests, we can be fairly certain that few of them had any idea of the controversies surrounding the use of tests in other countries.

The relatively small number of parents who received test results for their children said that these were helpful. Furthermore, about half the parents interviewed thought the provision of norm-referenced intelligence and achievement tests would be a change for the better in Irish education, and a large majority said they would be interested in receiving information on the performance of their children on such tests, if such information was available. These positive responses, however, were common to parents of children in all treatment groups; thus our findings do not permit us to say that the judgments were informed by actual knowledge of a testing program in schools.

Pupil-Level Effects

The effects of standardized testing are most widely debated in terms of their impact on pupils. We looked for evidence relating to such effects in a number of areas: pupils' perceptions of the standardized testing program, the extent to which different types and sources of information are perceived by pupils as affecting how they are doing in school, pupils' self-perceptions of their scholastic performance, and pupils' self-concepts.

In the school-level analyses, differences in test performance were not found to be associated with the type of test information that had been given to teachers. At the pupil level, however, differences were found between the performance of pupils in the diagnostic information group and pupils in other treatments. In the case of achievement test performance, a unique effect seems to be associated with the provision of diagnostic information. Pupils for whom such information, in addition to norm-referenced information, was available performed better than did pupils in all other groups. The performance of pupils in this group on the intelligence test was similar to that of other tested groups. Thus the effect was specific to the tests for which diagnostic information had been provided (i.e., the achievement tests).

These findings are not unreasonable. The point in providing diagnostic information is to make available to teachers information that is sufficiently detailed to help them in the identification of individual student learning difficulties. We have already seen that when such information is made available to teachers, they make more use of it than of simple, norm-referenced information. Our findings would seem to indicate that use pays off in terms of improved test performance of pupils.

These findings must be tempered by our failure to find any specific effect associated with the provision of diagnostic information in our school-level analyses. There are a number of possible explanations for this discrepancy. First, the larger number of degrees of freedom available for the pupil-level analyses meant that smaller differences between treatment groups would exhibit significance. Second, in our pupil-level analyses we departed from our experimental unit, which was the school. Third, aggregating scores to the level of the school may have masked within-school differences, differences that may have existed either between teachers or between pupils. Indeed one could argue that the teacher or the pupil is a more appropriate unit of analysis than the school to test the effects of the provision of test information. If one accepts this argument, then the pupil-level results may be regarded as being of greater import than the school-level ones, despite the departure from the study's experimental unit.

A further alternative treatment examined the use of criterion-referenced testing. Our investigation of this issue, however, was severely limited in a number of respects. It looked only at testing in the area of mathematics; it was confined to pupils at one grade level (sixth); the groups compared were not equivalent in mathematical achievement at the beginning of the treatment; and, of perhaps greatest importance, the information model we followed was the one we had used for norm-referenced tests. However, criterion-referenced information, if it is to be effective, should perhaps not all be provided at one point in time, but rather should be spread over a year, thus permitting the tests to serve a formative function (see Smith, 1976).

The results of our analyses of the effects of using criterion-referenced test results are complex and not very conclusive. Overall, students in the treatment that had received criterion-referenced and norm-referenced information tended to have a relatively high level of performance on the final, criterion-referenced measure. However, the performance of a control group, which was given no information, was on the whole better than the performance of groups that had received criterion-referenced and other kinds of test information. The high level of test performance of students with no information leads us to ask, as we did in the case of the final norm-referenced achievement test scores of students in the control group in the main study, if novelty and lack of information may not have acted as an incentive to teachers and pupils, while greater familiarity with testing and the study may have led to a certain complacency in test performance.

In our examination of students' self-ratings of their scholastic performance and of related behaviors, we found that students in the group in which teachers had received norm-referenced test information tended to rate themselves lower in a number of areas (spoken Irish, English composition, interest in school, keenness to do well in school, and originality) than did students in groups that had not received test information. We also found that students' self-ratings generally tended to be high in comparison with other rating criteria (test scores and teacher ratings). Perhaps the availability of test information had the effect of moving pupils' ratings somewhat toward those other criteria. However, a number of factors should cause us to hesitate before accepting this conclusion. For one thing, the finding applied only in some of the areas that were directly tested, while it also applied in areas not closely related to tested areas at all (e.g., originality). Thus the effect seems rather too diffuse and haphazard to be attributable to the test information with which teachers were supplied. Second, if test information affected students' self-ratings of their scholastic performance, we might have expected the effect to have also manifested itself in a closer congruence for the information group between pupils' own ratings and teachers' ratings of their scholastic achievement and, even more so, between the pupils' ratings and their test scores. However, the availability of test information did not seem to affect the amount of agreement between these sets of ratings; indeed, we obtained one significant difference that actually suggests the opposite. Finally, an examination of students' self-concepts, a measure of which was composed of students' views of themselves as students and of their perceptions of their performance levels in various scholastic areas, revealed no statistically significant differences that could be associated with testing or the availability of test information to their teachers.

A consideration of the role of norm-referenced information alone and of such information combined with diagnostic information indicates that, in many respects, the effects on pupils of the two conditions were similar. In common with the norm-referenced information group, pupils in the diagnostic information group exhibited lower self-ratings of their scholastic performance than did pupils in control groups. Indeed, the tendency was more extensive in the diagnostic group than in the norm-referenced group. There were, however, some differences between the norm-referenced and diagnostic groups. In some cases, particularly in matters not directly related to tests or testing, the diagnostic group was more like the untested and no-information groups than like the norm-referenced information group. In other cases, as we saw when we considered teacher-level effects, the provision of diagnostic information seemed more powerful in its impact than did the provision of norm-referenced information on its own. On the whole, the impact of diagnostic information seems more specific, more focused on factors closely related to student achievement.

Testing and the Expectancy Process

Our study afforded the opportunity to examine the expectancy or "Pygmalion" effect popularized by Rosenthal and Jacobson (1968). Unlike Rosenthal and Jacobson, we did not attempt to mislead teachers about their pupils' ability or achievement. The information we supplied described, as it does in the normal school setting, the pupils' *actual* test performance. Our design also allowed for a control group in which teachers did not have access to test information. Rosenthal and Jacobson, because the test results they provided were inflated, were able to examine only the expectancy "advantage" situation—that is, the situation where the test information was more favorable than the teachers' perceptions of a pupil. In a normal testing program, however, one would also expect instances in which the test information would be less favorable than the teacher's perception, in which an expectancy "disadvantage" could occur. Our use of the normal school setting allowed us to look at both types of situation.

We examined our data in search of an expectancy effect in several ways across grades over four different constructs (general ability, mathematics, English reading, and Irish reading) and by various pupil characteristics (gender, socioeconomic status, and location of school). Our analyses clearly show that, for the total sample we examined, expectancy processes were at work, both when teachers had test information and when they had not. While our results are not uniform across all grades or constructs, the clear trend of our data indicates that when teachers were given test information, their ratings of pupils tended to move in line with that information. On the other hand, when test information was not available, pupils' end-of-year test performance tended to align with teachers' initial perceptions of the pupils' achievement and ability.

Our results relating to gender indicate that while the expectancy process operated according to our model for both genders, test information and teacher perceptions did not interact in precisely the same way for boys and girls. We found that teachers, when presented with test information, altered their perceptions of their pupils' ability and achievement in line with that information more frequently in the case of boys than of girls. However, boys appeared to be less responsive than girls to the perceptions, and presumably to the expectations, of their teachers. This was so whether or not those perceptions and expectations were informed by test information. Different experiences in school on the part of boys and girls in pupil-teacher interactions, particularly ones related to evaluation, may account for the gender differences we found in the expectancy process.

When we examined the expectancy process in different school locations, we found some evidence that test information had a stronger impact on the expectancy process in urban than in town or rural schools. Results of analyses in which pupils were stratified by socioeconomic status provided little support for the claim that test information is likely to be most effective (and, the literature would argue, most deterimental) in the case of children from low socioeconomic backgrounds.

While the provision of test information tended to benefit pupils whose test scores were higher than their teachers' assessments of their ability or achievement, it tended to work to the detriment of pupils for whom the teacher's original assessment was more favorable than the test results. But further, our results also clearly show that when test information is *not* available, an analogous process comes into operation. If a teacher has a low opinion of a pupil and does not have access to test information that would have shown the pupil in a better light, this situation tends to work to the pupil's "disadvantage." Conversely, if a teacher has a favorable initial opinion of a pupil but is kept in the dark about the pupil's relatively poorer test performance, the uncorrected expectation tends to "benefit" the pupil.

What can we say about the net effect on pupils of the provision of test information? The literature tends to emphasize the negative—the expectancy disadvantage—outcome. Our cross-lagged partial correlation model does not distinguish between advantage and disadvantage. For some indication of the extent of advantage and disadvantage, we need to look at the discrepancy data using collapsed test scores. When we do, we see that the presence of test information, on balance, works to pupils' advantage. When we examine shifts in teacher ratings that became more favorable over the course of the year, we find that the provision of test information led to a significantly higher proportion of such shifts at all grades. On the other hand, when we look at teachers' ratings that became less favorable over time, we find that such shifts could not be attributed to the receipt of test information. An estimate of the "net advantage" associated with the receipt of test information indicates that between 4 and 11 percent more favorable shifts occurred among teachers who received information than among those who did not. The teachers in our study, like Salmon-Cox's (1981) American teachers, would seem to have dealt with discrepancies between test scores and their own assessments of pupils by giving pupils the benefit of the doubt raised by the discrepancy. In this situation a test score that indicated performance below that which a teacher had expected on the basis of classroom performance would tend to be discounted. However, if a pupil scored higher than expected, the test score would serve as a "red flag," indicating that the teacher had missed something.

When we look at the impact of the provision of diagnostic information on the expectancy process, we find that it did not have a unique impact on subsequent pupil test performance beyond that of norm-referenced information on ability and achievement. Additional analyses by gender, location, and socioeconomic status do not alter this conclusion. Similarly, we do not find any evidence of a unique expectancy effect when the kind of test information is limited to either achievement or ability tests.

We believe that the expectancy effects that we obtained are quite striking when one considers the numerous factors that were at work to limit their demonstration. First, initial teacher perceptions and initial test scores showed strong agreement. While there was some room for test information to influence teacher perceptions, the amount was not great. Second, we know that not all teachers attended to the information that was provided to them. Our best estimate is that only about half the teachers could be classified as "test users." Third, the test information that we provided was not generally communicated to parents, pupils, or other teachers. In twenty schools test results were not passed on at all; in forty-six schools they were passed on to other teachers; in thirty-nine schools to some parents; and in thirty schools to some students. Between 40 and 48 percent of sixth graders in the final year said they had been told their test results. Clearly, in this situation the potential impact of test information on pupil behavior and subsequent test performance is limited.

Despite these mitigating factors our results provide quite strong evidence that expectancy processes were operating in our classrooms. And this was so whether or not test information was available. Further, our results show that whether or not test information is available, the expectancy process works to the "advantage" of some pupils and to the "disadvantage" of others. However, on net, more pupils seem to be at an expectancy "advantage" than "disadvantage" when their teachers have test information than when they have not. Finally, our results demonstrate that the expectancy process works in a relatively small proportion of cases.

ISSUES IN INTERPRETING FINDINGS

Several issues relating to our test program and the experimental context in which it was carried out need to be considered in attempting to assess the import of our findings. These issues relate specifically to the experimental conditions in which our data were obtained, the fact that the study was carried out in Ireland, and the nature of the testing program.

The fact that we examined the possible effects of standardized testing experimentally had an important advantage. When considering the problem of assessing the effects of testing, we noted that the practice of testing had grown up in a haphazard way over the past fifty years in countries such as the United States and Britain. It is now so widespread that one could not obtain evidence on effects of testing that would be based on a comparison between a group of schools, teachers, and pupils that had been exposed to testing and a similar group that had not been exposed. An advantage of carrying out our study in Ireland was that we could constitute such comparable groups and thus form a basis for the drawing of inferences that would be based on a true experimental design. In practice, it became clear that there were also disadvantages associated with this approach. One set of disadvantages arose from the control of the experimental treatments, while another related to the degree of congruence between testing as part of an experimental program and testing as part of a normal, school-based program.

From the beginning of the study, we encountered problems in setting up the treatments. The fact that at the time the study began, statistics on schools were out of date and characteristics of schools in the system were changing almost daily as a result of a government policy of amalgamation of small schools created serious problems in the selection of schools for our sample. Many schools that were selected had to be replaced at very short notice. While the amalgamation policy slowed down considerably as the study progressed, cases still occurred in which participating schools closed, became larger or smaller, or amalgamated with other schools. The end result of all these problems was that our sample of schools did not remain stable throughout the study; in particular, its balance in terms of school location and gender composition (the stratifying variables for our sample) and school size and type of administration (matching variables for our sample) was disturbed.

We had expected that, during the course of the study, problems would arise from the attrition of schools and the nonresponse on specific instruments of teachers and pupils. Attrition, however, was not a serious problem. The continued participation of schools was extremely good for a study that made fairly heavy demands on teachers over a relatively long period of time. Response to instruments, particularly ones completed by classroom teachers, was less satisfactory.

Perhaps a more central issue in terms of our experiment, however, was that of treatment implementation (see Fullan and Pomfret, 1977). Having some sense of the extent to which test results were attended to and used by teachers is clearly important for the interpretation of our findings. If we find that teachers never even read the students' test results, we would hardly expect to find any discernible effects associated with testing. While this might be an interesting finding about teachers' reactions to test results, it could hardly be regarded as throwing much light on the effects of testing on students, parents, or even teachers.

Our measures of teachers' overt use of materials suggest that, depending on the measure used, around 50 percent, possibly as high as 70 percent, of teachers, could be regarded as test users. Other data we obtained on communication of test information between teachers, students, and parents suggest that this is not an unreasonable estimate. Thus we saw that about 80 percent of sixth-grade pupils told their parents about the testing program. Forty-five percent of sixth-grade pupils in the group that tested and received norm-referenced information said they were told their test results by teachers. Of those, approximately 70 percent talked to their parents and to classmates about their results; interestingly, however, only 23 percent talked to their teachers. The reports of teachers basically confirm these figures; of the 45 percent who said they told at least some pupils their achievement test results, about half told all their pupils. Smaller numbers said they told pupils their results on the intelligence tests. Almost half the teachers said they communicated achievement test results and somewhat over a quarter that they communicated intelligence test results to some parents, even though most of these told only a few. These data combine to present a picture of test results being used by about half the teachers to communicate information about pupils, evidencing a seriousness in their perceptions of the results.

These data perhaps do not indicate a degree of implementation as high as one would have liked in an experimental study. Furthermore, they point to variance within the experimental treatments. In terms of replicating a typical, school-based testing program, however, our experimental situation was probably not too different from that in any school-based program, in which we would expect some teachers to attend to results and others not, some to use results in a variety of ways and others not at all. To the extent that our experimental treatments reflected a typical school testing program, our findings are of particular relevance to a policymaker who is interested in the overall impact of a testing program, the operation of which, he or she can assume, will include deficiencies in implementation and application. Thus, the results of our analyses speak directly to the question: What effects is the introduction of a testing program likely to have on schools, teachers, parents, and students?

However, if our primary interest is in the effects of testing per se, we should focus not on our treatment groups as constituted in the experiment, but rather on teachers who actually used tests, since the responses or behavior of teachers or their students who paid no attention to test results is not going to provide us with any relevant information. Since we used membership of the originally constituted treatment groups as the criterion for inclusion in analyses, thus including all degrees of use and nonuse of tests, our findings are likely to provide an *underestimate* of the effects of testing per se.

The second factor relating to the experimental conditions under which our study was carried out concerns teachers' perceptions of the testing program. We were interested in instituting, insofar as that was possible, a normal, school-based testing program. In fact, the program had its origins not within the schools themselves, but in a research organization. Assessing what precise effects this may have had on schools and teachers is difficult. Certainly, we know that some teachers did not view the testing program as one that had been designed primarily to be of benefit to them. Some perceived it as part of an experiment, others as part of a test-standardization program, and others as an exercise in test development. Probably our strongest evidence on reactivity to the experimental situation is to be found in the high achievement test scores of the control group of children at the end of the study. This group, we suspect, was affected by the fact that pupils were taking tests for the first time. Students in the other groups, and their teachers, had no doubt grown accustomed to testing. Besides, over the period of four years, they may have come to accept that test results would not be used in any negative way by the research body that organized the study. Teachers are typically apprehensive at first about the test performance of their pupils; experience of the investigation in the groups that were tested over a period of four years should have done much to allay any fears teachers might have had.

There are, unfortunately, no simple answers to the problems that the experimental examination of phenomena gives rise to. If one chooses not to adopt an experimental approach, then one loses certain possibilities of examining an issue in a controlled way. If, on the other hand, one chooses to adopt experimental procedures, one inevitably departs to some extent from the reality that one tries to represent.

Whether effects of testing would be stronger or weaker in a nonexperimental situation is difficult to say. We have seen some evidence that suggests that strong effects can be induced by reactivity to an experimental situation. On the other hand, one might argue that if teachers adopted a testing program on their own initiative, they would show greater involvement in the working of that program and particularly in the use of test results. If that were so, we would expect to find stronger effects in such a program than we found in our study.

In considering our findings, it is important to bear in mind that our study was carried out in Ireland and thus raises the question of the relevance of the findings to countries that have a longer tradition in the use of standardized tests. At the beginning of our study we encountered set-up problems relating to the development of tests, the printing of machine-scorable answer sheets, and the training of teachers in test administration and interpretation. Further, we are conscious of the fact that the study ran only four years, a fairly short time in which to introduce and establish an educational innovation. At the same time, certain movements that were supportive of the development of standardized testing were in evidence from the beginning of the study. When the study began teachers were already starting to use a standardized procedure to assess reading achievement. At the high school level, standardized tests were also being introduced for educational and vocational guidance, and third-level training courses for guidance teachers to service this operation were available. Despite these trends the extent of standardized testing in schools, particularly at the elementary level, was quite small.

In light of this situation, finding a great deal of similarity between Irish and American teachers in their attitudes toward and opinions about standardized testing may seem surprising (Cahill et al., 1977). Whether one takes Goslin's (1967), Stetz and Beck's (1978) or Salmon-Cox's (1981) American teachers as the comparative group, the similarities are striking. Indeed, it is interesting within the American context to note that even though the American testing scene has altered markedly since Goslin's survey, principally because of the use of tests for accountability (e.g., program evaluation and allocation of funds), teachers' attitudes toward the use of standardized tests within the classroom have not altered greatly. Teachers, whether in America in the 1960s or 1970s or in Ireland in the 1970s, have very similar views about the place and uses of tests in the classroom. Obviously what is common in the work of teachers, in their tasks as classroom managers, instructors, and evaluators, far outweighs differences in background, whether they be temporal or geographical. Teachers' perceptions of their work also seem largely impervious to controversies about standardized testing that arise from time to time. These considerations suggest that we should not regard our results as being peculiar to teachers in the Irish educational system or even to teachers who have only recently become familiar with the practice of standardized testing.

A final issue to be considered in interpreting our findings is the fact that our treatment was planned as a classroom-based testing program. Tests were administered by teachers to their own students and results were returned directly to the classroom teachers, who had control over their further dissemination. Some teachers in fact communicated the results to other teachers, pupils, and parents, but this was the choice of individual teachers. In the original design of our study, we had planned to give test results directly to parents. However, teachers' opposition to this plan soon became apparent, so this treatment had to be abandoned. If we had given test results to parents, the effects probably would have been stronger than the ones we found. If test results had been available to other parties—administrators, schools' inspectors—the impact of the testing program also would probably have been more obvious. The provision of test results to parents and administrators could easily lead to interpretations that would involve notions of accountability.

The nature of our testing program also limited the use that could be made of test results to make radical decisions about students, such as selection for or exclusion from a particular course or type of school. The test results could have been used to assist in tracking and placement decisions at the level of the school if teachers had pooled their information about students. However, most schools seem to have a policy (at least implicit) of not tracking students, and the availability of test information did nothing to alter it.

Our findings clearly should not be generalized to the use of tests in contexts other than the classroom or for purposes other than the provision of information to teachers on pupil performance. The context that we examined is an important one and one that is commonly found. A great deal of test use is in the immediate context of the classroom. However, if test scores were used to assess teacher accountability or to select or certify students, we would expect to find evidence of a much stronger impact.

CONCLUSION

Several conclusions and generalizations may be made on the basis of our findings. At a general level we can say that standardized testing tends to be used to support, rather than to disrupt, existing school and teacher practices. In our study very little effect on school organizational or assessment practices was found; in retrospect, this is perhaps not surprising in a program that was centered on classroom teachers. It is perhaps more surprising that observed effects did not extend to parents or, except in a somewhat inconsistent way, to the overall test performance of pupils. That teachers, parents, or pupils do not manifest effects over a large range of variables lends support to the view held by many commentators that the information obtained from standardized testing has to take its place among a great many other kinds of evaluative information that are available to teachers. Thus, standardized test results would not appear to have a great deal of salience in the teacher's information web. Besides, test information in most cases serves to confirm the evaluations of pupils' ability and achievement that teachers have already formed. Thus, it will be the exception rather than the rule for a teacher to be confronted by information from tests that might lead him or her to believe that some modification of his or her perceptions or practice should be considered.

A standardized testing program centered on the teacher is, not surprisingly, likely to have its widest impact on the teacher. While that impact will not involve any radical change in the teachers' evaluative system, in which the teacher perceives him- or herself as playing the primary role, familiarity with standardized tests tends to be accompanied by favorable attitudes toward tests. In particular, familiarity leads teachers to perceive tests as being more accurate, while at the same time, and perhaps surprisingly, such teachers perceive the role of tests in labeling students or as providing a rationale for neglecting students as less significant than do teachers without testing experience.

Standardized testing, despite teachers' positive attitudes, is not likely to play any major role in their conscious organizational or assessment practices. The availability of test information does not lead to increased streaming or within-class grouping; however, if teachers already form instructional groups within their classes, test information is likely to play a role in the allocation of pupils to those groups. It may also play a role in retention practices in schools.

The gap between teachers' attitudes to tests and their reported use of them may seem surprising. Perhaps tests are highly regarded because they basically confirm teachers' own judgments. In a profession in which relatively little professional interaction between practitioners or with other professionals exists, this may be of considerable significance for the teacher. Or teachers may in fact make more use of tests than they are consciously aware. Our findings indicate that teachers' perceptions of pupils are affected by test information, perhaps to a greater extent than they realize. Furthermore, test information is somehow mediated to students and may affect their scholastic performance. This does not happen in the case of all students, or even most students, but it happens to a greater extent than one would predict from a consideration of teachers' reported uses of test information. These findings, while they indicate the role of test information in influencing teachers' expectancies, perhaps even more significantly underline the influence of teachers' expectancies on pupils' scholastic performance in a more general way. Whether or not test information is available, teachers appear to form expectations for pupils that can affect how pupils perform scholastically.

Whether the influence of tests in altering teachers' perceptions of pupils is beneficial or not is difficult to assess. Certainly, we know that teachers' ratings of pupils are more often raised than lowered when they have access to test information. If higher ratings lead to higher expectations and ultimately to superior scholastic performance, then test information would appear to be beneficial more often than not.

The precise type of norm-referenced test information that is available to teachers does not seem to be an important factor in determining most effects of testing. However, there are some indications that the provision of diagnostic information on pupil achievement in addition to norm-referenced information is more powerful than the provision of norm-referenced information alone. No particular effects seem to be associated with the provision of criterion-referenced information if that information is based on a single test administration in which performance on a large number of objectives is assessed. We suspect that the administration of criterion-referenced tests covering a more limited number of objectives spread over the school year would be a more effective procedure.

In conclusion, the picture that our findings suggest is one in which standardized testing seems to have been easily assimilated into the operating evaluative system of the classroom. In many cases test information apparently tended to support the existing perceptions and practices of teachers. In some cases test information did have unique and specific effects. However, our findings provide no evidence to support the position that standardized testing, when based in classrooms under the control of teachers, differs in kind in its effects from any other evaluative procedure available to the teacher.

REFERENCES

Adams, G.S. 1964. *Measurement and evaluation in education, psychology, and guidance.* New York: Holt, Rinehart & Winston.

Airasian, P.W. 1979. A perspective on the uses and misuses of standardized achievement tests. *NCME Measurement in Education* 10(3): 1–12.

——, T. Kellaghan, G.F. Madaus, and J.J. Pedulla. 1977. Proportion and direction of teacher rating changes of pupils' progress attributable to standardized test information. *Journal of Educational Psychology* 69: 702–09.

Anastasi, A. 1954. *Psychological testing.* New York: Macmillan.

Anderson, S.B., S. Ball, R.T. Murphy, and Associates. 1976. *Encyclopedia of educational evaluation.* San Francisco: Jossey-Bass.

Archer, P. 1979. A comparison of teacher judgements of pupils and the results of standardized tests. Unpublished doctoral dissertation. University College Cork.

Asbury, D.F. 1970. The effects of teacher expectancy, subject expectancy, and subject sex on the learning performance of elementary school children. Unpublished doctoral dissertation. Ohio State University, Columbus.

Austin, M., and C. Morrison. 1963. *The first R: The Harvard report on reading in the elementary schools.* New York: Macmillan.

Bartel, N.R., J.J. Grill, and D.N. Bryen. 1973. Language characteristics of black children: Implications for assessment. *Journal of School Psychology* 11: 351–64.

263

Beaton, A.E. 1980. Measuring differences among groups. Unpublished paper.

Beck, M.D., and F.P. Stetz. 1979. Teachers' opinions of standardized test use and usefulness. Paper presented at the annual meeting of the American Educational Research Association, San Francisco, April 1979.

Beez, W.F. 1970. Influence of biased psychological reports on teacher behavior and pupil performance. In M. Miles and W.W. Charters, Jr., eds. *Learning in social settings.* Boston: Allyn & Bacon.

Beggs, D.L., G.R. Mayer, and E.L. Lewis. 1972. The effects of various techniques of interpreting test results on teacher perception and pupil achievement. *Measurement and Evaluation in Guidance* 5: 290–97.

Bell, R., and N. Grant. 1977. *Patterns of education in the British Isles.* London: Allen & Unwin.

Bloom, B.S. 1969. Some theoretical issues relating to educational evaluation. In R.W. Tyler, ed. *Educational evaluation: New roles, new means.* Sixty-eighth Yearbook of the National Society for the Study of Education, Part II. Chicago: NSSE.

Bosma, B. 1973. The NEA testing moratorium. *Journal of School Psychology* 11: 304–06.

Brady, E.H. 1977. To test or not to test. *American Educator* 1(1): 3–9.

Brickell, W.W. 1962. Organizing New York State for educational change. Albany, N.Y.: State Department of Education.

Brickman, W.W. 1946. Preparation for the Regents' examination. *School and Society* 64: 263.

Brim, O.G., Jr. 1965. American attitudes towards intelligence tests. *American Psychologist* 20: 125–30.

——, D.C. Glass, J. Neulinger, I.R. Firestone, and S.C. Lerner. 1969. *American beliefs and attitudes about intelligence.* New York: Russell Sage Foundation.

Brookover, W.B. 1959. A social psychological conception of classroom learning. *School and Society* 87: 84–87.

Broome, B.J. 1970. An investigation of the effects of teachers' expectations on the achievement in reading of first-grade boys. Unpublished doctoral dissertation. Louisiana State University and Agricultural and Mechanical College, Baton Rouge.

Brophy, J.E., and T.L. Good. 1974. *Teacher-student relationships: Causes and consequences.* New York: Holt, Rinehart & Winston.

Cahill, V.M., P.W. Airasian, T. Kellaghan, and G.F. Madaus. 1977. Cross-cultural comparison of attitudes toward standardized intelligence tests. Paper presented at New England Educational Research Organization meeting, Manchester, N.H., May 1977.

Carter, D.L. 1970. The effect of teacher expectations on the self-esteem and academic performance of seventh-grade students. Unpublished doctoral dissertation. University of Tennessee, Knoxville.

Claiborn, W.L. 1969. Expectancy effects in the classroom: A failure to replicate. *Journal of Educational Psychology* 60: 377–83.

Clark, K.B. 1963. Educational stimulation of racially disadvantaged children. In A.H. Passow, ed. *Education in depressed areas.* New York: Bureau of Publications, Teachers' College, Columbia University.

Close, J.S., T. Kellaghan, G.F. Madaus, and P.W. Airasian. 1978. Growth in mathematical attainments of pupils. *Irish Journal of Education* 12: 3–21.

Cohen, D.K. 1972. Does IQ matter? *Commentary* (April): 51–59.

Connell, C. 1978. The going gets tough for educational testers. *The Boston Globe,* November 12, p. C16.

Cooper, M., and M. Leiter. 1980. Teachers on testing. In C.B. Stalford, ed. *Testing and evaluation in schools: Practitioners' views.* Washington, D.C.: National Institute of Education, U.S. Department of Education.

Coopersmith, S. 1967. *The antecedents of self-esteem.* San Francisco: W.H. Freeman.

Cronbach, L.J. 1949. *Essentials of psychological testing.* New York: Harper & Row.

——. 1975. Five decades of public controversy over mental testing. *American Psychologist* 30: 1–14.

Cullen, K. 1969. *School and family. Social factors in educational attainment.* Dublin: Gill & Macmillan.

de Rivera, M. 1974. Testitis: A technological affliction. *Childhood Education* 50: 217–21.

Digman, J.M. 1963. Principal dimensions of child personality as inferred from teachers' judgments. *Child Development* 34: 43–60.

Dockrell, W.B., ed. 1980. *The impact of tests on education.* Princeton, N.J.: International Association for Educational Assessment.

Dusek, J.B. 1975. Do teachers bias children's learning? *Review of Educational Research* 45:661–84.

——, and E.J. O'Connell. 1973. Teacher expectancy effects on the achievement test performance of elementary school children. *Journal of Educational Psychology* 65: 371–77.

Dweck, C.S. 1976. Children's interpretation of evaluative feedback: The effect of social cues on learned helplessness. *Merrill-Palmer Quarterly* 22: 105–09.

——, and E.S. Bush. 1976. Sex differences in learned helplessness: 1. Differential debilitation with peer and adult evaluators. *Developmental Psychology* 12: 147–56.

Dyer, H.S. 1977. Criticisms of testing: How mean is the median? *NCME Measurement in Education* 8(3): 1–9.

Ebel, R.L. 1966. The social consequences of educational testing. In A. Anastasi, ed. *Testing problems in perspective.* Washington, D.C.: American Council on Education.

——. 1977. *The uses of standardized testing.* Bloomington, Ind.: Phi Delta Kappa Educational Foundation.

Educational Research Centre. 1977. *Drumcondra Attainment Tests, Level III, Form A: Mathematics, Irish, and English. Administration and technical manual.* Dublin: Educational Research Centre, St Patrick's College.

——. 1978a. *Drumcondra Attainment Tests, Level I, Form A: Mathematics and English. Administration and technical manual.* Dublin: Educational Research Centre, St Patrick's College.

——. 1978b. *Drumcondra Attainment Tests, Level II, Form A: Mathematics, Irish, and English. Administration and technical manual.* Dublin: Educational Research Centre, St Patrick's College.

——. 1979a. *Drumcondra Attainment Tests, Level I, Form B: Mathematics and English. Administration and technical manual.* Dublin: Educational Research Centre, St Patrick's College.

——. 1979b. *Drumcondra Attainment Tests, Level II, Form B: Mathematics, Irish, and English. Administration and technical manual.* Dublin: Educational Research Centre, St Patrick's College.

——. 1980a. *Drumcondra Attainment Tests, Level III, Form B: Mathematics, Irish, and English. Administration and technical manual.* Dublin: Educational Research Centre, St Patrick's College.

——. 1980b. *Drumcondra Criterion Referenced Mathematics Test, Level 6. Manual.* Dublin: Educational Research Centre, St Patrick's College.

Findley, W.G. 1963. Purposes of school testing programs and their efficient development. In W.G. Findley, ed. *The impact and improvement of school testing programs.* Sixty-second Yearbook of the National Society for the Study of Education, Part II. Chicago: NSSE.

Finn. J. 1972. Expectations and the educational environment. *Review of Educational* Research 42: 387–410.

Fiske, D.W. 1967. The subject reacts to tests. *American Psychologist* 22: 287–96.

Fleming, E.S., and R.G. Anttonen. 1971. Teacher expectancy as related to the academic and personal growth of primary-age children. *Monographs of the Society for Research in Child Development* 36 (5, Serial no. 145).

Flook, A.J.M., and U. Saggar. 1968. Academic performance with, and without, knowledge of scores on tests of intelligence, aptitude, and personality. *Journal of Educational Psychology* 59: 395–401.

Flowers, C.E. 1966. Effects of an arbitrary accelerated group placement on the tested academic achievement of educationally disadvantaged students. Unpublished doctoral dissertation. Teachers' College, Columbia University, New York.

Fullan, M., and A. Pomfret. 1977. Research on curriculum and instruction implementation. *Review of Educational Research* 47: 335–97.

Garner, J., and M. Bing. 1973. The elusiveness of Pygmalion and differences in teacher-pupil contacts. *Interchange* 4: 34–42.

Gay, G., and R.D. Abrahams. 1973. Does the pot melt, boil, or brew? Black children and white assessment procedures. *Journal of School Psychology* 11: 330–40.

Gephart, W.J. 1970. Will the real Pygmalion please stand up? *American Educational Research Journal* 7: 473–75.

Goldsmith, J.S., and E. Fry. 1971. The test of a high expectancy prediction on reading achievement and IQ of students in grade ten (or, Pygmalion in puberty). Paper presented at the annual meeting of the American Educational Research Association, New York, February 1971.

Good, T.L., and J.E. Brophy. 1973. *Looking in classrooms.* New York: Harper & Row.

Gorman, W.G. 1968. The construction and standardization of a verbal reasoning test for age range 10 years, 0 months, to 12 years, 11 months, in an Irish population. Unpublished doctoral dissertation. University College Dublin.

Goslin, D.A. 1963. *The search for ability: Standardized testing in social perspective.* New York: Russell Sage Foundation.

——. 1967. *Teachers and testing.* New York: Russell Sage Foundation.

——, and D.C. Glass. 1967. The social effects of standardized testing in American elementary and secondary schools. *Sociology of Education* 40: 115–31.

Greaney, V., and T. Kellaghan. 1973. *Otis-Lennon Mental Ability Test (Irish Version), Elementary 1 Level, Form J.* Dublin: Educational Research Centre, St Patrick's College.

Green, R.L. 1975. Tips on educational testing: What teachers and parents should know. *Phi Delta Kappan* 57: 89–93.

Haggerty, M.E. 1918. Specific use of measurement in the solution of school problems. In G.M. Whipple, ed. *The measurement of educational products.* Seventeenth Yearbook of the National Society for the Study of Education, Part II. Bloomington, Ill.: Public School Publishing Co.

Hein, G.E. 1975. Standardized testing: Reform is not enough. In M.D. Cohen, ed. *Testing and evaluation's new views.* Washington, D.C.: Association for Childhood Educational International.

Herndon, T. 1975. Standardized tests: Are they worth the costs? Paper read to the Commonwealth Club, San Francisco.

Hoffman, B. 1962. *The tyranny of testing.* New York: Crowell-Collier.

Holt, J. 1968. *On testing.* Cambridge, Mass.: Pinck Leodas Association.

Houts, P.L. 1975a. A conversation with Banesh Hoffman. *National Elementary Principal* 54: 30–39.

——. 1975b. Standardized testing in America, II. *National Elementary Principal* 54(6): 2–3.

Husserl, E. 1969. *Formal and transcendental logic.* Trans. by Dorian Cairns. The Hague: Martinus Nijhoff.

Ingenkamp, K. 1977. *Educational assessment.* Slough, Berkshire: NFER Publishing.

Investment in education. 1966. Report of the Survey Team appointed by the Minister for Education in October 1962. Dublin: Stationery Office.

Ireland: Department of Education. 1971. *Primary school curriculum. Teacher's handbook.* 2 vols. Dublin: Department of Education.

Jackson, P. 1968. *Life in classrooms.* New York: Holt, Rinehart & Winston.

Jensen, A.R. 1980. *Bias in mental testing.* New York: Free Press.

Jose, J., and J. Cody. 1971. Teacher-pupil interaction as it relates to attempted changes in teacher expectancy of academic ability and achievement. *American Educational Research Journal* 8: 39–49.

Karier, C.J. 1973. Testing for order and control in the corporate liberal state. In C.J. Karier, P.Violas, and J. Spring, eds. *Roots of crisis: American education in the twentieth century.* Chicago: Rand McNally.

Kellaghan, T. 1976. Drumcondra Verbal Reasoning Test. In O.G. Johnson, ed. *Tests and measurements in child development: Handbook II.* Vol. 1. San Francisco: Jossey-Bass.

——, and D. Brugha. 1972. The scholastic performance of children in a disadvantaged area. *Irish Journal of Education* 6: 133–43.

——, and V. Greaney. 1970. Factors related to choice of post-primary school in Ireland. *Irish Journal of Education* 4: 69–83.

——, and J. Macnamara. 1972. Family correlates of verbal reasoning ability. *Developmental Psychology* 7: 49–53.

——, J. Macnamara, and E. Neuman. 1969. Teachers' assessments of the scholastic progress of pupils. *Irish Journal of Education* 3: 95–104.

——, G.F. Madaus, and P.W. Airasian. 1979. *Teachers' perceptions of test-taking behavior of pupils.* Washington, D.C.: National Institute of Education, U.S. Department of Health, Education, and Welfare.

——, G.F. Madaus, and P.W. Airasian. 1980a. *Standardized testing in elementary schools: Effects on schools, teachers, and students.* Washington, D.C.: National Institute of Education, U.S. Department of Health, Education, and Welfare.

——, G.F. Madaus, and P.W. Airasian. 1980b. With the assistance of P.J. Fontes and J.J. Pedulla. The effects of standardized testing. Report submitted to the Carnegie Corporation, the National Institute of Education, the Russell Sage Foundation, and the Spencer Foundation. Educational Research Centre, St Patrick's College, Dublin, and School of Education, Boston College.

——, G.F. Madaus, P.W. Airasian, and P.J. Fontes. 1976. The mathematical attainments of post-primary school entrants. *Irish Journal of Education* 10: 3–17.

——, and E. Neuman. 1971. Background characteristics of children of high verbal ability. *Irish Journal of Education* 5: 5–14.

Keshock, J.D. 1970. An investigation of the effects of the expectancy phenomenon upon the intelligence, achievement, and motivation of inner city elementary school children. Unpublished doctoral dissertation. Case Western Reserve University, Cleveland.

Kirkland, M.C. 1971. The effects of tests on students and schools. *Review of Educational Research* 41: 303–50.

Knill, F.P., Jr. 1969. The manipulation of teacher expectancies: Its effect on intellectual performance, self-concept, interpersonal relationships, and the institutional behavior of students. Unpublished doctoral dissertation. University of Cincinnati.

Lawler, J.M. 1978. *IQ, heritability and racism.* New York: International Publishers.

Lazarus, M. 1975. Coming to terms with testing. *National Elementary Principal* 54(6): 24–29.

Leiter, K.C.W. 1976. Teachers' use of background knowledge to interpret test scores. *Sociology of Education* 49:59–65.

Lewis, B. 1977. Testing: A parent's point of view. In R.M. Bossone and M. Weiner, eds. *Proceedings from the National Conference on Testing: Major issues.* New York: Center for Advanced Study in Evaluation, Graduate School and University Center of the City University of New York.

Long, B.H., and E.H. Henderson. 1974. Certain determinants of academic expectancies among southern and non-southern teachers. *American Educational Research Journal* 11: 137–47.

Lukas, C., and C. Wohlleb. 1973. *Implementation of Head Start planned variation: 1970–71.* Cambridge, Mass.: Huron Institute.

MacCorquodale, K., and P.E. Meehl. 1948. On a distinction between hypothetical constructs and intervening variables. *Psychological Review* 55: 95–107.

Madaus, G.F. 1979. Testing and funding: Measurement and policy issues. *New Directions for Testing and Measurement* 1: 53–62.

——, P.W. Airasian, and T. Kellaghan. 1971. The effects of standardized testing. *Irish Journal of Education* 5: 70–85.

——, and J. Macnamara. 1970. *Public examinations. A study of the Irish Leaving Certificate.* Dublin: Educational Research Centre.

——, and J. T. McDonagh. 1979. Minimum competency testing: Unexamined assumptions and unexplored negative outcomes. *New Directions for Testing and Measurement* 3: 1–14.

Mahler, C., and H. Smallenburg. 1963. Effects of testing programs on the attitudes of students, teachers, parents, and community. In W.G. Findley, ed. *The impact and improvement of school testing programs.* Sixty-second Yearbook of the National Society for the Study of Education, Part II. Chicago: NSSE.

Manis, M. 1955. Social interaction and the self-concept. *Journal of Social Psychology* 51: 362–70.

Maxwell, M.L. 1970. A study of the effects of teacher expectation on the IQ and academic performance of children. Unpublished doctoral dissertation. Case Western Reserve University, Cleveland.

McElligott, T.J. 1966. *Education in Ireland.* Dublin: Institute of Public Administration.

McKenna, B.H. 1975. A tale of testing in two cities. *National Elementary Principal* 54(6): 40–45.

Meichenbaum, D.H., K.S. Bowers, and R.R. Ross. 1969. A behavioral analysis of teacher expectancy effect. *Journal of Personality and Social Psychology* 13: 306–16.

——, and T. Smart. 1971. Use of direct expectancy to modify academic performance and attitudes of college students. *Journal of Counseling Psychology* 18: 531–35.

Meier, D. 1973. Reading failure and the tests. An occasional paper of the Workshop Center for Open Education, New York.

Mercer, J.R. 1973. *Labeling the mentally retarded.* Berkeley: University of California Press.

Merton, R.K. 1968. *Social theory and social structure.* New York: Free Press.

Merwin, J.C. 1973. Educational measurement of what characteristics of whom (or what) by whom and why. *Journal of Educational Measurement* 10: 1–6.

Meyer, W., and G. Thompson. 1956. Sex differences in the distribution of teacher approval and disapproval among sixth-grade children. *Journal of Educational Psychology* 47: 385–96.

Montague, A., ed. 1975. *Race and IQ.* New York: Oxford University Press.

Morris, T. 1968. Education. In V. Mealley et al., eds. *Encyclopedia of Ireland.* Dublin: Allen Figgis.

Morrison, A., D. McIntyre, and J. Sutherland. 1965. Teachers' personality assessments of primary school pupils. *British Journal of Educational Psychology* 35: 306–19.

Mostue, P. 1979. The construction of a self-concept scale. Unpublished manuscript. School of Education, Boston College, Chestnut Hill, Mass.

Murphy, C. 1980. *School report. A guide for parents, teachers and students.* Dublin: Ward River Press.

Neander, J. 1973. Objektivierte Lernerfolgsmessung in der Gesamtschule—Fortschrift für wen? *Deutsche Schule* 1: 35–47.

Neulinger, J. 1966. Attitudes of American secondary school students toward the use of intelligence tests. *Personnel and Guidance Journal* 45: 337–41.

Nibley, A.M. 1979. The evils of testing. *Boston Sunday Globe,* January 7, pp. A11, A12.

O'Meara, J.F. 1944. A critical study of external examinations and of their influence on secondary education. Unpublished master's dissertation. University College Cork.

Palardy, J.M. 1969. What teachers believe, what teachers achieve. *Elementary School Journal* 6: 370–74.

Parsons, T. 1959. The school class as a social system: Some of its functions in American society. *Harvard Educational Review* 29: 297–318.

Pedulla, J.J. 1976. The influence of standardized test information on teachers' ratings of their students. Unpublished doctoral dissertation. Boston College, Chestnut Hill, Mass.

Pellegrini, R.J., and R.A. Hicks. 1972. Prophecy effects and tutorial instruction for the disadvantaged child. *American Educational Research Journal* 9: 413–19.

Perrone, V. 1977. *The abuses of standardized testing.* Bloomington, Ind.: Phi Delta Kappa Educational Foundation.

Pidgeon, D.A. 1970. *Expectation and pupil performance.* Slough, Berkshire: NFER Publishing.

Pitt, C.C.V. 1956. An experimental study of the effect of teachers' knowledge or incorrect knowledge of pupil IQs on teachers' attitudes and practices and pupils' attitudes and achievement. Unpublished doctoral dissertation. Columbia University, New York.

Quinto, F. 1977. Why standardized tests fail the accountability test. In R.M. Bossone and M. Weiner, eds. *Proceedings from the National Conference on Testing: Major issues.* New York: Center for Advanced Study in Education, Graduate School and University Center of the City University of New York.

Ravitz, M. 1963. The role of the school in the urban setting. In A.H. Passow, ed. *Education in depressed areas.* New York: Bureau of Publications, Teachers' College, Columbia University.

Resnick, L.B. 1977. Matching tests with goals. *Social Policy* (September–October): 4–10.

Rist, R.C. 1970. Student social class and teachers' expectations: The self-fulfilling prophecy in ghetto education. *Harvard Educational Review* 40: 411–51.

———. 1977. On understanding the processes of schooling: The contribution of labeling theory. In J. Karabel and A.H. Halsey, eds. *Power and ideology in education.* New York: Oxford University Press.

Rosenthal, R., and L. Jacobson. 1968. *Pygmalion in the classroom.* New York: Holt, Rinehart & Winston.

Rotter, J.B. 1954. *Social learning and clinical psychology.* Englewood Cliffs, N.J.: Prentice-Hall.

Ryan, C. 1979. The testing maze. A national PTA white paper, January 1979.

Salmon-Cox, L. 1981. Teachers and standardized achievement tests: What's really happening? *Phi Delta Kappan,* 62: 631–634.

Samuda, R.J. 1975. *Psychological testing of American minorities: Issues and consequences.* New York: Dodd, Mead.

———. 1977. Critical concerns in the testing of minorities: Time for new initiatives. In R.M. Bossone and M. Weiner, eds. *Proceedings from the National Conference on Testing: Major issues.* New York: Center for Advanced Study in Education, Graduate School and University Center of the City University of New York.

Sanders, J.R., and W.L. Goodwin. 1971. Exploring the effects of selected variables in teacher expectation of pupil success. Unpublished manuscript. Bucknell University, Lewisburg, Pa. (ERIC Document Reproduction Service No. EJ 080 591).

Sandlin, A.A. 1959. Factors influencing curriculum in Oregon schools. Eugene: University of Oregon.

Scanlon, R.L. 1973. The perceptual press of classroom constraints. *Irish Journal of Education* 7: 29–39.

Schwartz, J.L. 1975. Math tests. *National Elementary Principal* 54(6): 67–71.

Serebriakoff, V., and S. Langer. 1977. *Test your child's IQ.* New York: David McKay.

Shepard, L. 1979. Purposes of assessment. *Studies in Educational Evaluation* 5: 13–26.

Silberman, A. 1976. Tests: Are they fair to your child? *Woman's Day*, November, pp. 54–62.

Simon, B. 1971. *Intelligence, psychology and education. A marxist critique.* London: Lawrence & Wishart.

Smith, D.E.P. 1976. *A technology of reading and writing, Vol. 1. Learning to read and write: A task analysis.* New York: Academic Press.

Snow, R.E. 1969. Unfinished Pygmalion. *Contemporary Psychology* 14: 197–99.

Sorotzkin, F., E.S. Fleming, and R.G. Anttonen. 1974. Teacher knowledge of standardized test information and its effects on pupil IQ and achievement. *Journal of Experimental Education* 43: 79–85.

Stetz, F.P., and M.D. Beck. 1978. A survey of opinions concerning users of standardized tests. Paper presented at the annual meeting of the National Council on Measurement in Education, Toronto, March 1978.

Thorndike, R.L. 1968. A review of Pygmalion in the classroom. *American Educational Research Journal* 5: 708–11.

Tolman, E.C. 1932. *Purposive behavior in animals and man.* New York: Appleton-Century-Crofts.

Torshen, K. 1969. The relation of classroom evaluation to students' self-concepts and mental health. Unpublished doctoral dissertation. University of Chicago.

Traxler, A.E. 1958. Are the professional test-makers determining what we teach? *School Review* 64: 144–51.

Tyler, R.W. 1966. What testing does to teachers and students. In A. Anastasi, ed. *Testing problems in perspective.* Washington, D.C.: American Council on Education.

——. 1968. Critique of the issue on educational and psychological testing. *Review of Educational Research* 38: 102–07.

——, ed. 1969. *Educational evaluation: New roles, new means.* Sixty-eighth Yearbook of the National Society for the Study of Education, Part II. Chicago: NSSE.

——, and S.H. White, chairmen. 1979. *Testing, teaching and learning. Report of a Conference on Research on Testing.* Washington, D.C.: National Institute of Education, U.S. Department of Health, Education, and Welfare.

U.S. Department of Health, Education, and Welfare: National Institute of Education. 1979. *The National Conference on Achievement Testing and Basic Skills,* March 1–3, 1978. Washington D.C.: National Institute of Education, U.S. Department of Health, Education, and Welfare.

Vernon, P.E., ed. 1957. *Secondary school selection. A British Psychological Society Inquiry.* London: Methuen.

Weber, G. 1974. Uses and abuses of standardized testing in the schools. Occasional Papers No. 22. Washington, D.C.: Council for Basic Education.

Weckstein, P. 1973. Legal challenges to educational testing practices. Harvard Center for Law and Education, *Classification Materials* (1973): 186–98; (1976 supplement): 37–38.

Williams, R.L. 1971. Abuses and misuses in testing black children. *Counseling Psychologist* 2: 62–77.

Willis, S. 1972. Formation of teachers' expectations of students' academic performance. Unpublished doctoral dissertation. University of Texas at Austin.

Womer, F.B. 1969. Test use. In R. Ebel, ed. *Encyclopedia of educational research,* 4th ed. New York: Macmillan.

NAME INDEX

SUBJECT INDEX